International Development:
Challenges for a World in Transition

POVERTY and INEQUALITY

Prepared for the Course Team by Hazel Johnson, Paul Mosley
and Wendy Olsen, with contributions from Ruth Pearson

Cover Women's micro-credit savings scheme, near Kenifra in Morocco.

The Open University
Walton Hall
Milton Keynes
MK7 6AA
United Kingdom

First published 2002

Edited, designed and typeset by The Open University

Printed in the United Kingdom by The Alden Group, Oxford

ISBN 0 7492 3787 2

This publication forms part of an Open University course U213 *International Development: Challenges for a World in Transition*

Details of this and other Open University courses can be obtained from the Course Information and Advice Centre, PO Box 724, The Open University, Milton Keynes, MK7 6ZS, United Kingdom: tel. +44 (0)1908 653231, email ces-gen@open.ac.uk

Alternatively, you may visit the Open University website at http://www.open.ac.uk where you can learn more about the wide range of courses and packs offered at all levels by the Open University

If you have not already enrolled on the course and would like to purchase this or other Open University material, contact Open University Worldwide Ltd, The Open University, Walton Hall, Milton Keynes MK7 6AA, United Kingdom: tel. +44 (0)1908 858785; fax +44 (0)1908 858787; email ouwenq@open.ac.uk; website http://www.ouw.co.uk

1.1

Contents

1	**Introducing the *Poverty and Inequality* Theme** ***Hazel Johnson***	**7**
1.1	Studying this Theme	7
	Aims	8
	Learning outcomes	9
1.2	Institutional agendas and the global context: some background to Section 2	12
	Economic growth and inequality	12
	Globalization	14
	Debt and conditionality	16
1.3	Livelihoods and lived experiences of poverty and inequality: some background to Section 3	19
1.4	Action on poverty and inequality: policy agendas, voices and Section 4	25
	The policy agendas of major institutions	26
	Poor people and action	28
	Summary of Section 1	32
2	**International institutions and the fight against global poverty** ***Paul Mosley***	**34**
2.1	The origins of the poverty theme	34
2.2	Adjustment, 'new' and 'old' poverty	38
2.3	The transformation of the Bretton Woods institutions	43
	The 1990 World Development Report and the IMF	43
	Changing perspectives on poverty policies in the 1990s	47
	Measuring and evaluating poverty reduction	52
	The 2000/2001 World Development Report and the IMF	59
2.4	International institutions and non-governmental organizations	65
2.5	Poverty agendas into the twenty-first century	69
	Summary of Section 2	75
3	**Understanding livelihoods and lived experiences** ***Wendy Olsen and Hazel Johnson***	**76**
3.1	Introduction: data, concepts, policy and action	76
	Analysing lived experience of poverty and inequality: an example	78
3.2	Analysing data about poor people	86
	Types of data about poverty	87
	Data are representations not facts	90
	Representing poverty through participatory approaches	93
3.3	Finding out about lived experience among the poor in rural India	95
	The survey: Wendy Olsen's own account	95
3.4	Inequality between households	102

3.5 Livelihood practices and lived experience 111
Assets, exchange entitlements and vulnerability 111
Cash income: gender inequalities within households 116
Interviewing rural women 119
Analysing rural women 124

3.6 Summary and conclusions 134
Summary 134
Conclusions 138

4 **Action on poverty and inequality** ***Hazel Johnson*** **139**

4.1 Studying this section 139

4.2 The scope of action 139
Perspectives: rights, capabilities and markets 140
Levels and spaces for action 141
Linkages between actors and actions 144

4.3 Analysing action 147
Individual action for private needs or ends 148
Collective action for private ends, and collective action for collective ends 154
Links between types of action 160

4.4 Evaluating action on poverty and inequality 165
Evaluation 1: interpretation through claims, concerns and issues 168
Evaluation 2: assessment by using explanatory concepts 172
Evaluation 3: political assessment of action 185
Evaluating action: processes and models 196

4.5 Conclusions 199
Summary of Section 4 199

5 **Rethinking poverty and inequality** ***Hazel Johnson*** **200**

5.1 Questioning Section 2: international institutions and the fight against global poverty 200
Context 201
Standpoint 201
Power relations 202
Gender 202

5.2 Questioning Section 3: understanding livelihoods and lived experiences 203
Context 203
Standpoint 204
Gender 204

5.3 Questioning Section 4: action on poverty and inequality 205
Context 205
Standpoint 206
Power relations and gender 206
Public action 207

5.4 Transformation 207

5.5 Reviewing the learning outcomes of this Theme 208

Appendix 1 Readings 210

Appendix 2 Suggested answers to activities 240

Appendix 3 Further reading 254

Appendix 4 Glossary 255

References 260

Acknowledgements 265

1 Introducing the *Poverty and Inequality* Theme

1.1 Studying this Theme

In the *Introduction to Poverty and Inequality* in Part 1, we laid the foundations for studying and understanding poverty and inequality. We looked at different ways that poverty and inequality can be conceptualized and analysed, and studied some of the issues involved in measuring and presenting data on poverty and inequality. In addition, in the last part of the section we considered what might be done about poverty, and looked in particular at public action and empowerment approaches. As a quick reminder, in Box 1.1 we have summarized key points from Part 1 that we would like you to keep in mind during your study of Part 2.

Box 1.1 Summary of key points from *Introduction to Poverty and Inequality*

The analysis and understanding of poverty and inequality have economic, moral, political and technological dimensions. Poverty is a multi-dimensional phenomenon: it includes and affects many facets of people's lives. In other words, poverty is as much about the quality of life and well-being as about access to assets and income.

Poverty is not just an issue for the poor. Poverty and inequality affect the capacities of societies to develop in multiple ways. Understanding and acting on poverty requires being able to analyse processes that create or reinforce poverty at different levels* – from the effects of political, technological and economic changes globally, to the dynamics of access to and control over resources, goods and services in local communities.

*In *Introduction to Poverty and Inequality* we called these levels global, national and local. In Part 2, we also refer to macro, meso and micro levels, and to the spaces in which action takes place.

There are many ways of conceptualizing poverty, and definitions are located in different social and historical contexts. In other words, how we define and measure poverty is socially constructed, and will lead to different ways of analysing poverty and developing policy. Recognizing the social construction of poverty as a concept also acknowledges the role of standpoint. Poverty may be perceived and acted on differently depending on the social and historical context, whether the actor is poor, wealthy, an academic, policy-maker, activist, etc.

Some key concepts for analysing poverty outlines in Part 1 were:

- low income
- multiple deprivations
- failure of capabilities and lack of freedoms
- social exclusion
- an outcome of particular types of social relations or structures
- as a residual phenomenon, or being 'left out of development'.

These conceptions have some overlapping areas. They may, however, lead to different understandings of how poverty is caused and what its effects are.

It is not always easy to measure poverty and inequality. Statistics are not necessarily reliable or comparable, and the data used have conceptual underpinnings and underlying assumptions that need to be understood. Quantitative data can help to show general patterns and trends over time. They cannot necessarily tell us why poverty or inequality occurs.

Inequality is different from poverty but closely linked to it in that poverty is often (but not necessarily) a manifestation of inequality. However, as with analysing poverty, we need to be clear about underlying concepts and assumptions. We need to distinguish between means and outcomes, as people are not created with an equal endowment of capabilities and resources. In terms of means, one way of understanding equality/inequality is through the concept of individual rights. Such a conception does not take into account the outcomes for society as a whole. Thinking about outcomes requires looking at the distribution of goods and services in society as a whole, and is likely to lead to very different policies based on a perception of equality based on individual freedoms in all spheres.

Measuring different variables, such as income and access to health, education and technologies, can demonstrate different types of inequality between people. Some of these may be positively correlated with each other. It is also possible to look at trends and patterns over time, both between groups of people within populations and between countries and regions. As with poverty, these measures do not in themselves explain why there is inequality (or changes in inequality).

Ways of analysing and understanding poverty and inequality will result in different policy outcomes and ways of acting on poverty. However, policies and actions also depend on who the actors are, what their interests are, and what resources they can command (human, political and economic) to bring about particular outcomes. The empowerment approach to the reduction of poverty and inequality overtly acknowledges the relative disadvantages that poor people face in terms of influencing action and outcomes.

Aims

The Part 1 *Introduction to Poverty and Inequality* was a launch pad for your study of the *Poverty and Inequality* Theme in Part 2. In Part 2, the focus is more on policies, practices and types of action on poverty.

The overall aims of the Theme in Part 2 are thus to:

- examine policy agendas, livelihoods and lived experiences, and courses of practical action;
- provide conceptual and analytical tools and skills for thinking critically and constructively about poverty and inequality in the twenty-first century.

Learning outcomes

The following are the anticipated learning outcomes for Part 2, which we would like you to check again at the end of your study of this Theme.

Knowledge and understanding

You should be able to demonstrate knowledge and awareness of:

1 The multi-dimensionality and historical and cultural specificity of poverty.

2 Key institutional poverty agendas and alternative anti-poverty strategies.

3 Different perspectives on and types of data used to analyse and understand poverty, at macro and micro levels.

4 Kinds of action that might be taken to reduce poverty and inequality.

5 How new thinking on poverty and inequality can contribute to reframing development in the twenty-first century.

Cognitive and key skills

You should be able to:

6 Reflect critically on the policy agendas and proposals on poverty of some of the major institutions.

7 Outline the main policy options available for reducing poverty and assess their effectiveness.

8 Understand and apply key economic concepts used in the analysis of poverty.

9 Outline different perspectives on investigating the lived experience of poor people.

10 Handle quantitative data on the assets and livelihoods of rural households in a developing country context (plot Lorenz Curves, analyse household data, make simple calculations, present data).

11 Analyse and interpret qualitative (interview) data using interpretative and explanatory approaches.

12 Identify the linkages between actors, the levels and spaces in which they act and their perspectives on action.

13 Differentiate different types of action on poverty and inequality.

14 Draw simple maps of linkages between types of action.

15 Analyse and evaluate action on poverty and inequality using three different approaches (interpretative, explanatory/conceptual and political).

16 Appreciate the role of models in developing courses of action.

17 Make arguments supported by evidence about policies and actions on poverty and inequality.

18 Write a short piece of critical analysis.

Study guide

The study for this Theme takes place in weeks 22–26. The components of the Theme are the unit texts, a video and an audiocassette. At the back of these units are three appendices: Appendix 1 contains some short readings that you use in Sections 1 and 4; Appendix 2 comprises suggested answers to some of the activities; Appendix 3 includes some suggestions for further reading. Appendix 4 contains a Glossary of terms used in Section 2. There are no additional audiovisual notes because the video and audiocassette are integrated into the sections of the Theme. You will notice that the teaching in this Theme is quite activity centred. Some of the activities are very short and a few may take up to an hour. They are designed to help you achieve the learning outcomes of the Theme.

The structure of the Theme is in the following chart:

Study week	*Section*	*Title*	*Other media*	*Study time (hours)*
22	1	Introducing the *Poverty and Inequality* Theme	Audiocassette Video	6
22–23	2	International institutions and the fight against global poverty	Audiocassette	14
23–24	3	Understanding livelihoods and lived experiences		21
24–26	4	Action on poverty and inequality	Audiocassette Video	21
26	5	Rethinking poverty and inequality		1
26	TMA	TMA	May use video and/or audiocassette	7

Your own interest in poverty and inequality may stem from the debates and campaigns around related issues such as the indebtedness of poor countries, the campaigns around the terms and conditions of world trade, and local concerns of homelessness, regional unemployment and social exclusion. You may also be from a country in which structural adjustment* programmes have been applied and their results for poverty hotly debated. Overall you are probably aware of some of the issues around the problem of poverty, including those that have been brought to the fore by the press, NGO campaigns and debates around the policies and actions of agencies such as the World Bank and the UK's Department for International Development (DfID).

*Structural adjustment is explained in the Course Book (Allen and Thomas, 2000), pp.301–304.

In a Theme of five weeks, we cannot cover everything to do with poverty and inequality. We have decided to look at the following aspects:

1 The changing agendas and policies on poverty in some of the major institutions such as the World Bank and the International Monetary Fund (IMF). These institutions have been key world players in terms of national policies in developing countries and their roles have been controversial and contested. However, the global poverty reduction targets agreed for 2015 indicate that their role deserves scrutiny.

2 How to understand the livelihoods of poor people. Here we teach some generic data skills for investigating and analysing livelihoods; we decided to do this, and to bring these skills alive, by focusing on lives and lived experiences in villages in Karnataka in India.

3 The nature of action on poverty and inequality. In this section, we pick up on the concept of public action that you first met in Part 1, and to look at how you might analyse and evaluate action on poverty and inequality, and its potential for bringing about longer-term change.

In this introductory section, we briefly present some of the background debates to these main areas of study. Our coverage is not meant to be comprehensive but to enable you to start appraising the issues. We include some activities around short articles and the audiovisual material for this Theme. As you study the different sections of the Theme, you should bear in mind the following questions. They will help you think about how a critical discussion of poverty and inequality can contribute to the overarching concern of the course to 'reframe development':

1 *Context.* What is specific about the context or contexts that you are studying? What difference does context make to how poverty and inequality occur? (In particular, think about 'old' and 'new' poverty here when you come to these concepts in later sections.) What difference does it make to how poverty and inequality might be addressed?

2 *Standpoint.* From whose perspective is the analysis of poverty and inequality being made? Whose voices are being expressed? Who is interpreting those voices (whether the voices of poor people, of governments, of different organizations working on poverty and inequality)? How does standpoint affect our understanding of poverty and inequality and what might be done?

3 *Power relations and gender relations.* How do the debates about action (including policies) on poverty and inequality address issues of power and social relations? How do they address gender?

4 *Public action.* What role can public action play in addressing poverty and inequality? How do the different types of action on poverty and inequality contribute to our understanding of public action?

5 *Transformation.* To what extent do ideas and practices around poverty reduction address poverty creation? To what extent are they actually or potentially 'transformative'?

Before continuing, we suggest you carry out the following activity. It will introduce you to some of the debates in this Theme.

Activity 1.1

The *Poverty and Inequality* audiocassette has two bands.

Listen to Band 1 and make notes on the key changes in thinking about poverty and inequality discussed in this band. Use your notes to think critically about the background debates introduced in this section.

(Spend about 15–20 minutes on this activity)

1.2 Institutional agendas and the global context: some background to Section 2

In Section 2, we look at the agendas of some major institutions, such as the World Bank and IMF, because they have been so influential in many parts of the world. However, the agendas of these institutions have been the source of much debate, contestation, lobbying and other campaigning. We are not going to repeat the discussion in Section 2 here. We look at some of the contextual issues at a macro level; these form part of the backdrop to what these major institutions do and to the global poverty reduction targets for 2015. The contextual issues we look at are economic growth and inequality, globalization, debt and conditionality.

Economic growth and inequality

Whether economic growth will benefit all populations, including the poor, within a given area or national boundary is a question that was raised in *Introduction to Poverty and Inequality*. That economic growth will or might benefit the poor presupposes that income or wealth generated is directed by one means or another into a number of possible channels – for example:

1 Productive investment in public and private enterprises that create adequately paid jobs to which poor people have access (and for which they have appropriate skills).

2 Education and training opportunities to enable poor people to gain access to new work opportunities.

3 Welfare support services and other forms of public provision.

4 Voluntary and non-governmental organizations that provide services and support projects to benefit poor people.

Such channels in turn might depend on a number of other elements – for example:

- Market signals or regulation that encourage productive investment in activities to which poor/unemployed people might have access.
- Differentiated policies on education and training for new work opportunities that enable the poorest, or those with least access, to benefit (i.e. to take into account differences related to gender or ethnic group, for example).
- A taxation system that directs part of the additional income into public provision and an infrastructure that allows a growth or extension of such provision.
- A growth in altruism and political will (such schemes as national lotteries have altruism as one of their goals, although income for lotteries is collected from the poor as well as the wealthy).

Such mechanisms can potentially help to reduce poverty (through public provision and enabling people to gain access to adequately paid work). They also involve redistribution, because they depend on income being channelled into other activities that would benefit and improve the incomes of poor people, rather than simply increasing the profits and wealth of investors or financiers, be they individual people or companies. The potentially redistributive effects would thus have an impact on inequality as well as poverty. However, the kinds of mechanisms and processes such as those above (and the willingness of governments and local authorities to legislate and act in particular ways) need to be in place for there to be an impact on inequality. Having such mechanisms in place cannot of course be assumed. In addition, it is often expected that economic growth will have a generally beneficial effect on poverty and inequality through a 'trickle down' effect. 'Trickle down' may or may not happen. A lot depends on the context and on who controls the benefits of economic growth, as indicated by Dan Murrow from the World Bank on the audiocassette. Moser on the other hand states that the poor cannot wait – a lesson to which she suggests the World Bank is now trying to respond.

There is thus an important relationship between economic growth, poverty reduction and inequality. Analysis carried out by Hanmer *et al.* (2000) has suggested that: 'High levels of income-inequality limit the poverty reducing effects of growth. Higher growth and pro-poor policies will improve poverty reduction prospects in both high- and low-inequality countries but high-inequality countries will need to grow twice as fast as low-inequality countries to halve poverty by 2015' (ibid., p.1). An even more serious critique of the 'trickle down from economic growth' view of poverty reduction is provided by Jesimen Chipika, a Zimbabwean economist who was a critical reader of this Theme when we were writing it. She points out that in the case of Africa:

> Poverty reflects the failure of development processes rather than being left out of development or the effects of development.
>
> The massive poverty in Africa is largely because development in general is not taking place rather than the benefits are not reaching certain segments of society.
>
> The trickle down view of development appears to assume unequal social relations as a given; however, the theory fails to address poverty and bring about development because it does not address the root cause of poverty and underdevelopment, which is unequal social relations.
>
> To the extent that poverty is the failure of growth effects to trickle down, there is an admission of the failure of development based on unequal social relations.
>
> (Chipika, 2001)

These are issues to reflect on as you proceed with your studies of subsequent sections of this Theme.

Globalization

The role of economic growth in reducing poverty and inequality also needs to be situated in the wider context of globalization. In the Course Book, p.348, McGrew defines globalization* as 'A process (or set of processes) which embodies a transformation in the spatial organization of social relations and transactions – assessed in terms of their extensity, intensity, velocity and impact – generating transcontinental or interregional flows and networks of activity, interaction and the exercise of power.' McGrew's analysis outlines three 'accounts' of, or perspectives on, the impact of globalization:

*Look back, if necessary, to the Course Book, Chapter 16, for McGrew's discussion of globalization.

- Neoliberal: a progressive force for creating prosperity through the market.
- Radical: exclusion and deepening inequality perpetrated through the activities of multinationals and the World Bank.
- Transformationalist: a change in world power, accompanied by changing roles of the state, private sector, NGOs and civil society, resulting in new concentrations of wealth and power in the South and increasing social exclusion and poverty in the North.

Each of these accounts has different implications for thinking about and acting on poverty and inequality. The neoliberal account supports the trickle down thesis. The radical account lies behind the wide-ranging protests against the meeting of the World Trade Organization in Seattle in 2000, and other protests at international gatherings (Figure 1.1). The transformationalist account lies behind some of the discussion in this Theme, where we address 'new' as well as 'chronic' poverty, in both Sections 2 and 4. It implies a need for action on poverty, social exclusion and inequality in North and South arising from changes in the structure of capital and markets worldwide.

Figure 1.1 Italian demonstrators try to break through a Czech riot police cordon near the conference centre in Prague, September 2000. Thousands demonstrated in the Czech capital to protest against the meeting of the International Monetary Fund and the World Bank.

There is, however, considerable debate* about the extent and nature of globalization, what it is, how it is happening and what its effects are on poverty and inequality as well as on culture and the environment. Part of the argument is about the nature of world governance, and the distribution and use of power, particularly with respect to decisions that may affect the livelihoods of millions of people. Massey (2000), writing after the Seattle protests in 2000, suggests: (a) we should not be counterposing global (as bad) and local (as good) but thinking about what kind of globalization (or global interconnectedness) is needed and wanted; (b) it should be the desirable outcomes of globalization that drive policies (for example, equality and environment, or quality of life and distribution rather than simply profits and growth); (c) power relations and the geography of power are fundamental aspects of a reformulation of globalization: globalization must thus be opened up to democratic processes, both at the level of protest and in international bodies (such as the WTO). These are issues that you can bear in mind in your study of both Sections 2 and 4 of this Theme.

*If you are in the UK, the World Development Movement can provide further information on campaigns if you are interested in this issue: e-mail wdm@wdm.org.uk For different perspectives, you might also contact the UK Department of Trade and Industry, (www.dti.gov.uk/ worldtrade); Focus on the Global South (www.focusweb.org) and Third World Network (www.twnside.org.sg)

Debt and conditionality

Debt can put a break on both economic growth and social welfare. This is of particular concern in the heavily indebted poor countries (HIPC). In Chapter 13 of the Course Book, Hewitt outlines the processes that led to the growth of indebtedness in many developing countries during the 1970s and 1980s. This story of the international debt crisis can be seen as an outcome of an increasingly interdependent global economy. It is closely linked to the fluctuations of economic growth in both rich and poor countries: the recycling of petro-dollars through the lending of Western banks to poor countries, the rising interest rates to control inflation in Western developed countries, and the difficulties of developing countries to export their commodities in time of world recession and to repay their loans. One of the responses to economic crisis in developing countries (and to some extent in developed countries) during the 1980s was for international institutions such as the World Bank and IMF to impose structural adjustment programmes. However, by the end of that decade, it was recognized that liberalization and the promotion of markets were not the answer alone (or even an answer) to the complex causes of poverty and the lack of access to (and even existence of) adequate services.

As with the governance of world trade, developing country debt has been the focus of extensive campaigning, notably by Jubilee 2000.* As with world trade, the economic arguments and related policies are subject to debate, particularly as to whether developing country debt should be cancelled completely, partially cancelled or rescheduled on more favourable terms. Jubilee 2000 would argue that much of the debt is unjust and that the costs of development (or lack of it) and indebtedness have arisen because of the behaviour of wealthy nations and multinational capital (what Hanlon, 2000, calls 'odious debt'). Box 1.2, extracted from a working paper series published by the international NGO World Vision, illustrates this position.

*Now called Jubilee Plus. If you are particularly interested in poor country indebtedness, you might like to visit the website of Jubilee 2000 (www.jubilee2000uk.org), also www.eurodad.org, and the World Bank (www.worldbank.org).

Box 1.2 A perspective on the debt crisis

The impact of the debt burden

Hundreds of millions of people living in poverty in low- and middle-income countries alike are paying the price for their countries' enormous foreign debts. These people did not benefit from many of the loans that gave rise to this debt. Few had any say in choosing the leaders who incurred these loans. Yet it is the poor who bear the brunt of repayment. Poor countries are trapped, making unending interest payments on their debts. In so doing, these nations must divert large amounts of scarce resources away from basic health care, primary education, and water, sanitation and food security. The debt burden thus inhibits human well-being and development needed to lift people out of poverty. As a result, the countries of sub-Saharan Africa, for example, spend more each year on repaying their debts than they spend on primary education and health care. In a recent survey of 27 of the poorest countries, only nine managed to spend more on basic social services than on debt servicing.

Foreign debt is not the sole cause of poverty in many developing countries. Nor would cancelling the debt automatically result in improved conditions for people living in poverty. But this ongoing indebtedness makes conditions worse for the poor. Debt cancellation – if carried out in ways that benefit the poorest people – could bring a new opportunity for many millions who are currently denied the most basic of human rights. It would also provide a real chance of meeting internationally agreed development goals, such as universal primary education by 2015, which are currently little more than a dream for many countries.

Who owes whom?

Over the centuries, vast quantities of minerals and other valuable resources have been plundered from developing nations by nations currently regarded as creditors. This includes millions of kilograms of gold and silver, and large numbers of priceless artefacts. This is a debt, now easily valued in trillions of US dollars (not including reparation costs), which the West has never repaid, or even acknowledged as a debt. Between the fifteenth and nineteenth centuries, an estimated 12 million slaves were forcibly removed from Africa, almost all by nations currently classified as 'creditors'. The removing of vast numbers of economically productive Africans led to a massive, highly destructive 'de-skilling' of African societies. The West, however, generated enormous wealth from the slave trade itself and from the millions of years of unpaid productive work extracted from slaves. The devastating impact of the slave trade on the individuals and families of those enslaved and on the wider society of which they were part, along with the personal, social and economic cost inflicted, and the cruelty with which slaves were treated was an enormous evil that has never been redressed. One recent estimate of the reparation necessary from Western Europe and the Americas for enslaving Africans while colonizing Africa is US$777 trillion.

A further issue to consider is the disproportionate amount of environmental damage that rich countries inflict on the planet compared with poorer countries. People in poverty are hurt first and worst when climate-related disasters strike. A recent report has calculated that the world's poorest nations are owed US$612 billion on their carbon dioxide account alone – because of their under-use or efficient use of fossil fuel resources. This is three times the amount owed by HIPCs. Rich-country demands for debt repayment, besides being morally illegitimate in the light of this large carbon dioxide debt, also undermine the ability of poor countries to achieve internationally agreed poverty reduction targets.

Source: Walker, B. (2000) 'A short history of the debt crisis' in Nyamugasira, W. and Walker, B. *The Poor Can't Wait: poverty and debt relief*, Working Paper No. 1, World Vision, Geneva, pp.12–14, 15–17.

The campaigns of Jubilee 2000 have helped put pressure on international lenders to provide debt relief for the HIPCs even though the implementation of relief has been relatively slow and subject to ongoing renegotiation. Overall debt cancellation is still under debate, as you heard in the discussion on the audiocassette associated with *Study Guide 1* ('Does Dropping the Debt Miss the Point?'). Tim Allen, who made that audiocassette, and Deborah Weinhold, for example, argue against overall cancellation and suggest that:

- It would be extremely difficult to make all lenders cancel all HIPC debt at the same time.
- It would be important to ensure that debt cancellation would not lead to refusal by creditors to provide new finance in the future.
- If new funds did not accompany debt cancellation, aid finance for the HIPCs would be much reduced.
- Debt cancellation might lead to corrupt use of the funds in some countries and not necessarily lead to an increase in well-being or social welfare.

Allen and Weinhold's conclusion is that debt cancellation has to be considered on a case-by-case basis (Allen and Weinhold, 2000). Whether or not one agrees with their position or that of Jubilee 2000, the role of debt cancellation in poverty reduction in specific cases would certainly need proper investigation.

Also under discussion is the role of conditionality in aid to poor countries. On the *Poverty and Inequality* audiocassette, Dan Murrow and Caroline Moser discuss a poverty reduction strategy that has been devised by the World Bank as a result of difficulties in addressing poor-country indebtedness; this strategy could be seen as a new form of conditionality (we come back to it in Section 4). However, some analysts have also put forward a view that conditionality cannot improve the effectiveness of aid and that aid should only be given to poor countries that have 'good policies' (Collier and Dollar, 1999). This position is discussed further in Section 2.

Activity 1.2

The purpose of this activity is to do some active reading around the issues just discussed in the course text. Listed below are articles that you might come across in your daily life, and here we give you an opportunity to think critically about their content.

Now read the following short articles in Appendix 1 of this Theme.

1. In Seattle, by Ainger
2. Protest against the protesters, by Brittan
3. The IMF's agenda, by Köhler

Compare the respective positions in these articles:

- What do they say about the relationship between economic growth and reduction of poverty?
- What do they say about the relationship between economic growth and inequality?
- How do they encapsulate the effects of globalization?
- What are their positions on debt and conditionality?

Compare your notes with those in Appendix 2.

(Spend up to 1 hour on this activity)

The three areas that we have briefly looked at here obviously do not exhaust the background of processes and activities which might result in an increase or a reduction in poverty and inequality. For example, we have not given separate space to a discussion of trade and investment, although it is part of our discussion of globalization (and in McGrew's chapter in the Course Book) and touched on in the articles in Activity 1.2. However, the issues we have looked at are part of the context in which policy development and contestation occur. It is thus important to study Section 2 of this Theme bearing these wider contextual issues in mind.

1.3 Livelihoods and lived experiences of poverty and inequality: some background to Section 3

At the other end of these global processes that produce and reinforce wealth, poverty and inequality, is the local context of people's livelihoods and livelihood strategies. This is the subject of Section 3. You have studied a certain amount of material on poor people's livelihoods in the Course Book already (notably in Chapters 3 'Understanding famine and hunger', 5 'Unemployment and making a living', 7 'Environmental degradation and sustainability', and 20 'Life in the cities'). You have also touched on the UK Department for International Development's framework for 'sustainable livelihoods' in *Introduction to Sustainability.*

For this Theme we need some additional analytical tools for understanding:

(a) why poverty and inequality may be created or reinforced through people's livelihoods; and

(b) the strategies that poor people pursue to maintain or improve their livelihoods, especially when they are faced with situations that may lead to further impoverishment.

In terms of the first issue, Bernstein (1992, p.24) outlined a brief set of questions that continue to be relevant for analysing livelihoods:

1 Who owns what or has access to what?

2 Who does what?

3 Who gets what?

4 What do they do with it?

*Endowments and entitlements: see Course Book, p.60, for definitions.

The first question concerns people's property and personal assets (what Amartya Sen calls endowments*). The second concerns the divisions of labour in work – between sector, by task and by other social criteria such as age and gender. It also concerns whether people are engaged in waged work or work for themselves. The third question is about remuneration of different people and types of work, in money or kind (including more intangible things such as forms of protection and favours as well as goods). The fourth concerns the distribution of output as a whole and what is done with it (e.g. does it go to consumption or to further investment? can producers expand their production or do they continue at the sample level of production?). Answering these questions will thus reveal information about poor people's endowments and entitlements (or lack of them), and the general distribution of property, assets, work opportunities and output. It will hence also indicate poor people's vulnerability to adverse changes in circumstances, such as losing access to small plots of land, a decline in real wages or rise in food prices. It may also tell you about the positive effects of some market changes or of policies directed to increasing endowments and entitlements.

Asking and answering these questions is to adopt a social relational approach to analysing livelihoods and helps to explain why poverty and inequality occur. For example, Jesimen Chipika's view is that 'The distribution of access to and control over assets and resources within countries is in most cases the primary source of poverty' (Chipika, 2001). However, to deepen this understanding, we also need to know how poor people negotiate their livelihoods and make choices and decisions about them, and the extent to which such possibilities are available. In other words, we need to know both about the structures that underpin people's livelihoods, on one hand, and about the actions that poor people take to try and maintain or improve them, on the other. We will come back to this relationship between structure and agency in Section 4.

As you have seen from chapters in the Course Book, the livelihoods of poor people are typically constructed from a diverse range of activities, which may include waged work combined with food production (Figure 1.2), petty trade, artesanal activity, informal production of consumer or intermediate goods, domestic service, etc. These activities

Figure 1.2 Cabbage production in Zambia. Cabbages can be both a food and a cash crop.

often have low productivities of labour and low value outputs in market terms, although their survival value to producers may have considerable importance.

Much has been researched and written about the survival and coping strategies of poor people – the means by which they try to gain a livelihood in highly adverse circumstances. At the end of the 1980s, Robert Chambers (1988) used a metaphor that is still useful. He distinguished 'foxes' and 'hedgehogs': foxes are those who are able to gain a livelihood from diverse sources, and hedgehogs are those who are locked into a single means of living. The choices and possibilities of foxes, while they may be severely constrained and offer limited income, are greater than those of hedgehogs. There is now considerable interest by policy-makers and investigators in the range of actions taken by poor people and their responses to changes in circumstances – in terms of their vulnerability, the risks they face (and are prepared to take) and the incentives that might induce poor people to undertake new (and possibly risky) initiatives (see Box 1.3 for definitions of *risk* and *vulnerability*). A characteristic of poverty is vulnerability to sudden shocks, such as an increase in food prices, drop in real wages, loss of work, illness, and social upheaval. Poor people thus face extreme risk with respect to their livelihoods. Risk mitigation thus forms part of the coping strategies that poor people adopt to protect themselves.

Box 1.3 Risk, risk exposure and vulnerability

As traditionally defined and measured, poverty is a static concept – a snapshot in time. But insecurity and vulnerability are dynamic – they describe the response to changes over time. Insecurity is exposure to risk; vulnerability, the resulting possibility of a decline in well-being. The event triggering the decline is often referred to as a shock, which can affect an individual (illness, death), a community, a region, or even a nation (natural disaster, macroeconomic crisis).

Risk, risk exposure, and vulnerability are related but not synonymous. Risk refers to uncertain events that can damage well-being – the risk of becoming ill, or the risk that a drought will occur. The uncertainty can pertain to the timing or the magnitude of the event. For example, the seasonal fluctuation of farm income is an event known in advance, but the severity is not always predictable. Risk exposure measures the probability that a certain risk will occur. Vulnerability measures the resilience against a shock – the likelihood that a shock will result in a decline in well-being ... [V]ulnerability is primarily a function of a household's asset endowment and insurance mechanisms – and of the characteristics (severity, frequency) of the shock.

Source: World Bank (2000a) *World Development Report 2000/2001: Attacking Poverty*, Oxford University Press, New York, p.139.

Another livelihoods concern for policy-makers is the role of labour markets. This concern is based on the fact that the main asset of poor people is their labour. Labour markets, as other markets, are unevenly developed in many parts of the world and within countries, which means either that limited opportunities for work, or for certain kinds of work, exist or that new work opportunities are not accessible to particular sectors of the population (often further differentiated by age and gender). In addition, the conditions of employment play a role in poverty creation and reinforcement, for example in informal contracting of poorly paid home-workers, or in the use of low-paid migrant labour. The relationship between the labour market and poverty creation is also associated with an absence of employment opportunities or the closure of businesses and relocation of capital. The latter is one of the causes of 'new poverty'.

A writer who has suggested a useful framework for thinking about the livelihood strategies of poor people is Caroline Moser (1998). Moser points out that the literature on poverty tends to address either debates on concepts and measurement, on the one hand, or poverty reduction strategies, on the other. Between these two arenas is a complex picture of the strategies that poor people adopt to protect their livelihoods. Moser proposes a way of analysing vulnerabilities and assets (her 'asset-vulnerability framework'), which we outline now and use again in Sections 3 and 4. Her ideas are also discussed on the audiocassette for this Theme.

Moser looks at four conceptual areas that enable us to analyse poor people's strategies:

1. *Vulnerability*, which she defines as 'the insecurity and sensitivity in the well-being of individuals, households and communities in the face of a changing environment [ecological, social, economic, political] ... and their responsiveness and resilience to risks' (Moser, 1998, p.3).

2. Poor people's *capacities/capabilities*, which are strongly associated with vulnerability (and resilience). You are now very familiar with this concept from your study of *Introduction to Poverty and Inequality*. Thus capacities/capabilities refer to the resources – material (economic), social (networks, influence), personal (education, motivation) – that people have, which are closely linked to the freedoms or opportunities to make choices outlined by Amartya Sen.

3. Closely related to capacities/capabilities is the concept of *assets*. Assets and entitlements are the 'means of resistance ... that individuals, households, or communities can mobilize or manage in the face or hardship' (Moser, 1998, p.3). Assets and Sen's concepts of endowments and entitlements overlap, as you can probably see. Threats to assets or people's capabilities to strengthen their assets are all part of their resilience to impoverishment.

4. The critical issue for poor people is how they are able to manage their assets, both in stable times and in times of stress. Thus there is a fourth conceptual area, that of *asset management strategies* (also sometimes called 'coping' or 'adapting' strategies). Moser distinguishes strategies as 'income-raising' or 'consumption modifying' (Moser, 1998, p.5). She also points out that multiple strategies may be used to manage assets. (Understanding how people's decisions and actions are established and prioritized may be an important foundation for policy development.)

Moser also distinguishes differences in the assets and vulnerabilities of people in the countryside from those in towns. For people who farm in rural areas, assets such as land and labour, entitlements such as crops for sale (and labour for sale), investments in physical and human resources, building up stores, and being able to make claims on others (such as neighbours and family) to provide support are all important. In towns, although some of these assets might also be critical for survival, Moser identifies three other areas of vulnerability: goods and services tend to be more commoditized in towns than in the countryside (where exchanges between people may not always enter the market) – urban people are therefore more subject to the effects of market changes (Figure 1.3); there are particular environmental problems with living in towns such as sanitation and waste disposal; and poor people in towns may be subject to greater social fragmentation and not have access to the types of social network and solidarity that exist in rural communities.

Figure 1.3 Managing assets and capabilities: making a living by providing a service – a hair salon in a poor urban area in Kenya.

These ideas are useful for thinking about poor people's roles in managing their own poverty and trying to reduce it. We need to be able to understand poor people's asset management strategies to have some idea of the possible effects of anti-poverty policy and interventions. However, this means that we need to be able to track how people's strategies change with changing conditions. Changes might be the result of wider social and economic processes, or might be from policy developments such as welfare provision. In the UK's DfID, there have been attempts to think about how livelihoods can become sustainable, as you saw in the *Introduction to Sustainability.* As with Moser, DfID's framework analyses people's vulnerability and assets (in which they include human, natural, financial, physical and social capital) and then uses this as a basis for looking at how structural changes and processes might influence livelihood strategies and outcomes (Ashley and Carney, 1999, p.47). There is increasing use of such frameworks that attempt to take a holistic approach to understanding livelihoods and planning interventions to improve them. Jesimen Chipika makes the following comment, which you can bear in mind when studying Section 2 as well as Section 3:

> The international debate on poverty is a bit off-target in emphasis, which is why the corresponding piece-meal solutions have been generally ineffective in reducing poverty ... I think what we need is a holistic solution or approach to addressing asset and resource control to encourage local empowerment, encourage good governance as well as addressing the international dimensions of globalization and debt.
>
> (Chipika, 2001)

We will come back to vulnerability, assets and entitlements when we analyse the livelihoods of Indian villagers in Section 3, and in Section 4 we will look at the, sometimes risky, initiatives that poor people are prepared to undertake to improve their economic circumstances. Activity 1.3 below gives you an opportunity to apply Moser's framework to the experiences of poverty in the video for this Theme. The video looks at situations where collective action has been taken to try and address poverty. Your responses to the activity will need to take into account the *context* of people's lives and how their assets and vulnerabilities are changing as a result of the interventions.

Activity 1.3

Now view the video for this Theme. It contains two programmes:

Small Change for a Better World: about micro-finance in Glasgow.

Funny Money: about social currencies in Quilmes, Buenos Aires, in Argentina.

Make notes on:

- The sources of vulnerability of the people in the video
- The nature of people's capabilities
- Their assets
- How they try and manage their assets.

Check Appendix 2 for our comments in answer to these questions.

(Spend up to 1 hour on this activity)

1.4 Action on poverty and inequality: policy agendas, voices and Section 4

You will remember that a key question for this course is: How might we analyse or understand what can be done – and what are people doing – about poverty and development?

This is a particularly important dimension to this Theme. Section 2 analyses the history of institutional policies on poverty, including what has worked, what has not and what might be useful approaches in the future. In Section 3 we implicitly address day to day action on poverty by analysing how villagers gain their livelihoods. Section 4 looks at examples of organized and purposive action, or public action, and their potential and limitations for reducing poverty and inequality. So here we want you to start thinking about the some of the issues.

The policy agendas of major institutions

What can be done about global poverty is a main issue on the agenda of more than one major international development organization. A key question is how economic growth and poverty reduction can go hand in hand, as the first does not necessarily lead to the second, but is seen as a necessary condition for the second. These ideas are embodied in the concept 'pro-poor growth', around which there is much investigation (reflected in the discussion in Section 2). In addition, there are the global poverty reduction targets – to halve world poverty by 2015 – agreed by international institutions and much commented on in international fora (with some pessimism that targets can be achieved). The World Bank (2000a, p.6) outlines the main elements:

1. Halving the number of those living on less than $1 a day
2. Ensuring universal primary education
3. Eliminating gender differences in primary and secondary education by 2005
4. Reducing infant mortality by two-thirds
5. Reducing maternal mortality by three-quarters
6. Ensuring universal access to reproductive health services
7. Implementing national strategies for sustainable (environmental) development in every country by 2005, so as to reverse the loss of environmental resources by 2015.

This is an ambitious list of targets, and there are several points to reflect on. One is the interconnectedness of some of these aims (for example poverty and education, or poverty and infant mortality; gender differences in education and maternal mortality; maternal mortality and access to reproductive health services; poverty and environment). The World Bank itself states:

> Each of the seven goals addresses an aspect of poverty. They should be viewed together because they are mutually reinforcing. Higher school enrollments, especially for girls, reduce poverty and mortality. Better basic health care increases enrollment and reduces poverty. Many poor people can earn their living from the environment. So progress is needed on each of the seven goals.
>
> (World Bank, 2000a, p.5)

The inter-relationship between these goals (for example changes in income with changes in infant mortality) can be investigated by plotting data graphically and analysing what correlations exist and how they might be explained. It may be that an increase in income will not alone lead to a decline in infant mortality, but that other processes or elements need to be in place, such as adequate healthcare or education. If so, the policy arena linking an increase in income (or a reduction in poverty) to a reduction in infant mortality is much more complex. An example that is often used in this discussion is that of the state of Kerala in south-west India, which has relatively low income per capita within an Indian context, but has extensive public provision in health care and education which has been associated in turn with a low birth and low infant (and maternal) mortality rate and high life expectancy. However, a key element in these achievements has been the role of public action, the history of 'voice' given to many women in Kerala and their position in the household, as well as the progressive nature of state policies. The context of policy affects outcomes.

A second point of reflection is that these goals focus on inequality as well as poverty. Although both the World Bank and DfID (2000b) see economic growth as key to poverty reduction, their documents also place importance on redistribution. The World Bank states:

> Attaining the international development goals will require actions to spur economic growth and reduce income inequality, but even equitable growth will not be enough to achieve the goals for health and education. Reducing infant and child mortality rates by two-thirds depends on halting the spread of HIV/AIDS, increasing the capacity of developing countries' health systems to deliver more services, and ensuring that technological progress in the medical field spills over to benefit the developing world.
>
> (World Bank, 2000a, p.6)

At this point, you might pause to ask yourself what measures and processes would in turn need to be in place for these proposals to reduce infant and child mortality rates to happen? How will the spread of HIV/ AIDS be halted? How will the capacities of countries' health systems be increased? What does it mean for technological progress to 'spill over'? It is important to be able to adopt a critical approach to reading texts and policy documents about poverty reduction and to look at the assumptions behind them. Again, our critical reader, Jesimen Chipika, commented: 'there is nothing magical about these targets. If consistent effort in the form of policies, programmes, real action and monitoring of these to address poverty are not pursued at national and local levels [i.e. as well as by international organizations], the targets are just a pipe dream' (Chipika, 2001).

A third point of reflection is the extent to which these goals are targets only for developing countries or are relevant for the 'developed' world. The World Bank includes Eastern Europe in its *World Development Report 2000/2001: Attacking Poverty*. There are issues to be addressed around gender differences in education and environment in countries like the UK (Figure 1.4), and more general concerns about poverty, often expressed in the concept of social exclusion, which has become a focus of debate and policy development.

Figure 1.4 To what extent do the global poverty reduction targets apply to areas of poverty in developed countries? Children playing in High View housing council estate, Penarth, South Wales – an area of poor housing and multiple deprivations.

Activity 1.4

To reflect on the role of context in policy agendas, now read the article by Maxwell and Kenway called 'Poverty in the UK: any lessons for the South?' in Appendix 1 (Reading 4). Just get the gist of this article – you do not need to learn its content.

Which particular aspects of the *context* in the UK support the reduction of poverty (and inequality)?

Look at Appendix 2 for our brief thoughts.

(Spend no more than 30 minutes on this activity)

Poor people and action

What role can and do poor people play in the reduction of poverty and inequality? In the rhetoric of the 'stakeholder society' and 'participatory development' of the late twentieth and early twenty-first century, this question has particular relevance. The question has increasingly been given a hearing in recent times because of the failure of many 'top-down' or non-consultative and non-participatory approaches to development. The gradual change in paradigm from state-led development after the Second World War to an increasing role for the private sector and civil society supported by an 'enabling state' has been accompanied in development discourses with a concern for the role of the poor and socially excluded in influencing policy and taking action.

Voices of the poor

An area of debate that has affected development organizations from large international institutions to local NGOs is whether and how to include the views of poor people in policy development and practice. Part of this debate has been about the role of participation and empowerment, which we will look at shortly. It has also involved trying to understand the experience of poverty from poor people's own perspectives. For example, interesting and debated volumes were produced by the World Bank in the *Voices of the Poor* series (Narayan *et al.*, 2000a,b),* using data from country participatory poverty appraisals around the world and from further consultations with poor people in 23 countries, including some in Eastern Europe. A fuller discussion of these studies is given in the second audio band in which you can hear Deepa Narayan, who was the team leader, explaining the background to the project and giving her view of its effects. An example of the kinds of understandings that were gathered is illustrated in Figure 1.5, which shows an analysis of the causes and effects of poverty by a women's group in Ghana. The volume from which it was taken underlines that poor people's own analyses of poverty show a 'circularity of causation' with causes and effects appearing on both sides (Narayan *et al.*, 2000b, p.251).

*The *Voices of the Poor* volumes are listed in the further reading in Appendix 3.

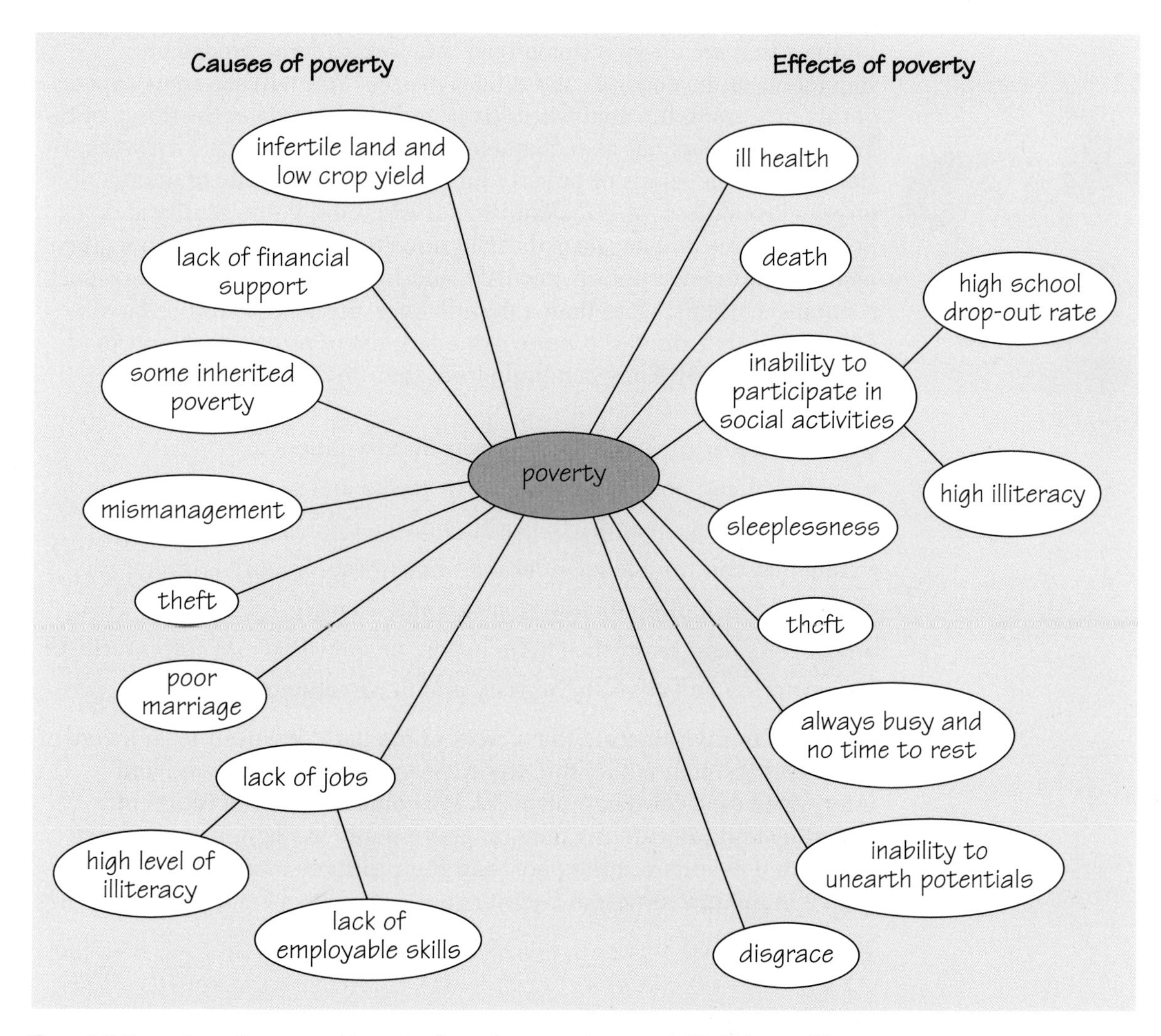

Figure 1.5 Perceptions of causes and impacts of poverty, women's group, Dobile Yirkpong, Ghana.

Such studies are attempts by outsiders to translate the experience of poverty to others by gathering information from those on the inside. Robert Chambers is one key analyst who has tried to understand poverty from the *inside* through participatory research methods. (His views were debated on the audiocassette 'Whose knowledge counts?'.) Chambers also had a hand in the *Voices of the Poor* series. However, he is aware that it is quite difficult to determine the extent to which listening to poor people influences the policies and practices of major institutions such as the World Bank, in particular as reflected in documents such as the 2000/2001 World Development Report with which the studies coincided. Chambers suggests that, although the World Development Report emphasizes the multi-dimensionality of poverty, it does not pick up on all the multiple dimensions revealed by poor people in the *Voices* studies. Nevertheless, this kind of work has encouraged further participatory initiatives in countries where the original studies were undertaken (http://www.odi.org.uk/speeches/booth8.html).

Such studies of people's experiences of poverty and inequality provide findings that are often systematized into forms of knowledge or statements and categories about poor people. You will see some aspects of this process in the analysis of lives and livelihoods in Section 2 of this Theme. Chambers has also characterized poverty from his own work. He states that dimensions of poverty include: lack of income or assets, physical weakness, physical and social isolation, vulnerability and powerlessness, and suggests that the priorities of the poor are: adequate incomes and consumption, security, and independence and self-respect (Chambers, 1988). More than a decade later, the *Voices* studies have come up with a similar, if more extended, list of priorities (Narayan *et al.*, 2000b, p.266). They conclude from their investigation that poor people want change from:

- material poverty to adequate assets and livelihoods;
- isolation and poor infrastructure to access and services;
- illness and incapability to health, information and education;
- unequal and troubled gender relations to equity and harmony;
- fear and lack of protection to peace and security;
- exclusion and impotence to inclusion, organization and empowerment;
- corruption and abuse to honesty and fair treatment.

However, in investigating the 'voices of the poor' we need to be aware of the lenses through which the experiences have been gathered and interpreted (and for what purpose). We come back to the issues of gathering and interpreting data on poor people in Section 3, while we return to the 'voices of the poor' and their influence on World Bank policy in the discussion in Section 2.

Participation

In parallel to these attempts to understand poverty and inequality from poor people's standpoints is the debate about the role of poor people's participation in development and their potential empowerment* through such participation. The rhetoric of participation is familiar at the beginning of the twenty-first century particularly in the term 'stakeholder' often used by politicians, and in the practice of consultations, focus groups, etc. We will leave aside the extent to which such practices enable greater openness and involvement in policy decisions, and can bring influence to bear on them in general terms. Participation in the context of action on poverty concerns whether poor people can have a role in defining and helping to carry out policies and projects directed to poverty reduction. It also concerns whether participatory action will change the social positions of poor people (a reduction in inequality through a process of empowerment) and lead to better development.

*Empowerment was addressed in Section 7 of *Introduction to Poverty and Inequality* – you may want to refer back to it. A definition of empowerment is on p.35 of the Course Book.

Such issues have been addressed by researchers since the 1960s and 1970s, including in the community development era in the UK, as you will have gathered from Marjorie Mayo on the audiocassette for this Theme. In the contemporary context, they are probably best known in Chambers' work. Chambers has argued for participatory approaches to investigating development and the definition of policies and projects. He has also argued for power reversals between researchers, policy-makers, development professionals and poor and socially excluded people – a process of 'handing over the stick'. You will have listened to the pros and cons of this debate in 'Whose knowledge counts?'.

Just as important is the role of poor people's organizations, which can act as sources of solidarity and mutual assistance as well as mechanisms for mobilizing people for development. They can also act as sources of resistance against unwelcome policies or forms of perceived or actual oppression. These roles are increasingly given prominence in the development literature and in policy proposals. In part this is linked to the growth in concern with how forms of community and social capital* can enable or enhance poverty reduction. It has been suggested, for example, that poor people tend to have forms of co-operation with each other (what is called 'bonding social capital'), a certain amount of links and ties with other groups and communities (bridging social capital), but few links with groups and organizations of higher social status, such as government (linking social capital) (World Bank, 2000a). Although such distinctions are bound to vary with context, they imply that a poverty-reduction strategy might include building bridging and linking social capital between organizations of the poor and other organizations. Such a process might include links with other civil society organizations as well as the private sector and government.

*For a definition of social capital, refer to the Course Book, p.37.

However, the concept of social capital has been hotly debated (as have participation and empowerment). It can be criticized for, among other reasons, being too imprecise a concept to capture the nature of social relations (especially power relations). Thus the assumed lack of bridging and linking social capital should not be taken simply as a 'problem' for poor people's organizations. Although this lack may be symptomatic of the isolation of such organizations and their relative lack of command over resources and powerlessness, it may also reflect a large gap between the interests of poor people and those which are vested in more powerful civil society, private sector and government bodies.

Activity 1.5

Listen again to Band 1 of the audiocassette for this Theme.

Make notes on the relationship between policy agendas, voices and participation in that discussion.

Check Appendix 2 for points we thought of.

(Spend no more than 30 minutes on this activity)

Summary of Section 1

This introduction has defined the aims and learning outcomes of the *Poverty and Inequality* Theme. It has also introduced the subsequent sections of this Theme by taking you through some of the debates and context in which they have been written. In doing this, we have touched on some key themes and concepts, which might be summarized as follows:

Section	*Themes and concepts*
Institutional agendas and the global context: some background to Section 2	Economic growth and inequality: 'trickle down' redistribution unequal social relations
	Globalization: neoliberal, radical and transformationalist accounts world governance power relations
	Debt and conditionality: unjust debt debt cancellation
Livelihoods and lived experiences of poverty and inequality: some background to Section 3	Creation/reinforcement of poverty through livelihoods: social relational approach endowments and entitlements distribution low productivity

	Livelihood strategies: 'foxes' and 'hedgehogs' vulnerability risk capabilities assets 'asset-vulnerability framework'
Action on poverty and inequality: policy agendas, voices and Section 4	International policy agendas: global poverty reduction targets interconnectedness of targets relative roles of growth and redistribution context and poverty reduction
	Action by poor people: voice outside and inside understandings participation power reversals social capital

At the beginning of this introduction, we also gave you some areas to reflect on as you study the following sections. They were:

- Context: here we have looked at some of the similarities and differences between developing countries and the UK context.
- Standpoint: we have seen the different perspectives of institutions such as the World Bank and the UK's DfID, NGOs and different analysts of poverty and inequality.
- Power relations and gender relations: this is not only an issue in relation to dominant organizations and voices in the debates and policies around poverty and inequality, but is also an issue for action at all levels, including household survival strategies.
- Public action: we have looked at different types of action on poverty and inequality, from campaigns on debt to participatory ways of engaging with the needs and interests of poor and socially excluded people.
- Transformation: we have seen some of the tensions that exist between addressing poverty and inequality as phenomena requiring particular policies to reduce them, and approaches that try to address the causes of poverty and inequality.

You may like to make a few notes on any further reflections on these dimensions before continuing.

2 International institutions and the fight against global poverty

There is a glossary of economic terms in Appendix 4 of this Theme, specifically for Section 2, in case you need it. The terms referred to in the glossary are in ***bold italic*** type in this section.

2.1 The origins of the poverty theme

The relief of global poverty – the main preoccupation of development institutions in recent years – is not a new theme. As far back as the 1950s, many institutions committed themselves to the cause of the poorest people, only for this commitment to be abandoned under the stress of the global crisis of the 1980s. With the return of a focus on poverty in the 1990s, the wheel has now come full circle. But with a difference: the new approach tackles what may be essentially the same problem, but the diagnosis of poverty, its distribution across the developing world, the geopolitical environment and the balance between state and private action have changed completely. As a consequence, world poverty is now being tackled in major institutions such as the World Bank and International Monetary Fund (IMF) (Figure 2.1) with a quite new range of policies from those encountered fifty and even twenty years ago. You have already encountered a brief discussion of some of the changes on Band 1 of the audiocassette for this Theme. This section examines this shift in policies, the ideas and evidence that motivated them and the results which they have so far delivered.

Figure 2.1 International Monetary Fund Managing Director Horst Köhler, right, greets Nicaraguan President Arnoldo Aleman prior to their meeting at the IMF in Washington, May 2000.

In early post-war diagnoses, such as the United Nations *Measures for the Economic Development of Underdeveloped Countries* (1951), poverty is seen as mainly a labour market or underemployment problem.* This in many ways is a surprisingly modern insight, since the studies by Sen (1983) and more recent authors have confirmed that the very poor and starving have nothing whatever to sell except their working time. Lacking ***physical capital***, ***human capital*** and ***social capital***, they are forced back on the sale of unskilled, and usually casual, labour. The United Nations report of 1951, co-authored by a group of five including two Nobel Prize-winners, Arthur Lewis and Theodore Schultz, states that 'the principal way to reduce unemployment and underemployment in the underdeveloped countries is through economic development' (1951, p.4). This has been interpreted by later generations as a belief that poverty could best be alleviated by policies to force economic growth, in particular high levels of ***capital investment***. However, the United Nations team is more specific:

*See Course Book, p.120, for a definition of underemployment. You can also refer to the discussion of employment and poverty in the *Transitions* Theme.

> In an economy which is overpopulated, the search should be for technologies which increase the yield of land per acre, or which enable large numbers of persons to be employed in ***secondary industries*** for a small expenditure of capital.
>
> (United Nations, 1951, p.7)

As we shall see, this is precisely the anti-poverty prescription adopted by the World Bank forty years later.

The 1950s and 1960s were very successful decades for world development: the world economy grew faster during that period than ever before (Figure 2.2). Cyclical booms and recessions there certainly were, but it was reasonable to believe that vulnerability to global depression of the kind which had occurred during the 1930s had been cured – and cured, specifically, by the return to a more free-market regime of trade and investment after the Second World War under the stewardship of the World Bank and the IMF. Formal data on global poverty were lacking, but it was already clear by the 1960s that the developing world was growing faster than the industrialized world, and, informally, there were encouraging signs on poverty as well. India – the country with probably the largest absolute number of poor people, then as now – was scarred by repeated famines throughout the colonial period, most dramatically in Bengal in 1943 when three million people died. But since 1943, there has been no famine in India. For thirty years after the Second World War, therefore, it was not unreasonable to suppose that policies of 'economic development', as the United Nations experts called it, were indeed reducing global poverty.

Two things changed this perception in the early 1970s. In the first place, this period marks the beginning of serious country-level studies of poverty and inequality in developing countries, one of which (Fishlow, 1970) revealed that in spite of rates of growth of national income in

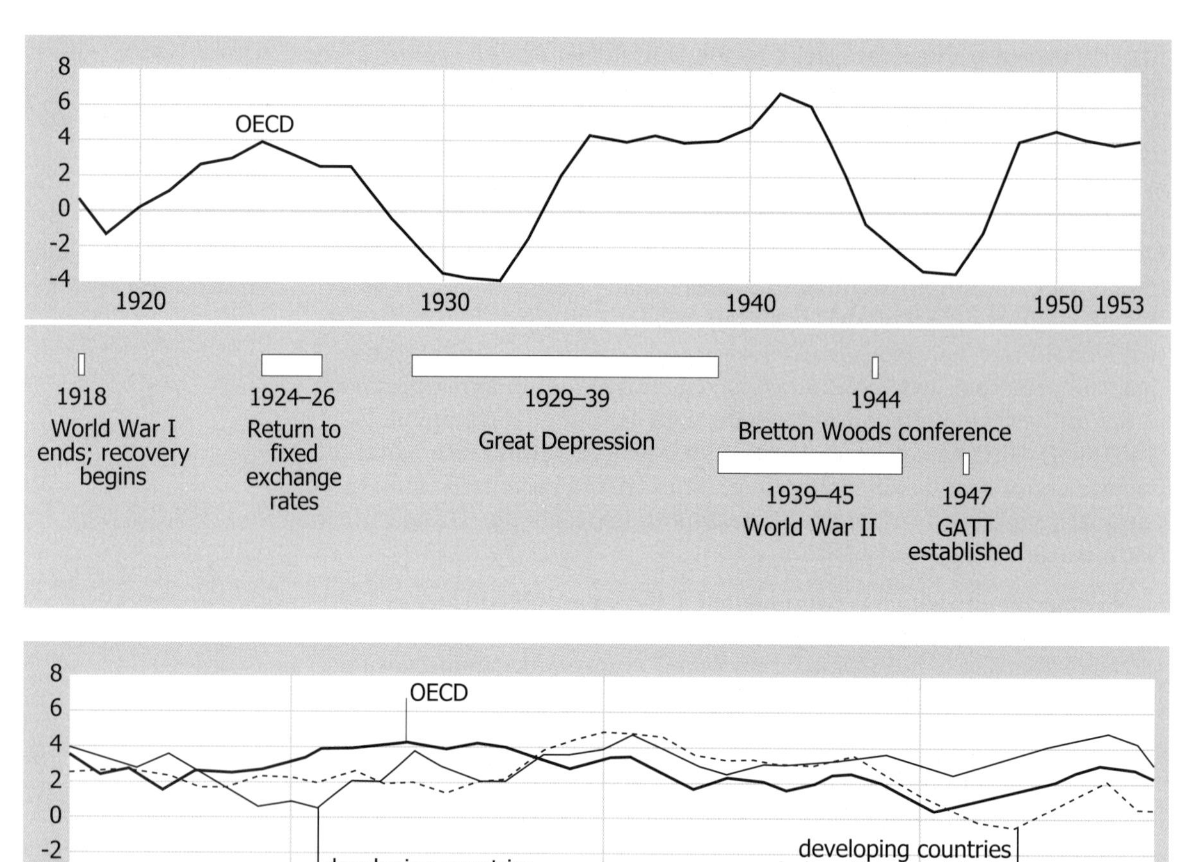

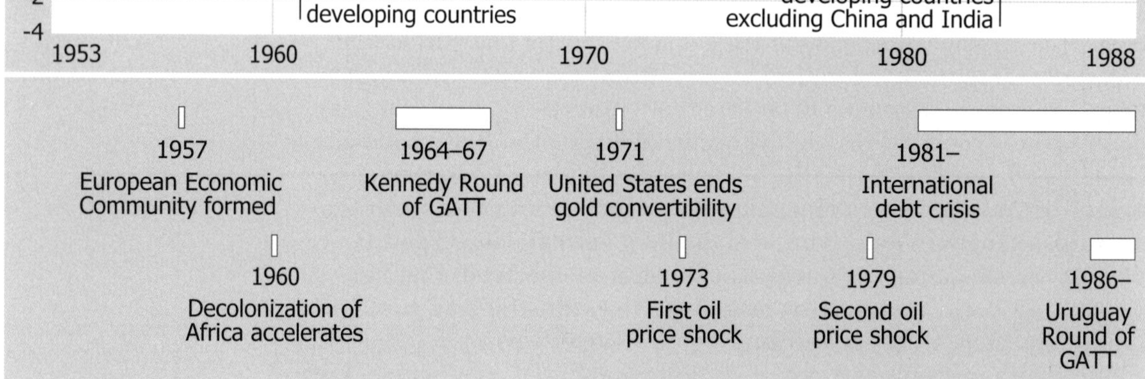

Figure 2.2 Per capita output growth in the OECD and developing countries (%, five-year moving average) and significant world events, 1918–88.

Brazil averaging over 7% since the 1950s, poverty and inequality were increasing. In the second place, famine, in Ethiopia and in Bangladesh, became once again a global issue at this time. These data made it clear that whatever benefits the forward momentum of the global economy was providing, it was certainly not eliminating poverty of the severest kind, and possibly was not even reducing it.

The reaction of the donor community was rapid. At the 1973 annual meeting of the World Bank in Nairobi, the Bank's President Robert MacNamara (Figure 2.3) committed the Bank to a reorientation of its

Figure 2.3 Robert MacNamara addressing a World Bank/IMF conference in Manila in April 1976.

strategy towards poverty elimination (Ayres, 1983). In Britain, for example, the White Paper *The Changing Emphasis in British Aid Policies: more help for the poorest* (1975) committed the government

> to give an increasing emphasis in our bilateral aid towards the poorest countries ...
>
> to promote situations in which British ***concessional aid funds*** can stimulate matching contributions of concessional funds from other governments, and to encourage the deployment of such aid through both multilateral and bilateral channels towards the poorest countries.
>
> The Government accepts that more should be done to ensure that a higher proportion of British aid should directly benefit not only the poorest countries but the poorest people in those countries. As most of these people live in rural areas, the third leg of our new aid strategy is not only to put a new emphasis on programmes orientated towards the relief of poverty but to give a special emphasis to rural development.
>
> (Overseas Development Administration, 1975, pp.7–8)

These approaches were given a formal underpinning by the World Bank/ Institute of Development Studies study *Redistribution with Growth* (Chenery *et al.*, 1975). That blueprint was willing to consider a number of anti-poverty options, including quite radical ones, such as land reform, but the policy instrument which came to be principally used by donors, as explicitly described by both the World Bank and the UK government above, in their shift to 'poverty focus' was a sectoral shift in expenditure – away from industry and towards agriculture. But an intra-sectoral shift is also visible: from heavy capital-intensive industry towards the newly renamed 'informal sector' of the urban shantytowns (ILO, 1973) and from estate and cash-crop agriculture towards food crops. One interesting aspect of the latter shift was the evolution of a strategy of 'integrated rural development', in which a range of public services – roads, health, education and farmer extension, irrigation, credit and so on – were supplied in co-ordinated fashion to underdeveloped rural districts. Bilateral donors bought enthusiastically into this approach, and many countries of Africa and South Asia came to be redivided between them in this new way: in Sri Lanka, for example, the Norwegians took on the south, Britain the east, the World Bank the south-west, and USAID the north-west. The integrated rural development experiment was never evaluated in a formal way – that is, in terms of the number of people it did or did not take out of poverty. However, in the perception of the donors, integrated rural development was a grand but ultimately unsuccessful vision (e.g. Cox, 1983; Symposium, 1988), eventually undermined by financial constraints and by the inability of governments of less developed countries (LDCs) to achieve integration in practice. But there is another view which has considerable relevance to present-day poverty strategies: in the words of Steven Wiggins (1986), 'concern for the rural poor evaporates very rapidly when hard-pressed administrators are still emptying their in-trays at 7 pm on Friday evening'. They often failed: money committed to rural projects was notoriously difficult to disburse, and this was seen by the said administrators, no doubt rightly, as a threat to the size of the aid budget. There were, therefore, internal as well as external reasons why the anti-poverty experiments of the 1970s eventually collapsed under their own weight.

Activity 2.1

Before continuing, ensure that you understand (a) the change in emphasis in aid policies after the early 1970s; (b) the reasons for a focus on rural development in the 1970s.

(Spend no more than 15 minutes on this activity)

2.2 Adjustment, 'new' and 'old' poverty

External reasons, however, appeared on the scene quickly, in the shape of the global economic and financial crisis of the early 1980s. Originally it looked like any other recession, triggered by the 'second oil price crisis' of 1979–80, but, as a look back to Figure 2.2 will show, it soon went out of control, and, in developing countries as a cluster, was as severe in impact as the great inter-war depression of 1929–35. What pushed it out of control was, in large measure, the reaction of northern governments and financial institutions to the crisis. Their fiscal reaction – certainly in Reagan's America, Thatcher's Britain and Kohl's Germany – was, this time, not to allow the cost of the oil price increase, or of the social security payments caused by recession, to be financed in an inflationary way: thus all budgets had to be cut. Their financial reaction, from New York to Frankfurt to Tokyo, was to pull out of the developing world on the perception that investing there was suddenly too great a risk. This atmosphere of retrenchment coincided with, and fed upon, the great global wave of disillusionment with government intervention in the economy, and desire for reform, that is described in Section 13.4 of the Course Book.* Its effect on international financial institutions – the IMF, the World Bank and aid donors – was to transform the manner in which support was given. Rather than providing project finance for development projects, including poverty-focused ones, donors increasingly came to provide policy-reform finance in support of the general wave of liberalization of government operations. In the World Bank and IMF, this was known as 'structural adjustment finance': aid conditional on liberalization of some specified cluster of markets (Box 2.1). This form of lending soon came to account for over a third of all the World Bank's operations, and in the process, as we shall see, brought it into conflict with the IMF.

*You can read these pages now to refresh your memory (pp.300–304).

Box 2.1 Conditionality

Conditionality (or, to give it its proper name, 'policy conditionality') is the practice of making a gift or loan of money conditional on the execution of particular actions. In the case of a loan by an ordinary bank, such as a mortgage, the condition consists of taking security, or collateral, to make sure that the loan is paid back. In the case of a loan or credit by the World Bank or IMF, the condition consists of required changes in policy – usually spending cuts in the case of the Fund, whereas the Bank will be more likely to ask for measures intended to expand productive capacity, such as privatization and export-promotion. Conditionality is controversial because the Bank and Fund's view of what policy reforms are needed may not coincide with the recipient government's – indeed, if it did, conditionality would be unnecessary. In addition, some conditionality, such as devaluation and the removal of food subsidies, has been accused of hurting the poor. So a great deal of conditionality, as some international financial institutions are now acknowledging, has been evaded (Mosley, Harrigan and Toye, 1995; World Bank, 2000a: Chapter 11), but in some form or another it continues, in our judgement, to be needed as a way of making aid and public expenditure accountable and effective. In particular it can be and has been used as a means of making public policy more pro-poor (for the Uganda case, see Box 2.5 below).

Activity 2.2

Listen again to the audiocassette programme for *Study Guide 1*, 'Does Dropping the Debt Miss the Point?'. In that programme, both Andrew Rogerson of the World Bank and Ann Pettifor of Jubilee 2000 speak in a gentle way of making sure that the proceeds of debt reduction are used effectively by developing countries. Rogerson says, 'Let's use this occasion to help developing countries to put into place ... better policies, strong institutions, a well-organized budget', and Pettifor says, 'We hope the donors will play a part in ensuring that proceeds of debt reduction shall be used for productive investment and poverty reduction.' Is this conditionality? If not, what is it?

(Spend no more than 30 minutes on this activity)

Comment

Our answer would be: yes, it is conditionality, but imposed with a velvet glove in the hope that the developing countries will feel they have initiated the reforms, rather than having them imposed on them.

Was the structural adjustment revolution intended to push poverty focus out of the window? The donors and international financial institutions were adamant that this was not their intention. The way the matter was put in Britain, for example by the Minister of Overseas Development speaking in Parliament on 20 February 1980, was 'to give greater weight in the allocation of our aid to political, industrial, and commercial considerations *alongside* [our emphasis] our basic development objectives'. The World Bank, in addition, forcibly argued that some poor people could expect to gain from adjustment, especially small-farm households and workers in export-based industries. What is certain is that bilateral aid budgets were cut, the language of poverty focus disappeared from common currency, and the conditions attached to developing countries' policies became exclusively preoccupied with creating an environment in which the private sector could prosper. Various pressure groups were formed at this time to put the case for the restoration of poverty focus into aid programmes, and to one of these (the Independent Group on British Aid, of which the author was a member), the Permanent Secretary of the Overseas Development Administration retorted, 'We wish you people would worry more about creating wealth, and less about how the cake is shared out' (Caines, 1983). And there is indeed a case for redistribution from growth, as put by Chenery and others in the mid-1970s. What really caused difficulty was that some parts of the developing world simply did not respond to the structural adjustment medicine. The countries of the Far East, such as Thailand and South Korea, responded the most quickly, and were virtually out of the World Bank's hands by the mid-1980s; Latin America responded more slowly; and Africa did not respond at all. Standards of living, averaged across Africa, declined continuously from 1980 to 1995, against the background of a post-war world used to continuous growth. It was here, and for a very different reason in Eastern Europe, that the 'social costs of adjustment' were greatest. In the process of this adjustment, the global map of poverty, and of solutions to it, were redrawn.

The first serious study of the poverty costs of adjustment was published, under the auspices of UNICEF, by Cornia, Jolly and Stewart in 1987. Its approach was to measure a large range of indicators of social and economic development – mortality, health, education, income, assets – across a sample of developing countries and see what had happened to these indicators over the decade of the 1980s. The shocking finding was that, in several countries of Latin America and almost universally in Africa, living standards had deteriorated, and not only had income fallen but, for the first time since the war, the human capital of these regions was deteriorating – falling educational standards, increasing morbidity (to which is now added the consequences of the AIDS epidemic) and even rising infant mortality. In previous recessions, these social indicators had kept rising even though income might be falling, but the 1980s' depression was different. As a consequence, the distribution of global poverty shifted rather sharply during the 1980s, as illustrated by Table 2.1, away from East Asia, which adjusted quickly out of the recession, and towards Africa, with South Asia more or less static. These trends were to continue during the 1990s, including deterioration in 'Europe and Central Asia' as a result of the process of adjustment in Eastern Europe. The human consequences of adjustment were more severe in Russia/Eastern Europe than elsewhere – consequences that are still being worked through.

Table 2.1 The composition of global poverty, 1980–98

Region	*Persons living on less than US$1 a day (millions; headcount index[a] in brackets)*				
	1980	*1987*	*1990*	*1996*	*1998*
East Asia and the Pacific	415.0 (31.1)	417.5 (26.6)	452.4 (27.6)	265.1 (14.9)	278.3 (15.3)
Europe and Central Asia	0.5 (0.1)	1.1 (0.2)	7.1 (1.6)	23.8 (5.1)	24.0 (5.1)
Latin America and the Caribbean	55.0 (14.5)	63.7 (15.3)	73.8 (16.8)	76.0 (15.6)	78.2 (15.6)
Middle East and North Africa	7.1 (3.0)	9.3 (4.3)	5.7 (2.4)	5.0 (1.9)	5.5 (1.9)
South Asia	465.1 (42.1)	474.4 (44.9)	495.1 (47.7)	531.7 (48.6)	522.0 (46.3)
Sub-Saharan Africa	170.5 (41.6)	217.2 (46.6)	242.3 (47.8)	289.0 (48.5)	290.9 (46.1)
Totals		1183.2 (28.3)	1276.4 (29.0)	1190.6 (24.5)	1198.9 (24.0)

[a] Percentage of people living on less than US$1 per day (measured in 1985 purchasing power parity (PPP) dollars; see also Box 1.3 in the Course Book).

Source: World Bank (2000a) *World Development Report 2000/2001: Attacking Poverty*, table 1.1, p.23.

The analysis of Cornia, Jolly and Stewart (1987) did not seek to define rigorously how much of the 'new poverty' (see Box 2.2) in Africa, South Asia and Eastern Europe was due simply to the effects of global recession, how much to extraneous events such as AIDS and how much to over-strict conditionality by the IMF and World Bank.

Box 2.2 'New and 'old' poverty

We use the term 'new poverty' to mean poverty caused by adjustment and thence by lack of global demand, rather than 'old' poverty caused by low productivity in the agricultural or urban informal sector. Much 'new' poverty, both in Africa and in Eastern Europe, occurs among former state employees made redundant by the adjustment process and unable to find jobs in the private sector. Iliffe's historical analysis of poverty in Africa (1987) distinguished between chronic and conjunctural poverty, which is very similar to the distinction made here between old and new poverty. The distinction is important because different policies are appropriate for dealing with the two types of poverty. New/conjunctural poverty can be counteracted by stimulation of global demand, whereas old/chronic poverty cannot be and requires to be dealt by actions on the ***supply side*** – such as land reform, public investment, technical education (see Tables 2.3 and 2.4 below).

There has been much controversy about this matter then and since (Sahn, 1996; Demery and Squire, 1996; Weeks, 1997). Many old and new critics of the Bank and Fund, and especially the rising influence of Northern and Southern NGOs (see the discussion in Section 2.4 below), began to weigh in against the 'Washington consensus'*, to the point of blaming it for increased child deaths across Africa and South Asia. Throughout the decade of the 1980s the Bank and Fund dug in against their critics, and appeared to wish to defend the structural adjustment strategy against all comers. The exact turning point, the publication of the Bank's first World Development Report on the poverty theme and its subsequent mainstreaming into the practice of the Bank and other institutions, did not occur until 1990. Beneath the ice, the waters were certainly moving: from 1987 onward the Bank was collecting the first significant data sets on poverty levels in Africa (the Social Dimensions of Adjustment Materials), and 1988 saw the setting up of a Programme to Mitigate the Social Costs of Adjustment (PAMSCAD) in Ghana and an Emergency Social Fund in Bolivia. These two operations followed the new model of grants by donors to private entrepreneurs for the construction of social infrastructure (roads, schools, hospitals) expected to be of benefit to poor people. They were to prove important additions to the arsenal of anti-poverty measures (see Table 2.3 below).

*See Course Book, p.40 and p.375.

We might end this discussion by asking why poverty trends in the 1980s and 1990s varied so much in different countries. Obviously part of the story is that some regions of the world, such as East Asia, grew faster than others, so that poverty fell faster there. But this is not the whole story – in much of Eastern Europe, such as Poland and the Czech Republic, there has been growth since the early 1990s, but poverty has risen. Why did 'new poverty' hit some countries worse than others?

Subsequent discussion on 'poverty elasticities' (see Box 2.3 below) will provide some data related to this question. However, part of the answer is that structural adjustment was spectacularly unsuccessful in Africa and in the former Eastern Bloc countries. In Russia, probably the worst case, poverty has risen from 2% before adjustment to between 20% and 40% (depending on one's choice of poverty measure) since.

2.3 The transformation of the Bretton Woods institutions

Exactly what was it that made the World Bank, after years of resistance, suddenly adopt a poverty agenda in 1990–91? Giovanni Andrea Cornia, one of the co-authors of the *Adjustment with a Human Face* study mentioned above, tells the following anecdote:

> We (UNICEF and others) were meeting with the President of the Bank to try and persuade him to adopt a poverty agenda, as we regularly did through 1988 and 1989. We expected a good lunch and little success from the meeting. We certainly got a good lunch – the menu read something like 'Steak Diane, $4; Tournedos Rossini, $4; Lobster Thermidor, $4.50'. I commented: "If it's all right to provide food subsidies here in the Bank, why is it wrong to do it in developing countries?" And do you know, I think the penny dropped at that point.

There is no doubt that Bank staff, over and above concerns of social conscience, felt embarrassed by the logical gap between the laisser-faire precepts in which they were seeking to instruct the developing world – in this case the elimination of food subsidies – and the practice in Western countries from which a lot of the instruction continued to come. (The decline of the Great Powers continues apace within the World Bank as elsewhere, and Smith, the commonest name in the Bank telephone book as late as 1986, has now slipped to third place behind Kim and Rodriguez, but cultural imperialism continues; see Section 2.5 below.) But it takes more than a lunchtime conversation to turn around the Bank juggernaut, let alone the Fund as well, which we shall see had also occurred by mid-decade. As we have seen, the waters were already moving within the Bank, and the turning point was the World Development Report (WDR) of 1990.

The 1990 World Development Report and the IMF

Often World Development Reports simply sit on the shelf and do not convert into changes of policy, but the 1990 World Development Report (WDR) was different. Why? There was certainly a perceived need to 'do something about Africa' given that, in spite of the Bank's protestations to the contrary (World Bank, 1994) it was clearly not responding to the structural adjustment medicine. It was actually the late 1990s before the Africa factor came together with a deeper analysis of inequalities (especially gender inequalities) to form a poverty programme to which all donors could sign up. But the 1990 report was the seed from which this programme sprang, and we must now examine it.

The 1990 WDR (World Bank, 1990) presents, in the best sense of the word, a common-sense approach to poverty alleviation summarized in Table 2.2.

Table 2.2 The 1990 World Development Report: a summary

Basic problem	*Antidote proposed in 1990 WDR*
Chronic poor have very little to sell, except labour	Labour-intensive growth path
Hence their productivity is low	Invest in the (physical and) human capital of the poor (education, health, micro-finance)
And conventional ways of enhancing it do not work for some poor (e.g. retired, disabled, subjects of discrimination)	Social safety nets, targeted on the socially excluded (typical measures: food subsidies, primary health centres)

The diagnosis is: the poorest have nothing to sell except their (often casual) labour; thus their productivity is low, and conventional ways of enhancing that productivity will leave some people still economically excluded. To that corresponds a prescription sometimes known as the 'three-legged stool':

1. *Labour intensity*, or patterns of expenditure with a strong tendency to take on labour. Small-farm agriculture and construction are particularly good at doing this.

2. *Investment in the physical and especially the human capital of the poor*, or measures by which poor people can increase their productivity – education (which often has to be targeted on girls, see below), primary health care, agricultural research and extension for small farmers, and micro-finance.

3. *Social safety nets* for those who have no access to the previous two measures – the old, the disabled and the socially excluded. In less developed countries these will typically not consist of computerized income support measures such as pensions, supplementary benefit to support incomes, and unemployment benefit; more important will be primary health, food subsidies and community development projects which will form a basis for intra-community redistribution.

Activity 2.3

Compare this prescription with the 1951 United Nations and 1975 World Bank approaches outlined in Section 2.1. To which approach do you believe it is most indebted?

(Spend no more than 15 minutes on this activity)

Comment

The emphasis on the labour market in WDR 1990 is strongly reminiscent of UN 1951 *Measures for the Economic Development of Under-developed Countries*, but this is quite compatible with World Bank 1975 *Redistribution with Growth*, as agriculture is very labour intensive. However, the WDR 1990 prescription – openly inspired by the success of East Asian countries in enabling the gains from growth to reach the many – is much less public-sector oriented than the *Redistribution from Growth* literature, and policies, of the 1970s; it mentions agriculture only in passing, and in this sense is more evocative of the 1951 United Nations than the 1975 World Bank approach.

Maybe the prescription is too inspired by the East Asian example. In poorer countries, several commentators have condemned the 'investment in the human capital of the poor' and especially the 'social safety net' nostrums as bland and politically infeasible. For example, Jesimen Chipika, critical reader for this Theme and an eminent Zimbabwean academic, says of the 1990 World Bank report:

> Unfortunately the '3-legged stool' prescription emphasizing labour intensity, physical and human capital development and social safety nets *does not* [emphasis in original] address the fundamental problem of extremely unequal access to assets and resources as the root cause of poverty and non-response to development programmes in Africa. Social safety nets are a disaster in Africa, partly because the poverty magnitude is too heavy to be captured in donor-underfunded social safety nets. I think, for [this] prescription to become a wealth redistribution tool, it has to be implemented *in heavy dose with inbuilt sustainability measures* [emphasis in original], not the current weak version. For example, local enterprise development through micro-finance support must be based on resource mobilization from the local financial sector with effective support from the donor community. Currently, in Africa, the reverse is true and programmes are therefore very vulnerable to donor conditionalities and subsequent withdrawals.
>
> (Chipika, 2001)

By 1993 the Bank's 'poverty report' had been mainstreamed: a Bank policy directive had required all countries desiring adjustment support from the Bank to be in possession of an anti-poverty strategy approved by the Bank, a *Poverty Reduction Handbook* had been produced (World Bank, 1993a) containing examples of good anti-poverty practice for NGOs to copy or adapt, and the Bank's policy conditionality had grown to embrace anti-poverty conditions (such as 'Set up Emergency Social Fund by January 1992' or 'Ensure ratio of social spending to GDP does not fall below 15%'). Many bilateral donors, including the UK Overseas Development Administration (now Department for International Development, DfID), quickly announced their intention to follow suit.

Around this time one notices something unprecedented, namely the emergence of the International Monetary Fund as a 'poverty lender' also.

This requires a little background.

Unlike the Bank, the IMF was not set up as a development institution, but simply as an emergency lender into a balance of payments crisis, in any country (for example Britain had a loan from the IMF in 1976). Under the 'Bretton Woods system' there was strict separation of powers between it and the World Bank, with the Fund having responsibility for the short term and for ***macro-analysis***, and the Bank having responsibility for the long term and for ***micro-analysis***.* All this changed with the onset of structural adjustment in the 1980s. The Bank's structural adjustment loans had macro-conditions attached in the area of ***exchange rates***, ***tax reform*** and ***public enterprise reform***; meanwhile the Fund, in pursuit of effective control over public finances, became interested in the micro-detail of ***agricultural pricing***, ***tariff reform*** and the composition of ***public expenditure programmes***. At times the two institutions would find themselves offering mutually contradictory advice, as when Morocco in 1985 was advised to raise ***tariffs*** by a Fund seeking to close the ***fiscal deficit***, and to lower them by a Bank seeking to encourage low-cost imports of equipment and other goods. In this entangled environment there arose a 'turf war' between the two institutions, which led both of them constantly to seek new spheres of influence. One of these, as its star rose again in the 1990s, was anti-poverty policy.

*To remind yourself about the discussion of the World Bank and IMF in the Course Book, see Chapter 9, pp.204–207; Chapter 13 also discusses these institutions and Bretton Woods.

Two particular stepping stones along the road to this involvement appear to have been the Fund's involvement in disarmament and the Enhanced Structural Adjustment Facility. The former arose directly from the Fund's attempt in the late 1980s to exercise control over individual budget components, rather than to set a target for the budget deficit and leave it to the client government to determine how to achieve it. The Fund began to look for areas of waste in national budgets which could be cut without cost to the national economy, and, in very many developing countries, the arms budget was an obvious candidate. To the fury of the World Bank, unused to being outflanked on the left by the Fund, the IMF was the first of the two to state this in public, at a press conference in February 1992, and by doing so it appears to have acquired a taste for humanitarian objectives. At the same time the Fund had become an aid donor through devoting a portion of its profits from gold sales to a concessional fund, the Enhanced Structural Adjustment Facility, or ESAF, which it disbursed to low-income countries on the basis of an expenditure plan agreed between Fund, World Bank and recipient government. This facility is very like conventional Bank finance:* long-term, concessional and poverty focused – indeed in 2000 it was renamed the Poverty Reduction and Growth Facility (PRGF). The Fund's rationale for broadening its operations in this way (Schadler and Bredenkamp, 1997) is to be able to provide resources over a long enough period to enable improvement in the ***structure of supply*** and public finances, without the political and economic disruption that would follow severe

*That is, the International Development Association (IDA) soft loans – see Course Book, Chapter 9, p.205.

short-term cuts in public expenditure. Evaluations by the author of this section (Mosley, 2001) suggest that the PRGF has had a positive impact on poverty by forcing poor countries to develop their own taxable capacity and thereby protect public expenditure against crisis-induced cuts, but the Fund's expertise has been challenged by critics (Collier and Gunning, 1999) within the World Bank. As we shall see, poverty reduction has become a heavily contested field.

Activity 2.4

As we saw above, the Bank and the Fund have moved from a simple to an expanded – and sometimes conflicting – set of functions over the last twenty years. Why do you think this has happened? (Refer back to the discussion in Chapters 9 and 13 in the Course Book if you wish.)

Do you sympathize with the idea that the Bank and Fund should be instructed to go back to their original functions (as at Bretton Woods in 1945)? Do you think this would be good for poverty reduction?

(Spend no more than 30 minutes on this activity)

Comment

Public bureaucracies, like private firms, have an inescapable drive towards empire-building. This leads them to diversify their functions, which may increase their own influence but may be bad for the world as a whole (this diversification is known as 'mission creep' in American English). For the World Bank and IMF, the process of mission creep is discussed briefly above and in Mosley, Harrigan and Toye (1995). Others (for example, Collier and Gunning, 1999; Meltzer, 2000) have argued strongly that mission creep should be stopped and that the Fund and Bank should revert to their original functions. The author of this section has, however, made the case that the Fund's increased concern with poverty reduction should be welcomed and preserved because that enables tax and public expenditure decisions to be taken with explicit reference to their poverty implications (Mosley, 2001).

Changing perspectives on poverty policies in the 1990s

As the 1990s progressed, three particularly important themes emerged to ornament and extend the deceptively simple analysis of the 1990 World Development Report. By 1995 development practitioners also had access to the following:

- A *macro analysis* of poverty, extending the original insight of Cornia, Jolly and Stewart that the social effects of adjustment depend on the type of policy adopted. In particular, flexible exchange rates are the most 'poverty-friendly' method of adjustment, because many poor people in export industries gain from ***devaluation***, and increases in tax rates are one of the most 'poverty-hostile', because most indirect taxes fall more heavily on the consumption of lower income groups.

- An *intra-household analysis* of poverty (e.g. Haddad and Kanbur, 1990; Agarwal, 1997), extending the question 'who are the poor?' into the analysis of who (men, women or children) gains and loses within the household. For example, one may use the approach of the World Development Report of 1990 to achieve labour intensity, but the achievement of labour intensity may be compatible with many males and no females being absorbed into the labour force, or with females within the labour force being forced to work longer hours for the same pay. Policy- and institution-building need to be aware of such biases.
- A *vulnerability-based analysis* of poverty, again taking off from the premise that poverty is more than the mere absence of material goods and services, and embraces a risk dimension. Risk analysis of poverty had made a brief but distinguished appearance in the 1970s in the context of small-farm household allocation decisions; the 'new risk analysis' picks up on a much broader range of the lived experiences of poor people to cover every kind of insecurity, including – as a particularly important cause of underdevelopment in many of the poorest countries – the risk of war (Cornia, Stewart and Vayrynen, 2001).

All of this new richness of approach makes it no longer possible for donors and international financial institutions to adopt a scattergun approach, taking aim at the ***headcount index*** of poverty and firing as hard as possible. Rather, they must choose between an unprecedentedly wide range of options, operating at several levels and taking note of locally specific differences in effectiveness between policy options as articulated in the priorities of the poor themselves. To help clarify what the range of options is, it will be useful at this point to list the spectrum of possibilities. Table 2.3 seeks to do this, distinguishing between three levels of intervention:

- the macro level of the entire economy;
- the meso level of the policies which operate on particular sectors, or transfer resources between sectors;
- the micro level of policies which operate to influence particular markets.

Figure 2.4 Interventions at the meso and micro levels can help generate income, from crop production to construction.

Table 2.3 Anti-poverty institutions and policies: a map

Level of intervention	*Approach required*	*'Recommendable' policies and institutions*	*'Best experience' cases*
Macro	(1) Carry out macro-economic stabilization so as to do least damage to poor	Adjust, via exchange-rate depreciation, erosion of public sector real wages, not dismissals of public servants or increases in indirect taxes	Uganda 1990–, Mauritius 1980–82, Indonesia 1980–97
	(2) Build up 'social capital' (WDR 2000/2001)	Establishment of reputation for trust by government (note: also measures at local level, see (4) (9) and (10) below)	
Meso	(3) Redirect resources to labour-intensive sectors (WDR 1990)	Avoid taxing employment; avoid subsidizing capital; promote small-scale enterprise, Green Revolution (see (8) below), primary health and education	South Korea, Indonesia, Thailand, 1970–
	(4) Poverty-conscious restructuring of public expenditures (Ferroni and Kanbur, 1990)	Within sectors, target labour-intensive crops, construction methods, industrial and energy technologies such as micro-hydro; support informal sector	
	(5) 'Multi-sector social funds' (donor-funded funds for reconstruction of social infrastructure such as schools, health centres, water supplies)	Must be demand-led; institutional autonomy required; co-ordination with line ministries needed	Bolivia: Emergency Social Fund
Micro	(6) Social safety nets (WDR 1990)/social risk management (WDR 2000/2001)	Self-targeting measures such as guaranteed availability of basic foods; also disaster relief and preparedness	Tanzania: Ngara refugee programme for Rwandese; Malawi: Mozambican refugee programme
	(7) Public employment schemes (Ravallion, 1991)	Labour-intensive public works	India: Maharashtra Employment Guarantee Programme; Zambia: World Food Programme

continued overleaf…

Level of intervention	*Approach required*	*'Recommendable' policies and institutions*	*'Best experience' cases*
	(8) Adoption of high-yielding food-crop varieties by smallholders (Lipton and Longhurst, 1989)	Applicable to all crops cultivable by smallholders but 'poor people's crops'. In dry areas, sorghum, millets, etc. especially relevant	Indonesia, China 1976–, India and Pakistan Punjab, Zimbabwe 1981–86, some high-density districts of Kenya, Uganda, Zimbabwe, South Africa
	(9) Asset redistribution (WDR 2000/2001)	Land reform, blended with pro-poor research, rural infrastructure reform, marketing etc (note: complementary factors of production (such as water rights) can also be transferred to the asset-poor through loan programmes, see (10)	South Africa 1994–; Malaysia: Federal Land Development Authority (FELDA) oil palm and rubber settlement schemes; Proshika (Bangladesh) for water rights redistribution
	(10) Downward extension of credit markets and other measures against financial exclusion (Hulme and Mosley, 1996)	Group lending (often female-biased); built-in insurance and savings and other risk management devices	Group schemes: Bangladesh: Grameen Bank and Bangladesh Rural Advancement Committee (BRAC); Bolivia: BancoSol, Programma para el Desarrollo de la Microempresa (PRODEM) and Asociación Nacional Ecuménica de Desarrollo (ANED); Indonesia: Bank Rakyat Indonesia (BRI) and Badan Kredit Kecamantan (BKK); South Africa: Small Enterprise Foundation
	(11) Broadening of base of educational and health programmes (WDR 1993, etc.)	Priority to primary sector; pro-female bias	

What options have the waves of anti-poverty strategy which we have so far considered chosen in relation to this list? A preliminary list of answers is given in Table 2.3, which sets out the main options available at the macro, meso and micro levels. In relation to each of the possible options, we ask, in the third column, 'What is the most effective way of implementing this strategy in principle?' and in the final column, 'Is there a case where the strategy has been effectively implemented in practice?'. In the case of the macro option 1, for example (***minimum social cost adjustment***), the approach suggested by available policy research indicates (column 3) that adjustment should mainly be done by means of changes in exchange rates rather than changes in taxation, and also (column 4) that this approach has been particularly effectively managed by the countries indicated in that column – Indonesia, Uganda and Mauritius. A typical strategy consists of a cluster of options – for example, the 'World Bank 1990' strategy which we examined earlier consists of a combination of options 3 (labour-intensive growth), 10 and 11 (investment in the human capital of the poor) and 6 (social safety nets).

Anti-poverty strategies chosen varied over time, as shown in Table 2.4.* Broadly speaking, the menu of the 1970s is more project-based, state-implemented and *dirigiste* (top-down): the menu of the 1990s is more market-based, NGO-implemented (as we shall see in Section 2.4) and outwith the direct control of the state and aid donors. But the menu is in continuous evolution, and the practitioners of the 'new poverty strategies' have had ten years of experience with which to evaluate those strategies. What have they learned, and what are the lessons for future anti-poverty action? We consider this issue in Activity 2.5.

*See also the Course Book, Tables 2.1 and 2.2, pp.29 and 43.

Activity 2.5

Examine the policy options listed in Table 2.3. Which of these options do you see as politically difficult, and which as politically straightforward, for the World Bank and the IMF to persuade developing countries to accept?

(Spend no more than 15 minutes on this activity)

Comment

In relation to this question we might ask whether there is any interest group which is likely to be hurt by the proposed action, and whether there are any developing countries in which this interest group has substantial power enabling it to resist change? For example, land reform and other forms of asset redistribution (option 9) are politically difficult, because they will obviously attract opposition from landowners, especially if they feel they will not be adequately compensated (as in Zimbabwe at the time of writing – August 2001). Recently, the World Bank has shown increasing awareness of political feasibility considerations, and there is a useful discussion of these issues in the most recent World Development Report, *Attacking Poverty* (World Bank, 2000a).

Table 2.4 Three waves of pro-poor development policy: preferred policy options

Numbers in bold relate to policy options indexed in Table 2.3 above.

Poverty strategy level of intervention	*United Nations, 1951*	*'Redistribution with growth' strategies of the 1970s*	*World Development Report 1990*
Macro	Maximize savings, thence investment rate	Aid donors: support poor countries only	'Least social cost' macro-adjustment measures **(1)**
Meso			Support labour-intensive sectors and strategies which encourage the use of labour (e.g. subsidize labour, not capital) **(3)** Restructure public expenditure so that it meets needs of poor people **(4)** Social funds/social safety nets **(5/6)**
Micro	Raise productivity of smallholders **(8)** and labour intensity of industry **(3)**	Support for informal sector Integrated rural development, of which employment guarantee schemes **(7)** are a component Land reform **(9)** – much advocated, but in practice usually financed from domestic sources, not aid	Investment in human capital of poor (i.e. primary health and education **(11)**, micro-finance **(10)**

Measuring and evaluating poverty reduction

*See Box 13.1 in the Course Book for details of composition.

In 1996 there was sufficient consensus around the poverty focus approach among donors to achieve joint acceptance by OECD* ministers of a set of long-term targets relating to extreme poverty (which must be halved by 2015), mortality, health and education. The World Bank has suggested that progress so far towards the targets is good on extreme poverty but poor on health (Figure 2.6). However, progress is very variable across regions. On the main target, the goal of halving extreme poverty by 2015, progress appears to be well above target in East Asia, more or less on target in South Asia and well below target in most of Eastern Europe and Africa. What is interesting, of course, is why achievement exceeds or falls short of target.

We measure achievement in terms of the 'poverty elasticity' (Box 2.3): the ratio of change in poverty over a specified time period to change in output, or the rate at which increased growth 'delivers' reduced poverty. (Note that this is basically an *economic* measure.)

Box 2.3 Poverty elasticities

The 'poverty elasticity' is simply the ratio of change in a selected indicator of poverty to change in output over a defined time period:

> Poverty elasticity = % change in poverty indicator ÷ % change in total output

For example: if poverty decreases by 10% while GDP rises by 5%, the poverty elasticity is 10/5 = −2.

(Note that if poverty declines as growth increases – the normal case – the poverty elasticity is *negative*, as in a negative correlation where one variable declines as the other increases; whereas in the converse case where poverty increases with growth the poverty elasticity is *positive*.)

Potentially, the poverty elasticity is a powerful tool for predicting the change in poverty which can be expected from a particular policy or institutional initiative: for example, a study by Hanmer and Naschold (2001), discussed below, used poverty elasticities for specific countries and regions to predict the likelihood of achievement of particular development targets. As we shall see in Section 2.5, they have also been used to evaluate alternative aid policies.

As may be seen from Table 2.5, poverty elasticities vary enormously across countries, and are perversely *positive* (i.e. poverty increases with growth) for many Eastern European countries in the second half of the 1990s. We now also know that they vary across time, which has not yet been properly analysed but puts at risk long-term predictions such as those of Hanmer and Naschold.

In addition, the data for Asia 1990–98 (the second and third columns) are a bit misleading because they are based on small samples and short time periods and do not have weighted averages. The figures for 1980–98 are more trustworthy in terms of indicating the trend during that period.

It is likely that national-level poverty elasticity will respond over time to some of the measures listed in Table 2.4. The key question of course is which. For Uganda and Tanzania, there is some evidence that poverty elasticity responds to the ***intersectoral mix of public expenditure*** (such as options 3 and 4 in Table 2.3). The 1990 World Development Report recommended that this mix should be shifted in a labour-intensive direction, while others have recommended that there should be shifts of expenditure within sectors, for example focusing on primary rather than secondary health care (Ferroni and Kanbur, 1990). Some examples of strategy on public expenditure in the case of Uganda are in Section 2.5, Box 2.5 below.

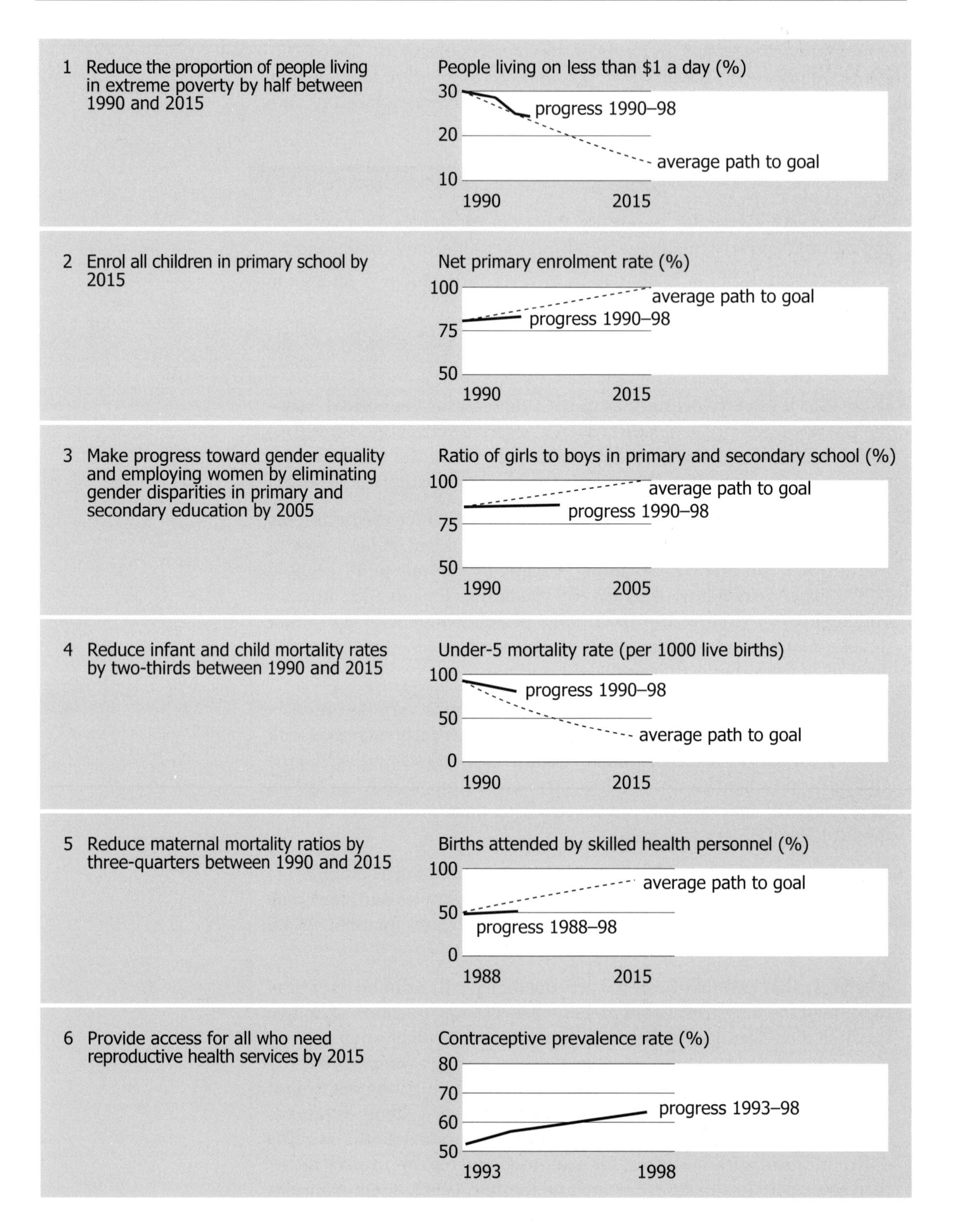
1 Reduce the proportion of people living in extreme poverty by half between 1990 and 2015
People living on less than $1 a day (%)
30
20
10
progress 1990–98
average path to goal
1990
2015
2 Enrol all children in primary school by 2015
Net primary enrolment rate (%)
100
75
50
average path to goal
progress 1990–98
1990
2015
3 Make progress toward gender equality and employing women by eliminating gender disparities in primary and secondary education by 2005
Ratio of girls to boys in primary and secondary school (%)
100
75
50
average path to goal
progress 1990–98
1990
2005
4 Reduce infant and child mortality rates by two-thirds between 1990 and 2015
Under-5 mortality rate (per 1000 live births)
100
50
0
progress 1990–98
average path to goal
1990
2015
5 Reduce maternal mortality ratios by three-quarters between 1990 and 2015
Births attended by skilled health personnel (%)
100
50
0
average path to goal
progress 1988–98
1988
2015
6 Provide access for all who need reproductive health services by 2015
Contraceptive prevalence rate (%)
80
70
60
50
progress 1993–98
1993
1998

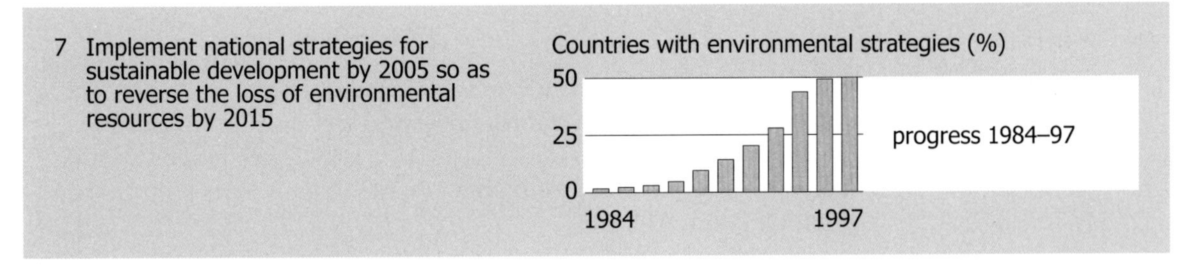

Figure 2.5 International development targets.

Table 2.5 Estimated poverty elasticities

	1985–89	1990–94	1995–98	1980–98	
		Using international poverty line[a]		*Using international poverty line*	*Using national poverty line*
Asia	–0.61	1.9	9.6		–0.86
Africa	–1.13	–1.4	–20.7		–0.79
Latin America	0.44	–0.78	–16.2		–1.76
Eastern Europe		–16.8	24.5	24.5	
All developing countries	–0.43	–2.46	–13.8	–0.47	–0.97
Number of observations	6	10	8	36	14

[a] ***International poverty line***: US$1/day (1985 PPP dollars; see Course Book, p.10–11).

Source: OU/Sheffield/Cambridge/Nottingham pro-poor growth project, funded by the UK Department for International Development (DfID): unpublished data, mostly derived from World Development Reports.

A study by Hanmer and Naschold (2001) sought to forecast which regions would be likely to achieve the development targets, and which policies might accelerate progress towards them. Apart from confirming that East Asia would be very likely, and Africa very unlikely, to achieve the targets, Hanmer and Naschold came up with one major finding: that progress towards the targets was strongly and negatively correlated with the level of *inequality* in a country: where inequality is relatively low (e.g. East Asia), progress is fast, and where inequality is high (e.g. Russia, South Africa and most parts of Latin America), progress is slow. This may look obvious but is not, and there is a large literature within the World Bank insisting that absolute poverty, not relative inequality, is the key policy target. So how are the two concepts connected in practice?

There are two likely connections:

- Where inequality is relatively low (as a consequence of the existence of a large and prosperous urban working class) there is the possibility of initially ***home-based industrialization*** and eventually ***export-based industrialization*** (as in East Asia), which has proved a much more effective model for reducing poverty than exports of primary products (as in Africa).
- Where inequality is relatively high, the potential is greater for tension between social groups. This may be papered over through ***inflationary expenditure*** by central government (as in Zambia and much of Latin America in the 1980s, or Russia in 1998) or it may emerge as open conflict (Peru 1985–95, South Africa from 1976 onward, Zimbabwe (Southern Rhodesia) in the 1970s and again today). Whichever way these latent tensions are responded to, production is disrupted, and the potential for poverty reduction is diminished.

This connection represents one of the key empirical lessons which have to be taken on board in planning the next generation of anti-poverty initiatives. Other lessons emerge from an audit of poverty-focused projects conducted in 1998–99 by the World Bank's Operations Evaluation Department (World Bank, 2000b). In particular, the Bank compared various qualitative dimensions of poverty impact in respect of the policy options listed in Table 2.3 as social funds (5), public employment schemes (7) and micro-finance (10). The evaluation did not try to assess impact in terms of a number, but rather looked for evidence of ***comparative advantage*** for particular policy instruments – which policy instruments are best at carrying out which jobs in which environments. The Bank's interim answers are set out in Table 2.6.

The lessons of Table 2.6 are experimental and qualitative: but they suggest that public employment schemes (option 7) are relatively good and micro-finance (option 10) relatively bad at reaching the poorest. They suggest that micro-finance and social funds (option 5) are relatively *sustainable,* i.e. potentially pay for themselves (this is a very important consideration in the reform of the welfare state in industrialized countries). Finally, they suggest that micro-finance and employment schemes can be *scaled up* in suitable conditions to reach a large number of beneficiaries, but cannot easily be *replicated* into culturally different environments. These comparisons illuminate some of the range of criteria that have to be satisfied in comparing across and choosing between anti-poverty policies.

Other lessons can be learned from the Operations Evaluation Department report, in particular a feeling that 'aid co-ordination has been weak, and over-heavy conditionality has undermined the ownership of anti-poverty strategies by recipient governments' (Evans, 2000). This lesson blends together two key themes of recent discourse on poverty – the conception,

Table 2.6 World Bank 'intuitions' on poverty impact of different measures

Criterion		*Social funds (option 5)*	*Micro-finance (option 10)*	*Public employment schemes/food for work (option 7)*
Targeting		Weak; non-poor do slightly better in demand-driven systems	Loan size an important indicator of how poor is the target group that will be reached	Self-targeting via low wage is effective
Institutional capacity	(i) Financial	Tend to be aid dependent	Good, usually high repayment	Tend to depend on 'external' finance
	(ii) Organization			Need a 'shelf' of plans, to avoid political pressure
Poverty effects	(i) Individual	Little known, but employment effects tend to be modest	Potentially good, but not for the very poorest. Positive private returns	Temporary relief of poverty. Need for complementary actions to get at causes
	(ii) Community	Little known except for improvement in social infrastructure	Indications of positive social returns	Stock of infrastructure improved. Some increase in local wages
Long-run and side effects		Capacity-building/ performance-based management	Can support/build local institutional capacity	Infrastructure side effects/some support for local organizations
Replicability, scaling-up		Replication possible, scaling-up and sustainability more problematic	Scaling-up possible, but replication very successful	Scaling-up possible, but difficulties in replication

Source: Adapted from World Bank *Development Assistance and Poverty Reduction*, Operations Evaluation Department (unpublished report).

going back to the work of Robert Chambers and others in the 1980s, that effective development strategies should be bottom-up and not top-down, and the sudden admission by the World Bank in the late 1990s, after twenty years of attempting to enforce conditionality, that it actually did not work very well (Mosley, Harrigan and Toye, 1995). This 'lesson', like those set out in Table 2.6, has been a key element, as we shall see, in the framing of anti-poverty strategies at the beginning of the twenty-first century.

Activity 2.6

Table 2.6 uses five criteria (targeting, institutional development, poverty impact, long-run and side effects, and possibilities for scaling-up) to choose between alternative anti-poverty options (social funds, micro-finance, public employment/food for work). From your study of this Theme so far (including the Introduction in Part 1) what other criteria do you think might be used?

Targeting (criterion 1) is the endeavour to confine benefits to the poor only. You read a discussion of a targeting approach in the UK in the article by Maxwell and Kenway in Section 1 of this Theme. You may also know of targeting from other parts of the world.

- How can targeting be done?
- What costs are associated with targeting?
- Finally, what are examples of using *financial sustainability* (ability to pay for itself) as a possible criterion for choice between anti-poverty options?

(Spend no more than 1 hour on this activity)

Comment

Some possible criteria are the concepts of poverty used by Judith Scott in the Introduction in Part 1. In addition to low income, these were multiple deprivations, capability failure, social exclusion, and relational and residual poverty. Thus criteria for choosing anti-poverty strategies might include whether incomes were raised, whether a range of deprivations was addressed, whether capabilities were enhanced, whether poor people were included in general processes of social life, etc. Thus, we could use these criteria to begin to assess the same policy instruments. To assess them, we might want to ask further questions about the instruments. You might want to jot down some thoughts from your reading in this course so far in relation to the questions listed in the table at the end of this comment (the audiocassette for this Theme might also be of help here).

You may also find Table 2.2 of 'main views of development' in the Course Book (p.43) useful in deciding how to evaluate anti-poverty policies.

In relation to the specific issue of targeting, Maxwell and Kenway discuss some of the foci (elderly, small children) and instruments (pension support, Sure Start) used in a UK context. They also discuss the administrative costs. To minimize these costs, an approach often adopted is 'self-targeting': the provision of benefits that only the poor will seek to take up, so that no means tests or other administrative costs of targeting arise. Soup kitchens, or work at a very low wage, or (arguably) the provision of very small loans, are examples of self-targeted benefits.

In terms of financial sustainability, the most self-financing anti-poverty option is micro-finance. There is a very large literature on this, and we come back to some of the pros and cons of micro-finance in Section 4 on 'Action on poverty and inequality'. You will have seen from the video and audiocassette for this Theme that micro-finance, if successful, ensures funds continue to be available. Public employment and food-for-work schemes are potentially financially sustainable, not necessarily in direct terms but because they generate other, linked, activity in the economy, as might social funds.

Criteria	*Questions to be asked*	*Social funds*	*Micro-finance*	*Public employment and food for work*
Increases incomes	Which groups benefit?			
Reduces a range of deprivations	How are such deprivations as ill health addressed by these instruments?			
Enhances capabilities	How are skills developed?			
Leads to social inclusion	How do poor people participate in local affairs and decision-making through these instruments?			
Changes social relations in favour of poor people	Do these instruments have redistributive effects?			

The 2000/2001 World Development Report and the IMF

When what one may call the 'second generation' of anti-poverty strategies was unveiled between 1997 and 2000 – for example, two UK White Papers published by the UK Department for International Development (DfID), and the World Bank's 2000/2001 World Development Report *Attacking Poverty* – there was therefore plenty of feedback from previous efforts to go on. We shall focus for the moment on the 2000/2001 WDR. In addition to absorbing the lessons mentioned above, this document began from a quite different vision of poverty and its alleviation from the 1990 Report. Rather than conceptualizing poverty as the *lack of particular material attributes*, such as income, the 2000/2001 report sees poverty in terms of a range of material and psychological characteristics of which an important one is *vulnerability*.* This vision, unlike what we have called the 'common-sense' vision of the 1990 report, is derived in large part from the testimony of poor people themselves, such as the Bulgarian who stated to the WDR team 'to be well is to know what will happen to me tomorrow' (quoted in World Bank, 2000a, p.135). Such a vision of what well-being is inevitably leads to a different set of anti-poverty prescriptions, targeted less at income and more at the concept of *livelihood security* – protection of assets, including social assets such as family and extra-family connections, against risks which threaten to damage them.

*Refer back to Section 1.3, Box 1.3, for the World Bank view of vulnerability and for Moser's definition of vulnerability a little later in that section.

Figure 2.6 World Bank President James Wolfensohn at the time of the WDR 2000/2001 fields questions during a press conference in Washington, April 2001.

A related component of the Bank's new vision is its insistence on *empowerment* as a dimension of well-being – again, there is an attempt to escape from a purely economistic concept of poverty as lack of income, towards a broader concept of poverty as lack of control over one's environment, physical and social. There is an overlap, on most definitions, with the concept of livelihood security, but whereas the focus there is on certainty of outcomes, the focus here is on the poor person's control over those outcomes.* Again, the new vision emerges from the testimonies of poor people, rather than that of the World Bank, which have been anthologized in the *Voices of the Poor* series, referred to in Section 1.

*Much has been discussed and written about the approach of the WDR 2000/2001. If you are interested in pursuing it further, one example is Hubbard (2001), listed in Appendix 3.

The Bank's new approach to poverty reduction (Table 2.7) thus emerges from a combination of empirical 'lessons' and a changed vision of what poverty is, with an emphasis on the latter. Like the 1990 Report, that of 2000/2001 rests on three pillars of wisdom, but whereas the legs of the stool in 1990 were labour intensity, investment in the human capital of the poor and social safety nets, those of 2000 are the somewhat snappier 'opportunity, security and empowerment'. As illustrated by Table 2.7, opportunity and security are the lineal descendants of 'investment in the human capital of the poor' and social safety nets respectively, but empowerment is a quite new theme. And labour intensity has disappeared off the map – though not because it has become any less true in the twenty-first century that the extremely poor derive most of their income from casual labour only. It remains the case, emphasized rather than downplayed by the 2000/2001 Report, *that the chronically very poor are those with no assets at all* – and therefore forced, by definition, to depend either on labour or on connections of some kind for their livelihood.

Table 2.7 1990 and 2000/2001 World Development Reports: themes and associated policy recommendations

1990		*2000/2001*	
'Pillars'	*Associated policies*	*'Pillars'*	*Associated policies*
Labour intensity	Small-scale industry; special employment measures; promotion of Green Revolution in small-farm agriculture		
Investment in the human capital of the poor	Promotion of primary health and education, especially amongst females; micro-finance	Opportunity	Micro-finance; land reform and other asset redistribution policies; fiscal, etc., measures to reduce inequality; 'pro-poor' public expenditure patterns
Social safety nets	Food subsidies, social funds	Security	'Tailor-made' social protection measures; measures to support asset diversification; insurance; 'international public good' defences against economic crisis, e.g. financial regulation; conflict prevention
		Empowerment	Democratization, decentralization; measures to build 'social capital'

Activity 2.7

Go back to the 'map' of policy options in Table 2.3. Once poverty is redefined (as in WDR, 2000a) in terms of the perceptions of the poor themselves, which of the policy options listed in Table 2.3 becomes more attractive, and which less attractive, once vulnerability rather than material poverty is used as the indicator of need?

(Spend no more than 10 minutes on this activity)

Comment

Measures which protect livelihoods and make them less insecure, such as insurance or savings (option 10) or irrigation and disease-resistant seeds (option 3), are clearly attractive. Social safety nets (option 6) can also reduce risk, while asset redistribution (option 9) such as land reform can change the social relations that make poor people vulnerable by improving their asset base. Often such processes need other infrastructure (roads, transport, credit) to be successful.

Two other themes of the 2000/2001 World Development Report deserve to be given emphasis, both of them new and old at the same time. The first is a discussion of, and an attempt to offset, *processes of impoverishment* rather than simply the state of being poor. The Report contains the following moving passage:

> Extreme poverty deprives people of almost all means of managing risk by themselves. With few or no assets, ***self-insurance*** is impossible. With poor health and bad nutrition, working more or sending more household members to work is difficult. And with ***high default risks***, ***group insurance mechanisms*** are often closed off.
>
> The poorest households thus face extremely unfavorable tradeoffs [i.e. 'options']. When a shock occurs, they must obtain immediate increases in income or cut spending, but in so doing they incur a long-term cost by jeopardizing their economic and human development prospects. These are the situations that lead to child labor and malnourishment, with lasting damage to children, and the breakdown of families.
>
> (World Bank, 2000a, p.146)

Some of the elements in this characterization are open to question. In particular, there is a lively debate about whether and where child labour causes 'lasting damage to children'.* But the important thing is the new focus on cumulative, indeed inter-generational, processes of impoverishment. Such a focus is also a feature of both historical and present-day research on poverty in industrialized countries (Horrell, 2000). In its application to the global poverty literature this focus is both new and old. The presentation of a vicious circle of ***decapitalization*** in *individuals* and *households* is new, but the more general concept of a vicious circle of poverty goes back to the 1950s, for example in Myrdal's 1957 'principle of circular and cumulative causation'. Rubbished by the neoliberal establishment of the 1980s, the concept of cumulative causation has now won back its place in the sun.

*You will come across the issue of child labour and its effects again in Section 4 on 'Action on poverty and inequality'. There is also brief discussion of child labour in the Course Book, pp.134–135.

The other 'new and old' element in the Bank's new poverty agenda is the case of asset transfer, such as land reform. Historically, land reform has been a key element in strategies of poverty reduction all over the developing world, often as a part of the decolonization process and in Latin America going back as far as the Zapata revolution in Mexico in 1911 (see Box 2.4). It appears in Table 2.3 as 'option 9', but again was pushed politically off-limits for the international financial institutions during the structural adjustment period of the 1980s. It has now regained its respectability (World Bank, 2000a), with the caveat that what is acceptable is *voluntary* and *compensated* transfers, as in South Africa at the present time, for example, rather than Zimbabwe.

Bilateral donors have, with exceptions, tended to follow rather than lead the World Bank view. Certainly the Bank was the leader in the return to poverty focus in the early 1990s, with even the Scandinavians following only slowly. But it was the UK Department for International Development (DfID)

Box 2.4 'The Zapata revolution' in Mexico

Emiliano Zapata was an agricultural leader in the south of Mexico who fought for land reform and social justice. In 1911, he drew up the Plan de Ayala which proposed that land should be nationalized (a reference to the strong North American interests and control over land), that lands seized by Mexican *latifundistas* (large landowners) should be returned to their rightful owners, and that a third of the remaining land held by the latifundistas be expropriated and redistributed. A violent struggle for land reform went on for 10 years, and was actually implemented in radical form in Zapata's own department of Morelos. Zapata was assassinated in 1919 and it was not until the presidency of Lázaro Cárdenas (1934–40) that a nationwide land reform was implemented (Galeano, 1973, pp.134–139).

which, in its first White Paper of 1997, anticipated the movement away from conditionality by announcing its intention to follow a policy of 'partnership' in which core support only – mainly to the health and education sectors – is given to non-trusted governments, with substantial debt relief and sector aid confined to those who already practise good policies. (On the ups and downs of conditionality, you may want to recall Box 2.1 above.) DfID also, in the same White Paper, announced its intention to favour governments which practised ethical trade and labour policies, even though implementation of this approach is complicated (DfID, 1997). This could be seen as a new form of conditionality. However, as just discussed, conditionality is difficult, and some 'unethical practices' such as child labour may, according to recent research, be positive rather than negative for the livelihoods of the poor (Basu and Van, 1998). In a second White Paper on globalization, of December 2000, DfID acknowledged that the significance of aid, its 'traditional' business, is declining in relation to other North–South relationships, including trade, investment and labour migration (DfID, 2000a). Its insistence that the maintenance of open markets in all these is good for the poor has brought it suddenly into conflict with the NGOs (see Section 2.4 below).

The status of the IMF's new poverty reduction mission is more interesting, because more contested. Until 1998 there was a reasonable measure of acceptance, even in the World Bank, that as the Fund found itself working in deficit countries with ever more fragile political systems and ever more fragile ***supply sides*** to their economy, it needed to make explicit provision for that fragility by extending the loan repayment term and the period over which budgetary balance could be expected to be attained. This is the thinking which motivated first of all the Fund's Extended Facility of 1974, and eventually also the ESAF/PRGF (Poverty Reduction and Growth Facility). Indeed, in Mozambique in 1996, it was the Bank that persuaded the Fund to extend the term of its recovery loan, in pursuit of what turned out to be a very successful process of poverty-reducing growth.

All this changed in the wake of the East Asian crisis of 1997–98, which in its turn spread to Russia and Brazil and, by contagion, became a global threat. So close did the world come at that time to the spectre of another mass default that in the winter of 1998–99 a procession of experts came to the microphone to argue that the Fund's long-term lending facilities (including the PRGF) should be cut back in order to preserve its essential mission of emergency balance-of-payments support. The US Secretary to the Treasury Laurence Summers, for example, argued:

> The IMF should focus on its core competency of preventing crises and mitigating them if they occur (by providing short-term financing for countries threatened by ***balance of payments problems***, financial contagion or market panics). The Fund should not be a source of low-cost financing for countries with ready access to private capital, or long-term welfare that cannot break the habit of bad policies.
>
> (Summers, 1999)

This message was supported by editorials in the UK press such as the *Financial Times*, the *Economist* and the *Independent,* and significantly by a senior member (P. Collier) of the World Bank's economics staff (Collier and Gunning, 1999). The recommendation that the Fund should abandon the function of long-term concessional lending (i.e. poverty reduction lending) also formed a key component of the argument of the American government's Meltzer report (of February 2000) on the post-crisis redesign of the international financial system.

In spite of this barrage, it is at the time of writing not at all clear what the Fund's future poverty stance will be. Its positioning as a key poverty reduction player was in many ways the personal initiative of its Managing Director during much of the 1990s, Michel Camdessus, who in his farewell speech at the United Nations Conference on Trade and Development (UNCTAD)* on 13 February 2000 described the Fund as 'the best friend of the poor' (Figure 2.7). His successor, Horst Köhler (see Figure 2.1 above), has less intellectual baggage requiring him to commit to this programme.* By contrast, the trauma associated with the East Asian/Russian/Brazilian crisis of 1997–99 is now further removed, and so the pressures pull both ways.

*See Course Book, p.201, for a map of the UN system of agencies.

*See Reading 3 by Köhler in Appendix 2.

The interesting feature of the developments described in this section, with particular reference to poverty, is that they all pull in one direction – that of increased and diversified responsibility, and reduced specialization, for all the players in the game. Under the Bretton Woods system of 1945, this specialization was very clear: the General Agreement on Tariffs and Trade (GATT)* would take responsibility for trade liberalization, the IMF would look after emergency balance-of-payments lending, the Bank with support from aid donors would look after long-term lending, and the NGOs were off the map. Now the IMF has moved into long-term and poverty lending (and become more like the Bank), the NGOs have moved into service delivery and advocacy (and become more like the Bank) and the Bank has moved into adjustment lending, trade liberalization, and short-term

*GATT was succeeded by the World Trade Organization (WTO) in 1995. See also Course Book, Chapter 13, Section 13.1, for a brief history of Bretton Woods agreements.

Figure 2.7 Former International Monetary Fund Managing Director Michel Camdessus addressing the UN Conference on Trade and Development (UNCTAD) in Bangkok in February 2000.

poverty reduction (and thereby become like the Fund, the WTO and an NGO all at the same time). It is this muddying of what was once a clean and simple division of labour that Summers was trying to undo. But on one view of the future, this muddying is an inevitable consequence of a struggle between bureaucracies for 'territory'. On this view, poverty (relief) has become a fashionable territory which any international financial institution neglects at its peril, and so those institutions find themselves obligated to colonize that territory and defend their gains. Is this imperative inescapable – and can it, should it, be regulated from outside?

It is time, for the moment, to leave this as an open question. In the concluding section we return to this question and to an associated one: amid all this competitive rush to embrace a poverty agenda amongst the different development institutions – some of it quite radical – what has happened to structural adjustment and liberalization? Has the 'Washington consensus'* collapsed, or is poverty focus simply a more rose-coloured way of expressing the same neoliberal ideology? After bringing on to the stage a new and increasingly important actor – the NGOs – we shall address this topic in the following section.

*'Washington consensus': see Course Book, p.40.

2.4 International institutions and non-governmental organizations

We cannot pretend here to give a complete account of the role of non-governmental organizations (NGOs) in the fight against global poverty, nor in their influence on policy development. This brief section scrutinizes the perceptions of, and relationships with, the international institutions we have discussed so far.*

*You can also refer to the short section on NGOs in the Course Book, pp.210–215.

Prior to the 1980s, many NGOs had a defined role in development as the managers of short-term relief projects – visualized as 'consumption' activities aimed at reducing the destitution of households afflicted by economic emergency, rather than as 'investment' activities which might hold out hope of improving a country's development prospects. The NGOs were thus often seen by the international institutions as a form of stop-gap, much as the IMF performed emergency support operations on macro-economies before handing over the 'rehabilitating patient' to the World Bank. The possibility that they could become involved in operations to achieve 'sustainable poverty reduction' was not foreseen; neither was their political, or advocacy, role that we see today.

As with the World Bank, the 1980s was the decade when everything changed, especially in the following four ways:

1 The Northern NGOs, in multiple, documented the costs of structural adjustment for the poor, and heavily lobbied the Bank (in particular) to get them mitigated, through debt relief, through a softening of policy conditionality and by standing out against the expenditure cuts imposed by the IMF – which they saw as their main adversary. In the process their 'advocacy function', hitherto a small and questioned part of NGO operations, moved centre stage, and in the process the NGOs, not accidentally, found themselves more and more at the top negotiating table.

2 Under the stress of adjustment, many governments (especially in Africa) savagely cut all kinds of developmental services – health, extension, education, agricultural credit and research, legal advice, etc. The southern NGOs picked up the mantle and thereby took over a number of state functions – to the point where, in Kenya and Bangladesh for example, the poor look more to them than to government for support. In Bangladesh, for example, one NGO (the Bangladesh Rural Advancement Committee, or BRAC) provides primary health care, vaccinations, adult education, legal advice, and advice on agricultural extension and environmental protection, on top of its basic function of the provision of financial services – all of them functions previously assumed by the state (Figure 2.8).

Figure 2.8 A self-employment centre run with small credit provided by BRAC. These Bangladeshi women joined a craft group to earn an income. However, participation has also increased their confidence and status.

3 This process was welcomed by aid donors seeking, as part of the process of structural adjustment, an 'exit route' in the shape of competition for inefficient and corrupt government services. Initially, of course, they had wished to privatize state functions and to turn them over to the private business sector. But services for the poor are not at all easy to privatize in the conventional way – no private company will find it lucrative to take them on. This left the door open for the entry of local and international NGOs with a charitable, pro-poor, not-for-profit function. (Jesimen Chipika, the Zimbabwean academic cited above, comments: 'I am more comfortable with the advocacy role [of NGOs] than I am with the service delivery outcome. In service delivery, while NGOs are said to be more effective in reaching the poor compared to conventional government institutions, reality is showing that NGOs are either too small for any meaningful developmental impact or have become huge inefficient bureaucratic institutions in themselves, chewing up a lot of money in administration rather than delivering the said services to the poor.') The growth, in the 1990s, of donor concern to build up a vibrant, participatory 'civil society' gave further impetus to this process: NGOs could be expected not only to take over some of the economic functions of the state, but also to develop the 'social capital', without which, especially in societies riven by civil conflict, a modern economy cannot be nurtured.*

*Some of these dimensions of the relationship between state and civil society were discussed in the World Development Report of 1997.

4 More recently, even the relief component of NGO operations became the object of additional patronage by donors, as a route towards internal security, now seen as a precondition of development. Especially in Africa and the Balkans, poor economic performance is now considered both a cause and a consequence of the breakdown of civil order, and NGOs are now conventionally entrusted with providing the kind of social and economic framework which will make conflict less likely. NGOs thus emerged into the sunlight of the 1990s' 'fight against poverty' with an augmented agenda, some of which they had sought, but some of which had been thrust at them willy-nilly. The expectation was that since 'NGOs had a comparative advantage in poverty reduction'* operating at their then scale they would be able to build effortlessly on that comparative advantage, in the process hitting grandiose targets like the '75 million poor families reached by micro-finance' of the 1997 Microcredit Summit. There is a severe lack of quantitative evidence on the efficiency of NGOs and the costs of scaling-up but the available evidence fails to support the hypothesis that, outside of direct famine-relief operations, NGOs reach a higher proportion of 'poorest' people or have greater impact at a given scale of operations than official agencies.

*If you are interested in NGOs and their role in poverty reduction and development more widely, and would like to explore these issues further, you can look at the references for Robinson and Riddell, 1992; Hulme and Edwards, 1992, 1996; and Lister, 2001 in Appendix 3.

This being so, the conventional wisdom that NGOs should expect, under poverty focus, to absorb a gradually increasing proportion of resources aimed at poverty alleviation needs to be questioned. In some activities, notably famine relief, micro-finance and some security-related operations, they do appear to have a comparative advantage, and in some other sectors across a limited set of countries (e.g. agricultural extension in East Africa, primary health care in Bangladesh). Gradually a shift is taking place from Northern to Southern NGOs, as capacity develops, with much project management within developing countries being devolved to local organizations – which of course leaves ambiguous the role of international NGOs beyond mere money-raising. In any case, the division of labour between NGOs and official agencies in any particular country is an empirical matter and there is little evidence to support the presumption that they are universally 'better at poverty reduction', either in style or in impact (Lister, 2001): comparative NGO/official evaluations are rare and badly needed. The issue is not addressed in the 2000/2001 World Development Report.

Recently the cosy relationship between NGOs and aid donors has soured over globalization (Figure 2.9). In the UK, for example, leading NGOs were requested by the Secretary of State for International Development Clare Short to 'grow themselves up' over their perceived disruptive attitude towards the World Trade Organization and the possibilities which globalization holds out for poor people (talk at House of Commons, 14 January 2000). The outcome of the relationship between NGOs and aid donors has importance for the possibilities of working out an agreed and fruitful division of labour within the poverty reduction process.

Figure 2.9 Should NGOs 'grow themselves up'? Direct Action Network (DAN) and the ad-hoc coalition of environmental and human rights groups protest against the World Trade Organization, Seattle, 23 November 1999.

Activity 2.8

For your personal reflection on some of the issues raised here, consider the following questions:

- Which of the anti-poverty options in Table 2.3 lend themselves to being operated by NGOs, and which can only be operated by government?
- In what areas of activity do you think NGOs have a comparative advantage?

You can also refer back to the Course Book, pp.210–215.

(Spend no more than 20 minutes on this activity)

Comment

On the first question, one possible criterion is scale: nobody has ever suggested that NGOs have a capacity for executing macro-economic policy, and in many ways they have thriven on seeking to implement the principle that 'small is beautiful'. But even within the category of smaller-scale operations, you may from experience or your own reading be able to sketch out the areas in which NGOs may have a comparative advantage over governments and large international institutions.

2.5 Poverty agendas into the twenty-first century

In this final section, by way of conclusion, we shift the focus from how international organizations' agendas *have evolved* to how they *should evolve in the future* – from a positive to a normative approach. We examine this question in relation to a widespread feeling of disappointment about what international organizations have achieved, and widespread debate, partly caused by this, about what their role should be in the future. On the first issue, the OECD in its comprehensive review *Twenty-Five Years of Development Co-operation* concluded that 'the most troubling shortcoming of development aid has been its limited measurable contribution to the reduction – as distinguished from the relief – of extreme poverty, especially in rural areas of both middle-income and poor countries' (OECD, 1986, cited in World Bank, 1990, p.127).

Is this still true? In many ways the stakes are higher now: we used to believe that poverty reduction was needed for its own sake, but in recent years the 'poverty discourse' and the 'security discourse' have become rolled together into an 'emerging development–security complex', as it has been called, so that we now expect the reduction of poverty and inequality to provide a peace dividend, as well as the other way about. 'Diplomacy' and 'development', once such uneasy bedfellows, are becoming intermingled.

On these issues, we can illustrate the debate by specific reference to the World Bank, which throughout its life has sought to lead both global discussion on poverty relief and efforts in that direction by bilateral aid donors – and increasingly NGOs. Four roles are feasible for the Bank in the twenty-first century, and in the final activity in Section 2 we invite you to consider the question of which role it should assume, together with the related question of how the battle against global poverty should be conducted. We have also suggested three roles for the IMF for you to consider.

Activity 2.9

Which of these roles do you favour for the Bank and Fund in the future? What additional evidence, over and above that provided in this section, do you need to help you make your decision?

Possible roles for the Bank:

1 The Bank as a bank: a profit-maximizing institution, investing in both public and private sector.

2 The Bank as emergency fund or source of infrastructural capital for poorer LDCs.

3 The Bank as a policy adviser or supplier of ideas and human capital.

4 The Bank as a component of a system of global governance in which it is a provider of ***global public goods*** (e.g. reduction of poverty and inequality, conflict reduction, environmental protection).

In thinking about these alternative roles for the Bank, how do you think the discussion in the audiocassette for this Theme reflects on them, particularly alternatives 3 and 4. Either listen to this band again if necessary or review your notes on it.

Possible roles for the Fund:

1 Emergency short-term lender.

2 Emergency short-term lender, *and* adviser on ***fiscal and monetary*** issues.

3 Emergency short-term lender, adviser on fiscal and monetary issues, *and* concessional 'poverty lender'.

(Spend no more than 30 minutes on this activity)

Comment

Our thoughts were as follows:

Bank 1: How much would the Bank add to what commercial banks offer? There is always the risk that, by putting profit first, the Bank would be forced to turn down risky projects in very poor countries and thus lose its distinctive role.

Bank 2: This is quite plausible and seems to represent the way that the Bank is going. But to make the Bank dependent on taxpayer contributions makes it vulnerable to sudden politically inspired cut-offs of money, especially from the US Congress. Finally, how sustainable would such a Bank be, and how susceptible to political pressures in the North?

Bank 3: This is the role that Bank staff really seem to enjoy (supported by the discussion on the audiocassette). But what is the comparative advantage of such a Bank in relation to merchant banks, universities, other international development organizations and NGOs in the case of poverty reduction?

Bank 4: Can the Bank, having been set up as a financial institution, effectively execute any of these roles?

Fund 1: What about the political fragility of weak states exposed to sudden public expenditure cuts? If they fall under the stress of a Fund adjustment programme, the new government will simply have to go back to the Fund in a year's time for more money – and nothing will have been mended.

Fund 2: This is a generally accepted role but it may have negative effects on poverty reduction. In particular, the Fund requires clients to balance their budget, which often requires the imposition of user charges on, for example, schoolbooks and medicines. If these are unpopular, who pays? There is also the '***moral hazard***' problem: if the Fund is always there, and all its clients know it, the clients may overspend and run the risk of another crisis like the East Asian crisis of 1998.

Fund 3: This is a role into which the Bank has been sucked through awareness that its ***stabilization*** operations were increasing poverty. Potentially this role for the Fund duplicates the second role proposed for the Bank.

Overall, deciding whether the World Bank should become 'even more like an aid donor', extending role 2 at the expense of the Fund's function 3, or whether these roles should be reversed (on the grounds that the Fund can make a greater contribution to poverty reduction by imposing fiscal discipline and attracting private capital than anything the Bank can achieve) helps to determine whether the Washington institutions between them can improve on the 'troubling' incapacity against chronic poverty, lamented by the OECD. Returning to the discussions about perceived changes in the Bank in the audiocassette, we can also note the support for alternative 3, or even alternative 4, for the Bank. We have not discussed the relatively recent advent of poverty reduction strategy papers (although we return to them in Section 4 of this Theme), however poverty reduction strategy papers are closely linked to the idea of the Bank having an advisory and interventionist role in poverty reduction. The *Voices* study carried out by the Bank reinforces this perspective.

Similar questions of overall strategy arise for aid donors. In a recent paper, the World Bank authors Paul Collier and David Dollar claim that:

> ...even with the present allocation [of aid], aid is effective in lifting around 10 million people per annum sustainably out of poverty in our sample of countries. With a poverty-efficient allocation, the productivity of the same volume of aid would nearly double, and lift 19 million people out of poverty.
>
> (Collier and Dollar, 1999, p.1)

This is a much more up-beat story than that told by the OECD. How is this supposed to happen? Collier and Dollar's story depends on four steps:

1. If aid stopped being given to middle-income countries (such as Russia and Israel) for political reasons, then poor countries would get more benefit from it.
2. Within those poor countries, aid only increases growth in countries where policies are 'good' (initially defined as conservative fiscal policy and open economy, now broadened to include a clutch of additional variables including the existence of an anti-poverty strategy).
3. Do not bother to try to improve policy by means of conditionality, as it does not work.
4. Therefore, confine aid to poor countries with good policies, and providing the poverty elasticities (Box 2.3 above) continue to turn out as estimated by Collier and Dollar, the prediction of 'poverty reduction of 19 million per annum' will come true.

Whether it will, indeed, come true, depends on whether some or all of the cluster of policies specified in Table 2.3 above are actually internalized by developing countries, and whether they work. About this we are still very ignorant, and such snippets of knowledge as we have (e.g. the instability of poverty elasticities) tends to put in doubt precise predictions like 'global poverty reduction of 19 million per annum'. There is no doubt that much progress in poverty reduction strategy has been made since the World Development Report of 1990. But much of it, as earlier argued, consists of progress in attaching policies to first principles (such as 'security' and 'empowerment'), rather than progress in getting those policies implemented, let alone demonstrating that they will lift 19 million or any other number of people out of poverty. Our own judgment would be, however, that in some areas Collier and Dollar's analysis is actually not optimistic enough. Specifically, conditionality sometimes works in reducing poverty – for example in Mozambique, Tanzania and Uganda. The Ugandan case is illustrated in Box 2.5. There are some coded indications that donors are now acknowledging this, and the repackaging of conditionality, under the guise of euphemisms such as 'dealing with poor performance', has been debated at many a recent workshop and seminar.

Box 2.5 Aid, policy and poverty reduction in Uganda

During the 'lost decades' of generally failed adjustment in the 1980s and 1990s, poverty rose dramatically across Africa as a whole (Table 2.1). But in Uganda, it fell just as dramatically: according to the latest estimate (Uganda, 2001) from 56% to 32% over the eight years from 1992 to 2000. Even the other fast-growing countries of Africa – such as Botswana, Lesotho and Ghana – have not seen poverty reduction of this magnitude. How has it been achieved?

The evidence points to the following factors as having been important:

Effective and stable policy. There has been a movement towards the free market – especially for coffee farmers, who now receive a far higher share of the export price than in the 1980s – but not a headlong rush. Even more importantly, public expenditure has been pro-poor (strategy 4 in Table 2.3 above) – focused on primary health and education, agricultural research and extension, and rural infrastructure.

Political stability and ethnic tolerance. Uganda, which has been under the same leadership since 1986, quickly invited back the Asians and their capital expelled by Idi Amin in the 1970s, and has avoided the racial scapegoating practised by the leaders of less successful African countries such as Kenya and Zimbabwe.

A constructive dialogue with aid donors – who tolerated President Museveni's flirtation with fixed exchange rates in the mid-1980s and with a coffee export tax in 1994, believing it more important to encourage a basically enlightened leadership to find its own salvation than to hassle it over details. Where conditionality has been used explicitly – as it frequently has, for example in setting up the Programme against Poverty and the Social Costs of Adjustment (PAPSCA) – it has generally been by the provision of carrots rather than sticks.

Luck – especially in avoiding drought and civil war, which between them have been responsible for so many of Africa's disasters over the past twenty years.

It will be clear from the above that much of the progress that has so far been made towards pro-poor growth has occurred through exit rather than voice or loyalty (Box 2.6). Indeed, the devolution of state functions to NGOs and the private sector has been one of the techniques of 'dealing with poor performance' which has carried through from the age of structural adjustment to the present. In the field of poverty reduction this approach, in countries such as Kenya, Zimbabwe and Bangladesh where NGOs are strong and the state weak, has already proved extremely fruitful. As government has retreated from the functions of agricultural extension, primary health, non-formal education and especially small business finance, so NGOs have enthusiastically taken these functions over.

Box 2.6 Exit, voice and loyalty

The terminology is from a book by Albert Hirschman (1970), which explicitly contrasted three alternative responses by individuals to failure or decline in an organization: 'exit' (leave it), 'voice' (try and mend it by constructive criticism) or 'loyalty' (try and mend it by defending it). In the context of economic decline in developing countries, the attempt to reform state institutions can be seen as voice and the attempt to find alternatives to them (through privatization or the use of NGOs) can be seen as exit.

Is the current wave of anti-poverty enthusiasm among development institutions sustainable? And will it crowd out the possibility of a neoliberal backlash, as in the 1980s the 'Washington consensus' crowded out much pro-poor action by international agencies? In recent years various authors, including the former Chief Economist of the World Bank (Stiglitz, 1998; also Gore, 2000), have declared the old 'Washington consensus' in need of serious updating, and overt cracks in it have appeared in public; for example the 2000/2001 World Development Report now insists on the need for direct controls on ***short-term capital movements*** in time of crisis (Stiglitz, 1998, p.181), which the IMF is still seeking to eliminate. What is very clear is that the markets for labour, for capital and for knowledge often fail, thus aggravating poverty – and that the conventional 'Washington consensus' solution of expecting liberalization and free market pricing to solve the problem is not going to come to grips with the challenge of poverty reduction (Williamson, 1990).

*'Post-Washington consensus': see Course Book, pp.352, 363, 396.

Stiglitz's 'post-Washington consensus'* insists, in addition, on 'sound financial regulation, competition policy, and policies to facilitate the transfer of technology and encourage transparency in public administration' (Stiglitz, 1998, p.1), and argues that the East Asian crisis of that year arose from neglect of some of these principles. But would those principles have been sufficient to produce the set of policies listed in Table 2.3, or for that matter the East Asian miracle itself? The answer is surely not: those policies arose from a mixture of political pressure towards egalitarianism and institutional creativity. Pro-poor growth does not emerge from a market process – even a regulated market process – alone.

We will illustrate by reference to two countries, Uganda and Bangladesh. In both countries a process of pro-poor growth is going on (e.g. Appleton, 2001), but in Uganda it is state-led (Box 2.5) whereas in Bangladesh it is NGO-led (Section 2.4 above). In Uganda the key policy instrument is pro-poor allocation of government expenditures (option 3 in Table 2.3 above) whereas in Bangladesh it is pro-poor allocation of *non*-government measures, in particular finance (option 10), but also health and education (option 11). None of these initiatives emerged from a market process, but free markets, especially the absence of controls on rural interest rates, are certainly helpful. In these countries, donors and international financial institutions can simply go with the flow, support the pro-poor actors and be reasonably confident of the outcome. The not yet resolved question is what they should do in a country such as Pakistan, with a history of undemocratic political systems, education and health systems are deeply unequal, and yet the possibility of influence still seems to exist. The Washington consensus has said 'liberalize', and this has not worked. The post-Washington consensus says 'liberalize with appropriate regulatory and governance reforms', and this does not appear to be working either. The Collier–Dollar approach would presumably say 'pull out, since conditionality is not working', but this would not resolve the problem either, since there are more developing countries like Pakistan than there are like Uganda or Bangladesh; and since the terrorist attacks on the US of September 2001, pulling out of Pakistan is not a politically feasible option. Whereas there may be a new, and in many people's view a very happy, consensus around the ultimate goal of poverty reduction, therefore, there is no consensus around the means by which progress towards this goal should be made.

Much though one may hope that these insights will be stable, it would be unwise to take this for granted. We have seen how the 1997/1998 East Asian crisis – which turned out to be remarkably short-lived – threw into doubt and instability the IMF's new anti-poverty role. We have seen how the global crisis of 1980, which was not short-lived, threw into reverse the anti-poverty efforts of all the major international institutions. With these hindsights it would be foolish to assume that the gains of the last ten years will automatically be built on in the twenty-first century. But with luck (avoidance of global crisis), and good management, they may be.

Summary of Section 2

1. In developing countries poverty was, until the early 1970s, expected to decline automatically with growth, requiring no separate anti-poverty policies.
2. Since the world discovered that this would not happen, there have been three waves of anti-poverty policies, or 'institutional agendas'. The first, in the 1970s, involved a focus on the rural development and the urban informal sector. The second, in the late 1980s and early 1990s, concentrated on labour intensity and the human capital of the poor. The third, culminating in the World Bank's World Development Report of 2000, redefines poverty in terms of a range of poverty indicators including vulnerability, and hence is focused on the security and empowerment of the poor rather than simply their economic well-being.
3. As these agendas have developed, so have the organizations putting them forward. All the actors examined here – aid donors, NGOs, the World Bank and the IMF – have experienced 'mission creep' over the last twenty years, adding many objectives to their agenda and deleting none. Inevitably, this has involved some inter-institutional conflict, and some nostalgia for the clean and simple division of labour between international institutions which existed after the Second World War. Nonetheless, some good things are happening. Poverty levels are falling in a number of countries, including in Africa now. These changes may even owe something to the 'new wave' of anti-poverty policies described in Section 2.3.

3 Understanding livelihoods and lived experiences

3.1 Introduction: data, concepts, policy and action

This section focuses on poor people's lived experiences. In particular, we want to understand the lived experiences of poor people by taking a close look at the kinds of data – both quantitative and qualitative – that are collected about their daily lives and livelihoods. By doing this we hope to develop your skills of data analysis and critique, as well as enable you to gain a deeper understanding of the nature and experience of poverty and inequality. We also think these skills will be useful for you when and if you do read other texts about the lived experience, such as the suggestions for further reading listed in Appendix 3 to this Theme.

There is more than one reason for a focus on lived experience. The first is to link the broad analysis of poverty and policies on poverty at one end of the spectrum to the experiences and practices of poor people at the other. As an individual, you might have had some first or second hand contact with poverty. At first hand, this might have been in places you have lived and worked, or possibly even in your own life or family history. At second hand, you might have read fictional or non-fictional accounts of poverty, or seen it represented on both feature and documentary film or in photographs and paintings. Thus you will come to this section with some idea about what the experience of poverty might be like for an individual, a family, a group of people or a community. You will also, through your study of this course, and almost certainly through the media and your wider reading, be aware of debates about how to improve the situation of poor people (as well as about policy measures to reduce poverty globally). For example, in the UK, we hear interviews with pensioners who have very little money but are ineligible for income support grants, and are therefore worse off than those with lower pensions. We hear about family tax credit, measures to get people into work, and debates about the abuse of state benefits. We notice the tension between how poor people describe their conditions and needs, and the actions of politicians and policy-makers in response to them. This can be a very emotive process, so one of the tasks of this section is to try and think more analytically about the experiences of poverty and inequality, so that we can assess what effects policies and interventions might have on people's lives in practice (the subject of Section 4 of this Theme).

A second reason is to gain more insight into the daily survival strategies and practices of poor people. Poverty is not a 'condition' but results from social processes and relations in which poor people are actors. Thus how people make sense of the processes and relations which make and keep them poor, and how they manage their livelihoods, also helps us to think more analytically about the effects of policies and interventions, as well as which types of action or intervention might be effective. (These aspects will be picked up again in Section 4.)

In this section of the Theme we cover the following aspects:

Section 3.1 We think about what it means to analyse lived experience by looking more closely at the story of Murari, whom you first encountered in the Part 1 *Introduction to Poverty and Inequality*. In particular, in answering the question 'Why is Murari poor?', we see how to extract and display different types of data; we also examine what concepts might be used to explain his (and his family's) poverty; and we also look at how this type of analysis might be useful for thinking about action on poverty.

Section 3.2 We consider the types of data* that are gathered about poor people and the ways that they are gathered, to understand more about poor people's lives. You might wonder what this discussion has to do with understanding poor people's lived experiences – however, it is important to have a sense of how analysts and policy-makers approach data gathering and how they make sense of those data. In part this is about how people use data to explain poverty and inequality and how they use them to shape policy. There are many debates about how to understand the different realities of poverty and inequality.

*Data are usually referred to in the plural because the word *datum* is the original Latin for a single piece of information.

Section 3.3 We then look at how some data were gathered about households in villages in Andhra Pradesh in India. In this section, we provide the researchers' own account (one of whom is an author of Section 3), and some of the issues and challenges they encountered in deciding which data to gather and how to go about it.

Section 3.4 Here we start to look at the households' lived experiences directly. In particular, we look at the issue of inequality and how inequality between households can be measured, in this instance in relation to the land they had access to. In another context, this might be income or housing, or access to education and healthcare.

Section 3.5 In this subsection we analyse the lived experiences of a few households by looking at some quantitative data that were collected about them, in particular their crops and income. As well as differences between the households, we are also able to see differences in male and female earnings within households and reflect on the implications for gender relations. We complement the quantitative data on the households by hearing the voices of some of the women who live and work in them. We can see how their interviews add to our understanding of their lived experiences, and we also look at selected methods for making sense of such data.

Section 3.6 In this final subsection, we summarize Section 3 and draw some overall conclusions. Here we indicate some lessons for analysing and interpreting lived experience in other parts of the world. You might want to reflect on our discussion of the data on lived experience in India in relation to your own context, or one that is familiar to you.

Please note that this section is 1.5 weeks' study time, or 21 hours' study. As some of the subsections of this section involve thinking with, and carrying out, short exercises on data, it is wise to break up your study. Don't try to go through Section 3 all in one go. Here is a rough guide to the study time of each subsection so that you can pace yourself (we also suggest you make breaks in your study of Section 3.5):

The rest of Section 3.1 (2.5 hours)

Section 3.2 (1.5 hours)

Section 3.3 (2 hours)

Section 3.4 (3 hours)

Sections 3.5.1 and 3.5.2 (3 hours)

Sections 3.5.3 (2 hours)

Section 3.5.4 (4 hours) (split it up if necessary, between 'explanation' and 'interpretation')

Section 3.6 (0.5 hour)

Note that this is only 18.5 hours in total but it may take you a bit longer. We suggest that you use the summary in Section 3.6 to remind yourself of the main lessons of this section of the Theme, particularly if you use this section in your TMA or when revising for the examination. It may also be useful to read the summary of each subsection before you study the subsection itself.

Analysing lived experience of poverty and inequality: an example

What does thinking analytically about lived experience involve? First we need to have a means of understanding and interpreting the stories of people's lives. This may involve using analytical categories or concepts, or having a theory or framework that we want to test against information about people's lived experiences. Second, we need to look at different kinds of data about people's lives. Depending on the questions we want to ask, this might include their assets, their incomes and means of livelihood; how many people there are dependent on these sources of income; how it's distributed amongst them (and how that is decided); what other sources of support people have access to; what their access is to services and to networks in the community; what voice they might have to influence change; what their sense of their own well- or ill-being is, and so on. You can see that, as we extended this list, we moved from 'measurables' or data that can be quantified, such as assets and income, to more diffuse aspects of people's lives, such as networks, influence and well-being, that are more difficult to measure. Although certain aspects of people's lives are not necessarily easy to measure in practice (for example because people often do not want to disclose information about their incomes or property they hold), you can also see from this list that we would need data that are quantitative and data that are qualitative.

The two kinds of data together provide a much more complete picture than data of just one kind.

Let us see how this might work in practice by looking at an example that you are already familiar with. In *Introduction to Poverty and Inequality*, Judith Scott asked you to look at the story of an Indian labourer, Murari, from the point of view of how different ways of conceptualizing poverty might help interpret the causes and consequences of his (and his family's) situation. The story is reproduced below in Activity 3.1 for ease of reference. This time we're going to look at the story as a piece of data. We will first analyse the data (raising some questions about the limitations of the data provided in this story in the process), then link our analysis to the concepts of poverty used by Judith Scott in *Introduction to Poverty and Inequality*. Finally, we will try and think through some of the implications of our analysis for policy intervention.

We may look for two kinds of data: quantitative and qualitative.* As suggested above, we also need to have a sense of the questions we want to ask and the categories of data we want to 'collect'. In this instance, our question is:

*Quantitative and qualitative data were explained in *Introduction to Poverty and Inequality*, Section 5.

> 'Why is Murari poor?'

To try to answer this question, we need to break it down into smaller questions that may explain Murari's poverty. The kinds of questions we suggest below are closely linked to those outlined in the discussion of livelihoods in Section 1 of this Theme. As you will see, they also relate to Moser's asset-vulnerability framework, which we also looked at in Section 1. We will see that some of these questions might be answered with quantitative data and others might be better answered with qualitative data.

Thus we might ask:

(a) What are his assets?

(b) What is his income (in cash and in kind)?

(c) What are his source(s) of income (or where does he get his income from)?

(d) What are the conditions under which Murari obtains his assets and income?

(e) What is the relationship between his flows of cash and flows in kind?

(f) What are the constraints on earning further income or being able to realize assets?

(g) What are the constraints on being able to find other sources of income?

Notice that these are all 'what?' questions, while we actually want to achieve an answer to a 'why?' question. This is because we want to gather data about Murari's livelihood situation that we think can help answer the 'why?' question. However, in order to answer 'Why is Murari poor?' we will need to try to draw connections between the answers to our 'what?' questions to build an explanation. We may also find that there are other questions we need to ask to explain Murari's poverty, and that other types of data are needed than those in the story.

Activity 3.1

Re-read the account of Murari below and make notes in answers to the seven questions above:

Then compare your notes with our analysis below.

(Spend no more than 30 minutes on this activity)

The story of Murari

Murari is a 30-year old man who is presently living in the village of Kedarkui [India] with his family. He began his period of contractual labour in agriculture five years ago for a dominant Thakur caste farmer. The Thakur also acts as moneylender in many of the surrounding villages. Five years ago Murari took out a loan of approximately Rs.1000 that he needed for an unexpected emergency. As a term of the loan, Murari was compelled to work for the Thakur farmer as an agricultural labourer on the moneylender's land for a wage of only Rs.5000 a year. This Thakur farmer/moneylender provided Murari and his family with accommodations, food, and some money for miscellaneous expenses, while keeping account of everything that was provided.

At the end of the first two years, Murari owed Rs.2500 to the Thakur. After two years of labour he owed 250 percent more to the Thakur than he had initially borrowed due to the interest incurred on the loan, charges for food and accommodation, small loans provided on an ongoing basis, and so on. However, despite this dismal situation Murari was not able to leave the Thakur's farm in search of more profitable work. If he attempted to leave, or flee, it is reported that the moneylender would track him down and the consequences would undoubtedly be serious. After five years of work as an agricultural labourer and house servant for the Thakur, Murari owes over Rs.8000. Murari and others like him find that they are virtually powerless once they enter the vicious circle of contractual labour, where they are compelled to concede to the tyranny and exploitation of the moneylenders. But for many of the poorest villagers, there are no alternative sources of loans and in certain circumstances they have no choice but to accept the exploitative terms of the local moneylenders.

(Narayan *et al.*, 2000b, p.63)

Comment

You will probably have noticed already that answering some of the specific questions involves mainly quantitative data, while as we proceed in trying to answer the overarching question 'Why is Murari poor?' we also need some qualitative data to begin constructing an explanation. It is often difficult to construct an explanation on the basis of quantitative data alone, which tend to answer 'what?' questions but may not alone reveal the social processes of 'how' and 'why' things occur. Although qualitative data can be used in a descriptive rather than an explanatory way, combining quantitative and qualitative data usually provides the richest picture of people's livelihoods and clues as to why they are in poverty.

Let us see what the answers to our questions might look like.

What are Murari's assets? On the surface, it appears from these data that the only asset Murari possesses is his own labour. (You will remember from Sections 1 and 2 the idea that labour is the main asset of poor people – and that therefore threats to health and the ability to use one's labour are risks that poor people tend to try and mitigate.) There are, however, some unanswered questions about assets in this story. For example, there are no data on the members of Murari's family and their labour. We have a story only of Murari's personal situation, although, in practice, different members of the household from relatively young children to elderly people may be contributing their labour in different ways. So the assets of the household overall might include Murari's wife's labour and possibly that of at least one child or other relative. In addition, we do not know anything about any other assets, such as material possessions, education or networks. By implication from this story, we can probably assume that Murari and his family had very little of any of these.

So, to continue, *what is Murari's income (in cash and in kind), and what are his source(s) of income (or where does he get his income from)?* We have recorded our answers in Table 3.1. (Again, note that we do not know if any other members of Murari's family are bringing in income.)

Table 3.1 Murari's income and sources of income, in cash and kind

	Income	
Source	*Cash*	*Kind*
From higher caste Thakur farmer and moneylender for whom Murari works as agricultural labourer and house servant	Loan of Rs.1000 Wage of Rs.5000 p.a. Money for miscellaneous expenses Small loans	Food for family

What are the conditions under which Murari obtains his assets and income? We have included housing as an asset; however, given that Murari only had access to this housing as a function of his job, it may be more accurate to consider it as income in kind (and therefore to have included it in the income in kind column in Table 3.1). Again, we have included money and food as income in cash and kind. We can record the following conditions of indebtedness under which they were obtained, displayed in Table 3.2.

Table 3.2 The conditions under which Murari obtains his assets and income

Assets (?)	*Income (cash and kind)*	*Conditions*
	Loan of Rs.1000	Tied or bonded labour to Thakur farmer at low wage rate; high interest rate
	Wage of Rs.5000 p.a.	Wage rate influenced by initial debt of Rs.1000
	Money for miscellaneous expenses	Apparently part of favours from farmer but in fact included in farmer's accounts of what Murari owed him
	Small loans	Added to previous loan with interest
'Free' accommodation for family		Also appears as a favour to Murari and family but accounted by farmer as part of the debt
	Food for family	Accounted by farmer as part of the debt

'I like the illustration that most things given as gifts or help are in reality not that; they could in actual fact be 'poverty-chain-tighteners' i.e. the subtle or hidden dimensions of poverty' (comment from critical reader, Chipika, 2001).

What is the relationship between Murari's flows of cash and kind? Although we do not have precise data, we could broadly map them as in Table 3.3 over the five years covered in the account.

Table 3.3 Murari's income and outgoings over a five-year period

Incomings	*Outgoings*
Loan of Rs.1000	Interest on original loan
Annual wage of Rs.5000 (total of Rs.25 000 over 5 years)	
Income in kind	Interest on income in kind included with interest on original loan
	Murari's and family's expenditures on consumption needs other than provided by the farmer
	(A total accumulated debt of Rs.8000 over 5 years)

What are the constraints on Murari's earning further income or being able to realize assets? We now move more into the qualitative arena. From the data on Murari's livelihood displayed above, the critical constraint is his indebtedness. However, we gather from this account that there is an unstated, implied use of coercion to keep Murari and his family from escaping their situation.

What are the constraints on being able to find other sources of income? The account suggests that there are no alternative sources of loans. We know little about other sources of employment for Murari but his condition of increasing indebtedness has tied him into a situation from which it is difficult to escape.

There are some additional points to make about this example. These data were extracted from a secondary account: that is, they have already been processed and put into a story. If we had been collecting these data from Murari himself, which is what someone investigating the lived experience of poverty might do, we might have ended up writing a similar story. But we might also have asked different questions and constructed a different or more complex story. In particular, we might have wanted to talk to Murari's wife and possibly other members of the household, depending on its composition, about their labour use, income and assets, and especially the conditions under which they obtained any further assets and income. In particular, we might have found that it was not only Murari who worked for the Thakur farmer but that his wife might have had to provide domestic service in the house or other labour. So we might have wanted to hear her perceptions of the situation, which might have been different from Murari's. We might also have wanted to interview other debt-bonded labourers and members of debt-bonded households to gain a more general picture, including why they had entered (or been forced to enter) debt bondage in the first place.

However, what we have done in this case is to disaggregate a particular story to identify the nature and dynamics of Murari's poverty in so far as we can tell from these data. In addition, we have displayed some of the data in simple tables, which can be as effective as writing a story about them. If we were trying to document and display the experience of many debt-bonded labourers, we might use graphs and charts to show key variables and their relationships (for example, the relationship between incidence of landlessness and incidence of debt bondage), as well as summarize complex data in tables.

To what extent do you think Murari's poverty has been satisfactorily explained by analysing the data in the account? You will have your own views. Here we make just two points in answer to this question. First is to think about what other data might be needed to develop a more complete explanation. In addition to the kinds of additional data we have mentioned above, we might also want to look at the wider context, including land distribution, constraints on access to land and other assets, local labour markets and different opportunities for employment, and so on.

Second, as you know from *Study Guide 1* of this course, data alone do not explain phenomena. Concepts and theories are also needed. Analysing Murari's lived experience enables us to look at evidence that might help explain his poverty, and to relate the evidence to concepts and theories. For example, you will have noticed that, towards the end of the discussion of data above, we started to talk about 'debt bondage'*, as though debt bondage were the (or a) cause of Murari's poverty. In other words, we were beginning to suggest an explanation of Murari's poverty through the concept of debt bondage. We could have made a statement such as:

*Wendy Olsen has written the following paper on debt bondage: 'Contract Labour and Bondage in Andhra Pradesh (India)'.

> 'Debt bondage is the cause of Murari's poverty.'

We could even have started with this statement (rather than 'Why is Murari poor?') and looked for evidence to support it. In the process of gathering evidence, we might have modified, or reconceptualized, our original statement to say:

> 'Debt bondage is the result of Murari's poverty, not the cause, and serves to reinforce his poverty further.'

As you probably realize, both these statements about debt bondage are hypotheses,* which can be tested through the collection of data. In doing so, we might have begun to develop a theory of rural poverty in Murari's part of India.

*A hypothesis is a statement or an 'interim guess' (Robson, 1993, p.29) about a situation that can be tested by investigation. Evidence might support it or suggest strongly that it is incorrect.

As our next step, we review the conceptual analysis of Murari's story, which was provided by Judith Scott in *Introduction to Poverty and Inequality*.

Activity 3.2

Re-read Scott's analysis in Section 4.1 in *Introduction to Poverty and Inequality*, paying particular attention to the evidence she brings to bear on it.

(Spend no more than 15 minutes on this activity)

Scott applied a social exclusion and a relational approach to this account. In terms of social exclusion, Scott shows how Murari had no rights (supported by the data on debt bondage), no resources (supported by the data on no alternative access), and no relationships or networks to support him (he had his family, of course, but it could be deduced from this account that he had no one else to borrow from). Scott concludes that social exclusion is both a cause and an effect and is therefore a (self-reinforcing) process. In terms of social relations, she underlines the inequality of the relationship between Murari and the farmer/moneylender, which is based on a set of cross-cutting relationships of caste, employer/labourer, and creditor/debtor. In both these analyses, Table 3.2 above could have been used as supporting evidence.

As implied above, one might gather and analyse data on lived experience by starting with concepts or a theory of poverty in a particular context that we want to examine. For example, we might decide to examine one of the statements about debt bondage above, widening it to assess its applicability to Murari's village (or to several villages). We might explore how individuals and households experience debt bondage in this context. We might also gather data from landowners, village traders and others who provide credit and how they perceive their roles and relations to debtors. However, although gathering data on the lived experience of debt bondage will contribute to our understanding, it will not tell us all we need to know to explain its relationship to poverty. So we might develop a hypothesis about social relations in the village, for example about the relations between those who have access to land and other assets and those who do not (or who do not have adequate land or other assets to meet household needs). We might also gather data about the exchanges of labour, money and other goods between them, and the conditions under which they take place, the amounts of money in circulation through loans, what it is used for and what the interest rates are. We might gather data on contractual arrangements and the mechanisms through which some people are tied into debt relations with others, and so on.

How is gathering data and examining this kind of lived experience at the micro level useful in terms of policy development and intervention? In the instance of Murari, we have to be aware that we are only using one person's story. Usually the process of policy development and intervention is based on generalized phenomena and a much bigger database. However this account does indicate that Murari is not alone in his experience of debt bondage. It also suggests that there are no alternatives for the poorest villagers. So one might extrapolate some tentative conclusions from this account for policy development and intervention. For example, we might ask questions such as:

- In specific terms, what effect would establishing a micro-finance scheme in the area have on someone like Murari? Would he be able to repay his existing debt if he participated in such a scheme? Would he (and other members of his family) be able to use the scheme to build up assets (e.g. in land, or housing)? How might other members of his family benefit from such a scheme?
- In more general terms, how could debt bondage be abolished in reality as well as in the law? How would those currently in debt bondage be affected in terms of their livelihoods? What would the effects be for the demand and supply of labour in the countryside – i.e. what would happen to labour markets? How would both the Thakur farmer and Murari and his family be affected?
- We might go further and ask questions such as: What other sources of rural (farm and non-farm) employment could be created and what investment (and by whom) would be needed? What market conditions are needed and what regulatory environment would be appropriate? How would individuals and households in debt bondage benefit from such initiatives?

From this, we hope you can see that having data about lived experience enables us to build scenarios or ask 'what if?' questions about intervention and policy in terms of how people's lives might be changed, both in specific cases and for groups of people in the same social position. Understanding the lived experience of poverty and inequality is an essential ingredient in asking questions about the effects of policy instruments and development programmes and projects. This is not to say other kinds of data are unimportant. Quantitative and qualitative data of many kinds are needed to inform policy and action on poverty. The kinds of data collected depend on how problems are perceived, which depends in turn on standpoint* and implied theories of how the world works.

**Study Guide 1* defined *standpoint* as 'an attitude to or outlook on issues, typically arising from one's circumstances or beliefs' (Section 10).

In the following subsections, we will be considering further the lived experience of Indian households through looking at some survey and interview data collected as part of a research project in the state of Andhra Pradesh. This project was aimed at assessing the effects of structural adjustment reform policies in south India and offers useful evidence in exploring the experience of poverty and inequality among rural households. We will also develop further some basic data skills. As part of this process, our next step is to think a little bit more about some of the issues involved in gathering and using 'live data'.

3.2 Analysing data about poor people

The previous section showed that it is possible to think about data on lived experience in different ways. This applied to how we might analyse and display the data, the role of concepts and theory in interpreting and drawing conclusions from data, and how analysing lived experience might inform policy and action. It is not surprising that there are different views and interpretations of the realities of poor people, and that data about them are used in different ways to substantiate different claims and interventions. So one important aspect of this section of the Theme is to learn how data offer contestable representations of the lived situation, and that people writing about the lived experience of poverty and inequality have to choose what kinds of representations to put forward.

By representations we mean different pictures or interpretations of people's realities. The representations will be influenced by (a) their source and types of data; (b) the standpoint of those doing the analysis; (c) the concepts and methods used to analyse the data.

These issues about data are similar to those about concepts, a point initially raised in *Introduction to Poverty and Inequality.* Thus many concepts in development studies, notably poverty and empowerment, are contested terms. Some people think the answer to these arguments lies in getting accurate data, but in our view the 'answer' is more like a series of probing questions and multiple interpretations.

Types of data about poverty

In addition to interviewing poor people about their lives and livelihoods, or capturing their experiences on video or audiocassette, there are obviously other ways of gathering data about poor people, such as in censuses and surveys (Figure 3.1). In conjunction with data on lived experience, these different types of data can be used to provide policy-makers and activists with a more general picture of the causes and manifestations of poverty.

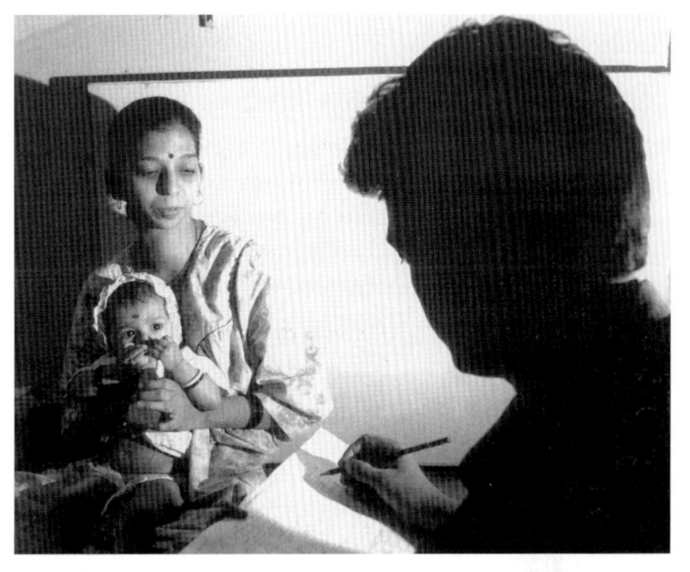

Figure 3.1 (a) A woman gives details about her family to a census official in Madras, 2001. (b) Interviewing a family for the census in Bombay, 2001.

Development data from local grassroots situations are often called 'micro data' to distinguish them from macro data representing the aggregation or averaging of numbers at regional or national level. However the two are closely related. In development work three types of survey are often used:

1. Surveys of government data that are collected under compulsory systems of rules. These include the census data and data about firms that are collected through the taxation department or ministry. Official data are often kept for internal use by government only, except for a few summary tables and graphs that are published in official documents such as a Review of Statistics, Statistics of Agricultural Production and Prices, and so on.
2. Independent surveys conducted by academics, consultants, and national and local organizations, such as firms or NGOs, for specific purposes. These data sets are sometimes of a higher quality than government data sets, but at the same time they are not done annually and, with each survey being unique and having different coverage, they are very hard to compare with each other.

3 Surveys that take up the official government publications and collate them into large international comparative tables. Foremost among these international comparative data sets are the World Development Report statistical appendix, the *Human Development Report* statistical tables, and the *International Financial Statistics* monthly issues and yearbooks.

Table 3.4 summarizes the characteristics, advantages and disadvantages of each of these three types of data set.

Table 3.4 Types of data set and their characteristics

Type of data set	*Characteristics*	*Advantages*	*Disadvantages*
Official government data	Compulsory forms concerning economic activity, demographic characteristics (e.g. census)	Consistent over time and often across different regions and countries; wide coverage; consistent format	Forms and categories may not change rapidly enough to accord with rapid social change; illicit activities are omitted
Independent or academic data sets	One-off or repeat surveys tailored to a specific purpose	In-depth coverage of the chosen subject area; careful testing and development	May be small scale and may not be repeated over time, making it hard to make generalizations or comparisons over time and space
International data sets	Gathered at the national unit of analysis,* these data sets have consistent measurement of the chosen variables	Enables international comparisons and inter-temporal analysis of trends and pattern at the global level	Neglects intra-national differences such as regional and class differences (worst for the large countries)

*The unit of analysis is the unit which is to be surveyed in a given data set. Units may be households, persons, firms, or nations, for instance.

The defining characteristic of the survey method is the desire for consistent measurement and representativeness. This aspect is not of such concern in qualitative data, such as oral histories, life stories, lived experiences and perceptions. The basic distinction usually made is as follows:

- Survey data are consistently recorded for a set of comparable cases and are usually subject to measuring by number.
- Qualitative data are based on words or images rather than numbers, generally arising from observing and interviewing people; they vary in form and substance across the different sources from which they come.

Note that, although different, each of these kinds of data has its own validity and usefulness. We return to the issue of validity below.

Activity 3.3

You have seen examples of quantitative and qualitative data before in this course. Refer to Chapter 5 of the Course Book. Tables 5.1 and 5.2 are survey data from a limited range of countries. Now look at the summary of Shahanara's Day as seen on p.110. This is an example of qualitative data, although the evidence does not come in Shahanara's own words. Instead the data were collected by an observer, as in Murari's story in Section 3.1. Later in this section, we will look at some qualitative data on lived experience in the first person. For now, just look at these different types of data and representation and consider what they tell you about the different dimensions of employment and unemployment.

(Spend no more than 15 minutes on this activity)

As we said above, quantitative survey and qualitative data are often combined to present a more complete picture of poverty and inequality, or to present different perspectives on the causes and manifestations of poverty. In the *World Development Report 2000/2001*, both survey data and qualitative data were used extensively (World Bank, 2000a). The report uses examples drawn from a databank of interviews and discussions with 64 000 people in poor countries. The detailed qualitative data from these interviews were analysed and published under the title *Voices of the Poor* (Narayan *et al.*, 2000a,b), which we have mentioned already in this Theme.

The differences between quantitative and qualitative methods and data are not always clear cut. For example, surveys also require qualitative concepts for data to be collected (for example, land tenure, literacy, healthcare). This means that concepts have to be operationalized in both quantitative and qualitative research to be able to collect data about them. The meaning of operationalization is outlined in Box 3.1 below.

Box 3.1 Operationalization

In this context, operationalization is the process of translation of a theoretical or abstract concept into an indicator that refers directly to something that can be recorded or measured. Operationalization often refers to defining a variable that measures a concept.

If you look at the back of any major published report, such as the *World Development Report 2000/2001*, you will find some 'technical notes' that explain how the concepts used in the quantitative tables have been measured. One example from the *World Development Report 2000/2001* is 'adult literacy rate': 'the percentage of people aged 15 and above who cannot, with understanding, read and write a short, simple statement about their everyday life' (ibid., p.319). The technical note goes on to explain that this measure is based on the notion of functional literacy and that controlled conditions are needed to measure it.

However, 'In practice, many countries estimate the number of illiterate adults from self-reported data or from estimates of school completion rates. Because of these differences in method, comparisons across countries – and even over time within countries – should be made with caution' (ibid.). So you can see that operationalizing concepts to collect quantitative data in surveys is not necessarily straightforward. In *Preparing for Development*, you will already have come across the idea of using proxy variables or indicators to measure something. An example might be to measure life expectancy or under-5 mortality rates as a measure of the health of a population.

In qualitative research, operationalization refers to a more substantive translation of concepts into language that is shared with respondents. For instance, 'empowerment' might be translated into a discussion about 'joining in', 'having a voice' or 'sharing decisions'.

In this section of the Theme, we will be considering different ways of operationalizing the concepts of poverty and inequality: that is, we will be looking at ways of measuring and exploring quantitative and qualitative data on these two concepts in the context of two Indian villages, and thereby also gain a picture of the lived experiences. First, however, let us consider some issues concerning validity, which are often raised in connection with survey data in particular.

Data are representations not facts

How do we know that the data collected on poverty and inequality (and especially on people's lived experiences) are valid data? For quantitative and large-scale data gathered through surveys, there are many statistical checks that can be carried out. However, in recent years there has been a growing debate about what constitutes validity (or valid data or valid knowledge), and as a result there is increased interest in 'epistemologies'.

An *epistemology* is a theory of knowledge or a theory of how we come to have knowledge of the world external to us. 'The term is used more loosely in sociology to refer to the methods of scientific procedure which lead to the acquisition of sociological knowledge' (Abercrombie *et al.*, 1994, p.147). There are debates about 'what form knowledge takes, the ways in which knowledge can be attained and communicated to others, and ultimately who can be a knower, and what tests and criteria must be involved in order to establish knowledge' (Hitchcock and Hughes, 1995, p.19). These debates can get us into quite deep philosophical waters. For example, in relation to our current subject, we might ask how we can really know about the lived experience of poor people. This is why discussion of epistemology tends to involve discussion of validity. Epistemological statements are those which support, or challenge, the validity of certain claims about our knowledge. As the title of this subsection suggests, data are representations not facts.

The most traditional epistemology in the social sciences is empiricism,* which argues that claims must be backed up with evidence. If you have a background in the sciences, you may think this is a perfectly valid way to proceed. Empiricists often seek generalized truths in the data they gather. A recent alternative epistemology in the social sciences, known as *standpoint theory,* suggests that there is more to validity than providing evidence for a claim. According to standpoint theorists, people have different starting positions which means that they perceive and know things differently. Some people start as middle-class youth in France, while others are working-class female garment workers in India, and so on. You will remember the discussion on standpoint in *Study Guide 1* and this issue has been raised in other Themes of the course.

**Empirical* refers to observations about the world as actually observed. *Empiricism* refers to a commitment to observation and making records as a way to provide evidence.

Evidence from personal narratives or accounts is considered important in explaining the knowledge that people have, and standpoint theorists expect claims to be challenged by others who have different experiences, and who are unfamiliar with the standpoint of the first author or speaker. A specific claim arising from standpoint theory is that women's experience of gender relations is fundamentally different from men's, and that one must ask women to explain and explore their experience of gender relations rather than expecting men to do so for them.

This brings us to a third epistemological position: *pluralism.* If a person thinks that it is possible to see the same thing from different perspectives, and that those perspectives may be associated with different notions of validity, then the person may have a *pluralist epistemology.* The pluralists have challenged notions of the universal and timeless validity of social research.

It is thus important to recognize that our understanding of the world and other people's lives is open to such problems as ethnocentrism or gender bias. For example, Diane Elson and others in the book *Male Bias in Development Economics* (1991) argued that there was an implicitly male standpoint in much orthodox development economics, and that theories might have to be re-worked from the ground up if gender were to be incorporated in them. In Elson's view, gender is not just a division of people into two sexes, but a profoundly powerful set of relations in society which influence how people see the world as well as how people are seen by others.

Those who are interested in standpoint approaches to development or in pluralist epistemologies tend to be more interested in the meaning of things for people participating in development than in generalizing about overall trends in development. Perhaps it is difficult to combine the two, which might imply that the notions of validity used for survey data would be different from the notions of validity applied to qualitative data. There is no settled answer to these questions. However, it is important for any researcher or development practitioner to offer evidence in connection with their claims. Then they may wish to be self-critical and to consider possible challenges to the interpretations that they make of the data. Thus it is possible to question empirical data from different viewpoints.

One of our critical readers for this Theme, Jesimen Chipika, had the following critical points to make about our ways of knowing. She was concerned with the policy and action implications as well as the theoretical issues. Summarizing her points, she states:

> *Empiricism:* It is true that empiricists say that data must be backed by observed, and generalizable, evidence. However, there is [also] a danger of misrepresentation in qualitative data, which can result in ... the use of indicative and exaggerated language based on small-scale data sets.
>
> *Standpoint theory:* While standpoint theory is true and useful for redressing inequality and designing targeted intervention, there is a danger of resource misallocation when every interest group is fighting for special status, especially where it is undeserved.
>
> *Pluralism:* It is important to see the same thing from different perspectives using different notions of validity, as in pluralism. Generalizations are not very useful for understanding problems and policy design. [However, t]he real challenge is to tell a consistently meaningful story for policy and action design from the different perspectives.
>
> (Chipika, 2001)

She also gave the following example from working with unemployment data:

> From my background in Economics plus a heavy dose of Statistics, I used to believe in data evidence until I began having insight into how published data are gathered in reality.
>
> Currently, being with the International Labour Organization, I can tell you that unemployment figures in developing countries are most problematic. The problem arises from different definitions in different surveys and between international definitions and the lived experience of unemployment.
>
> Most standard definitions of unemployment require that the person in the labour force must have been actively seeking employment in the last 7 days or sometimes last 12 months. This means that 'resigned' job seekers, who are the majority in our structurally problematic economies, are not part of the official unemployment figures.
>
> In Zimbabwe, for example, the latest Labour Force Survey of 1999 [at the time of writing] put the unemployment rate at 6–7%, which is ridiculously low. The misleading policy implication is that there is no unemployment problem in Zimbabwe. The lived unemployment experience in Zimbabwe is currently estimated at around 60%, showing that unemployment has reached crisis proportions for social stability to be expected in the nation.
>
> (Chipika, 2001)

You can reflect on this interesting perspective in the light of the previous discussion (including the issue of operationalizing concepts discussed in Box 3.1 above, and the data in Section 2 of this Theme).

Representing poverty through participatory approaches

In recent years the idea of externally organized data creation has been criticized by Robert Chambers (whose name you will have come across in various sections of this course, including in this Theme) and others who advocate participatory appraisal of poverty. Rather than creating survey data, or doing structured interviews leading to qualitative data sets, Chambers and others have recommended letting people speak for themselves (Chambers, 1994, 1997; Pretty, 1995; chapters in Thomas *et al.*, 1998). In the social sciences this distinction is often seen as parallel to the gap between economics and anthropology, where economics is seen as offering an 'outsider's' viewpoint on things whilst anthropology is seen as offering an 'insider's' viewpoint. Of course, there are problems with the notion of a single insider's view, because there is so much differentiation in any one village or town that there are sure to be multiple interpretations and multiple insiders' views. Nevertheless, Chambers insists that it is better to try to give local people a chance to speak.

Outsider research* takes an outsider's view and applies it to a situation. For instance, outsider research might apply a specific academic theory by estimating variables rooted in that theory and testing whether the theory's predictions are substantiated. On the other hand, insider research* explores the insider's viewpoints. The passage below from the work of J.C. Scott, who researched the everyday lives of peasant farmers in Malaysia in the 1980s, illustrates insider research:

*The technical names for outsider and insider research are 'etic' and 'emic' research.

> Two brief commentaries on the present state of affairs in Sedaka [Malaysia] will serve to illustrate how the facts reported … can take on widely divergent meanings …
>
> Pak Yah, a landless labourer with eight children, has always been hard-pressed to make ends meet. His situation is reflected not only in his house … but in his nickname. He is called *Yah-Botol* (Yah-Bottle). The reference is to the sound made by the bottle of cooking oil rattling in his bicycle basket as he pedals back and forth nearly every afternoon to his house near the far end of the village. It is at the same time a reference to his poverty, since he can seldom afford more than the 30¢ minimum purchase and must therefore buy oil daily. Unlike Razak, he is widely regarded as an honest and reliable worker. I have heard him complain bitterly before about the difficulty of finding work and about his futile efforts to rent in even a small piece of paddy land. On this occasion, however, he is even angrier than usual about having been denied any of the funds recently distributed by local United Malay Nationalists' Organisation (UMNO) leaders as part of the Village Improvement Scheme (RPK). Spurred on by a couple of neighbors (Nor and Mat 'halus'), who were also ignored at the handout, he launches into a more global assessment of the situation.
>
> 'The well-to-do are throwing those who are hard up aside. The more we want to lift ourselves, the more we are pushed down, the more cruel [they are to us]. They want to bury us.' As he says this last phrase, Pak Yah thrusts the heel of his hand toward the ground at his feet as if pushing

> something into the earth and adds, 'We want to be higher.' To illustrate what he means, he notes that in the past it was possible to get loans of rice from the well-off villagers. But now, he claims, they sell their rice for cash and then claim they have no money.
>
> This last charge, which I had heard several times before from other poor villagers, deserves some comment.
>
> (Scott, 1985, pp.141–142)

Scott goes on to discuss which generalizations are reasonable, based on fundamental disagreements he observed among villagers. Scott has shown great attention to detail here, and he respects the meanings that poor people attribute to the actions (or lack of action) in the villages. Scott's 1985 book is an 'ethnography': a long work of detailed description and analysis of a given locale using anthropological methods. Participatory research on poverty derives much insight from such methods. Its proponents argue that a relatively rapid, cost-effective way of doing participatory research would be to call meetings, ask for verbal contributions, and walk around a poor area with local people doing analytical exercises that help them to express their tacit knowledge of what is happening and how best to interpret it. Pure ethnographic research on poverty might have been mainly interpretative and descriptive in the past, but in recent years this approach has, for many people, developed into 'critical anthropology' in which lessons are drawn for development interventions and practical activism. There is much in common between critical anthropology and participatory development research, and both have made contributions to the poverty debate.

However, we should also remember some of the problems associated with gathering data on lived experience using participatory approaches. Chipika names a few in her comments on this Theme:

> When people are interviewed in a group, they can be unduly persuaded to go along with the opinion of the influential members ... even if on their own they would have thought differently ... Books have been written about rural development in which conflicting stories emerge concerning the same community depending on which group the researcher interacted with:
>
> - The local government officers ... report an efficient institutional set up, [while] the NGOs and some local people report the opposite.
> - The agricultural extension worker reports increasing food output while the environmentalist screams about extreme environmental degradation leading to unsustainable food production.
> - The local headman or councillor reports efficient channels of government food relief distribution for political reasons.
> - The local better-off farmer is worried about markets while the silent poor farmer is worried about everything.
>
> Most development social scientists will probably agree that no data collection methodology is sufficient on its own in exploring adequately

> the dynamics of development ... Quantitative research gives individuals a chance to answer independently (the silent poor/weak in society can be heard) concerning what they are experiencing … For example, Zimbabwe, for the first 5–6 years of independence, was hailed as a food success story until survey data unveiled massive household food insecurity and high levels of child malnutrition, overshadowed by pockets of success. This shows that the level of objectivity has serious implications for policy direction, magnitude and impact of intervention programmes. It is the researcher's task to draw on the general trends in the community under study and, together with participatory approaches, build a coherent story in the community.
>
> (Chipika, 2001)

We hope that this discussion in this subsection will make you more aware of how data on poverty are gathered and analysed, and that you will ask yourselves some of the questions raised here when you look at the data below (and how they were collected, which is described in the next subsection), as well as in other parts of this course.

3.3 Finding out about lived experience among the poor in rural India

Now we will look at the lived experience of poverty amongst households in two villages of Chittoor District, Andhra Pradesh, India. The data on these households were collected in a survey carried out by Wendy Olsen, one of the authors of this Theme, and her colleague, Uma Rani, in 1995 (Olsen and Rani, 1997). Uma Rani interviewed one person from each of 115 households in two villages. In this section, we look briefly at some of the issues involved in the collection of these data and the context in which they were collected. Then, in Section 3.4, we look at inequality in access to land and use of land amongst these 115 households. In Section 3.5 we turn our attention to the livelihoods of eight particular households by studying data that were collected in the survey on their land, crops' labour use and income. We also look at qualitative data from interviews with some of the women.

The survey: Wendy Olsen's own account

Collecting the survey data

In order to make a *random sample* in the survey (Box 3.2), we needed a list of the households in the study area. We obtained the local electoral registers, and we checked for changes to update the list by asking several local élite people to help us. We augmented the list by annotating it with an estimate of the land held by each household. Of course this implies switching from individuals as the *unit of analysis*, where each adult is listed on the electoral register, to the *household unit of analysis*, where each household is seen as owning a given amount of land. Local people had no problem grouping the adults' names on the list into their households and estimating the land held.

Box 3.2 Random sampling

Simple random sampling is when each person or unit has an equal chance of selection. However, populations being sampled often have distinct groups or strata that differ from each other on some key variables being researched. In this case, *stratified random sampling* was used, i.e. sampling each stratum separately. The researchers wanted to ensure that the rich households were included as well as poor ones, so they used stratified random sampling based on the amount of land held. Land was being used as an indicator of wealth.

Our personal approach, lengthy preparations, use of the local language (Telugu), and past experience in doing rural research made all this possible. If a tax inspector or other outsider wanted to ask for the same information, they might not get the truth. The land-holdings' information is particularly sensitive. We later checked the land-holdings' information by asking in detail about each plot during the questionnaire interview, and we found few gaps between the original estimate and the later figure. There is often a tendency for small and large farmers to underestimate their own land holdings, because of the risk of taxation or land ceilings which owners may feel as a threat. If you ask the questions in public and check them with knowledgeable local people, you may be able to find out these details without too much trouble. In some cultural situations, however, you simply cannot ask and you need to be sensitive to such issues.

It took several months for Uma Rani to complete the 115 questionnaire-based interviews. Rural people are often busy working, and some do not see the point of sitting down to explain (to them) rather obvious details about their farming and other work to an outsider. Again, you might imagine that if they were doing the research themselves, under a more participatory methodology, their motivation might be stronger (although participatory approaches can also be quite time-consuming both for researchers and other participants). However, we used a non-participatory method, and in the end Uma Rani often found that she had to go to the fields during the working day (clipboard in hand) and ask the man of the house to talk with her under a tree during the lunch break. She would then re-visit the household in the evening if necessary to fill in any additional details. The questionnaire was about ten pages long and Uma Rani also did various longer, less structured, interviews about moneylending, farming, cropping patterns, and other matters. In some instances we were both present and took detailed notes. A number of women were later interviewed at length from among the sampled households.

Why did Uma Rani talk to the 'man of the house'? We knew that we were interested in gender relations and women, but Uma Rani felt that to get the details of farming, animals, labouring, sharecropping, borrowing, and investments in wells, it was essential to talk with the men, not the women. Most men and women agreed with Uma Rani and sent her to find the head of household rather than talk with others about these matters. In other words in this region there was a widespread perception that the male head of household would speak on behalf of the household members about economic and poverty-related matters. However, in other parts of India and in other countries, one might find a number of female heads of household, single women living alone, or women sharing decisions and knowledge about their household. In many parts of Africa women would be seen as having the knowledge about farming that was here attributed mainly to men.

Classifying the households

In describing poverty we felt it valuable to contrast the main social classes in the study area. Social classes can be defined from within (as how people feel their society is stratified) or from without (as how an outsider would classify people). One social-class division, frequently used in Indian research on farming, is based on how much land is owned. Landless, marginal farmers, small farmers, and large farmers are four categories that partially define farming classes. However, these 'land size classes' have been debated in India. It was observed that some large farmers leave some land as fallow or waste, whilst many small farmers used their land intensively. Looking at land alone did not tell the whole story of social inequality, the nature of people's livelihoods and positions in society.

So this survey did not just look at land as the main determinant of people's social position in the villages. We also looked at people's labour relations: whether they used only their own labour on their farms, whether they hired labour, and whether they had to sell their labour. This approach is also based on people's relations to each other (in how they gained access to land, if they had land, in how their own labour was used, and in how they used others' labour). This approach was thus 'relational'. One advantage of this approach was that instead of placing merchants and teachers (who often have no land) with the 'landless' as if they were poor, we placed them in a higher social class *as if they employed others*.

We ended up with four social classes according to how people entered the local labour markets. These are outlined in Table 3.5. The proportion of each social class in our 'stratified random sample' of 115 households is in the pie chart in Figure 3.2.

It was possible to classify every household in the sample according to this scheme, because nearly everyone either had land, or was a tenant, or worked on the land as a labourer sometimes. There were a couple of households that did stone-breaking work, and they were classified as workers.

Table 3.5 The four social classes defined

Workers (*kuulies*)	At least one person in the household normally or usually works (e.g. as a farm labourer or construction worker) for others
Farmer-workers (*ryots*)	Some people in the household report themselves as working for others, but some also call themselves farmers (in Telugu, *ryots*)
Ryots (farmers not workers)	People in the household call themselves farmers (*ryots*) but no one works as a farm labourer or other employee
Supervisors only	People in the household employ others either to do their farm labour or household labour, and they do not work for others

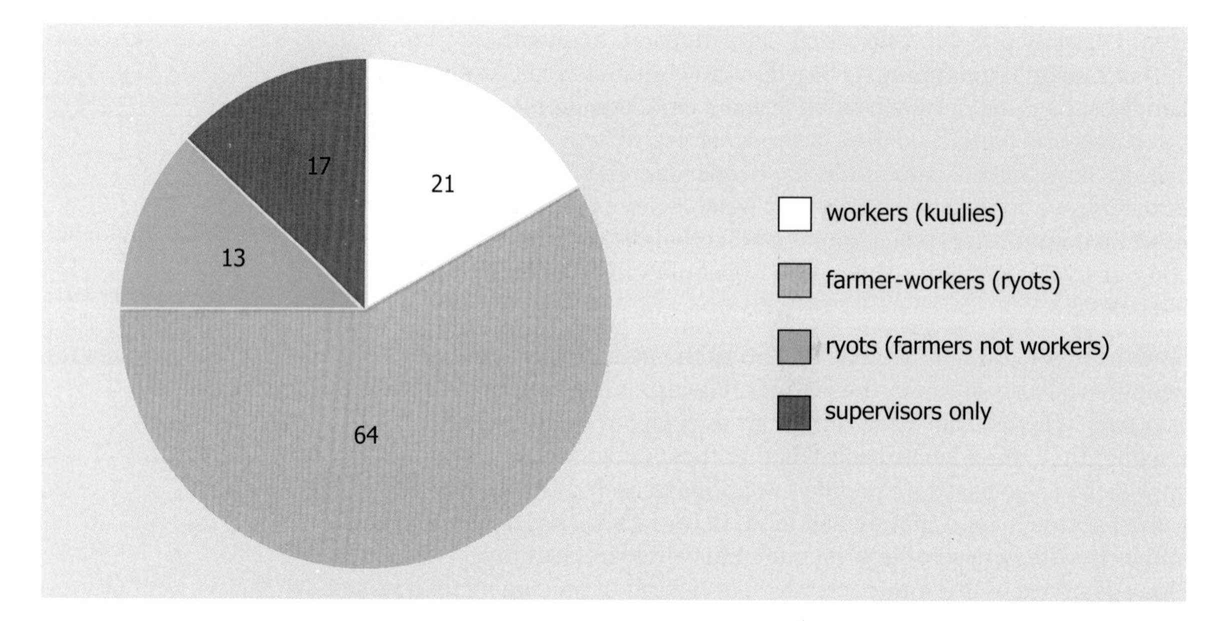

Figure 3.2 Pie chart showing distribution of households in survey. The figure shows the numbers of households of each type. (Data from fieldwork in 1995; Olsen, 2001.)

In the local language the words *kuulie* (worker) and *ryot* (farmer) are well established. Even when speaking in English or Urdu people still labelled each other using these words. On the other hand, 'supervisors' is a word the researchers introduced, whereas local people would call the members of these households either *bhuuswamivaaru* (landlords), *vysya* (merchants), or by their occupation, such as *mastaaru* (teacher) or simply 'teacher'. We grouped the supervisors together since they had in common that they always got other people to do the farm work for them, rather than doing it themselves. Some 'supervisors' had jobs and were therefore employees by standard Western class typologies, but there were so few contractual employees in the sample that it was hardly worth separating these white-collar employees (such as teachers) from the other supervisors of farm labour.

There is however an additional issue with class identification, one that has been made apparent, in particular by gender analysis. Gender analysis has shown us how individuals within households often have unequal relations to each other as well as to others outside the household. As well as taking gender differences into account, there are other issues involved in labelling a whole household as being in a given social class. For example, in this study, if there were individuals who owned some land and/or individuals who were tenants and/or individuals who were workers or labourers living in the same household, what social class would the household fall into?

Classifying households rather than individuals as if they could employ others or be employed is a sleight of hand that simplifies data. However, it does lead to the idea that households are individuals or are acting as individuals (just as firms are in micro-economics, and countries might be when discussing world trade). There is a danger of forgetting that it is individuals who have livelihoods and that it is people, not households, who do labour.

Thus in our study, we also looked for ways of modifying our categorization of households into social classes. To do this, we cross-tabulated data about the individuals within households. In this instance, we cross-tabulated their access to land with their use of labour (i.e. could employ others or were employed by others). We kept the categories simple. We cross-tabulated people who either held land as a tenant (i.e. rented land) or did not hold land as a tenant. (Those who did not hold land as a tenant would have either owned their land or would have had no land at all.) Some results of this cross-tabulation are shown in Table 3.6. From it you can see that we were able to be more precise about the social class characteristics of our households with respect to land as well as labour.

Table 3.6 Tenants and non-tenants by social class

Class by labour relations	*Not a tenant*	*Tenant*	*Total*
Workers (*kuulies*)	19	2	21
Farmer-workers (*ryots*)	28	36	64
Ryots (farmers not workers)	6	7	13
Supervisors only	17	0	17
Totals	70	45	115

You can probably see from this table that:

- most of those who said they were only employed by others did not rent land;
- those who described themselves as both farming and being employed by others were divided between renting land and not renting any (in the latter category, there may have been some farmers who had their own land);
- those who said they only farmed but did not work for others, were evenly divided between renting and not-renting land (in this case because they would have owned some);
- none of the supervisors rented land.

Activity 3.4

To finish this subsection, we suggest you carry out some short calculations from these data to see how using percentages as opposed to raw numbers can provide you with a different perspective on things.

You had to calculate percentages at different times in *Study Guide 1* (for example, Activities 22 and 26). This activity enables you to see what different ways of calculating percentages can tell you about a given set of data.

Using the data in Table 3.6, make column percentages (out of the total of 115 households) of the tenants and non-tenants in each social class.

Next work out what percentage of the households in each social class are tenants.

Then work out the column percentages of tenant farmers in each social class.

Put your results in the tables below.

Are you surprised by any of your findings? Why?

You should check the percentages in Appendix 2. Some of our comments are below.

(Spend no more than 1 hour on this activity)

Column percentages of tenants and non-tenants in each social class

Class by labour relations	*Not a tenant*	*Tenant*	*Total*
Workers (*kuulies*)	19 (%)	2 (%)	21 (%)
Farmer-workers (*ryots*)	28 (%)	36 (%)	64 (%)
Ryots (farmers not workers)	6 (%)	7 (%)	13 (%)
Supervisors only	17 (%)	0 (%)	17 (%)
Totals	70 (%)	45 (%)	115 (%)

The percentage of households in each social class that are tenants

Class by labour relations	*Total number in each social class*	*Number of tenants in each social class*	*Percentage of each social class that are tenants (rounded to nearest whole percentage)*
Workers (*kuulies*)	21	2	
Farmer-workers (*ryots*)	64	36	
Ryots (farmers not workers)	13	7	
Supervisors only	17	0	

The column percentage of tenant farmers in each social class

Class by labour relations	*Tenant*	*Percentage of tenants in each social class (rounded to nearest whole percentage)*
Workers (*kuulies*)	2	
Farmer-workers (*ryots*)	36	
Ryots (farmers not workers)	7	
Supervisors only	0	
Total	45	

Comment

The first table shows a distribution of tenants and non-tenants in each social class. It is best read vertically (by columns). Looking at the 'tenant' column, we can see, for example, that 39% of all households in the sample were renting land (100 × (45/115)). Most of the households that rented land combined farming with some waged work (31% of all the households), while only 2% of households were both tenants and predominantly worker households. There are two possible explanations: either the workers were too poor to rent land; alternatively, they owned land (unlikely!). Looking at the 'not a tenant' column, we can see that 61% of the households did not rent land. We can safely assume that, for most of these households, this was because they owned land. However, for the 17% of households that were both worker households and 'non-tenants' the opposite would have been true: in their case, the likelihood is that they could afford neither to own nor to rent land.

The second table shows the percentage of households in each social class that are tenants, and is best read horizontally (by rows). Thus 10% of workers were tenants, 56% of farmer-workers were tenants, etc.

The third table show the percentage of tenant farmers (or those renting land) that falls into each social class. Column 3 should be read vertically, and shows that only 4% of all tenants were workers compared with farmer-workers who were 80% of the tenants.

You can see it is possible to calculate and present these data in different ways, depending on what aspects you want to pick out and demonstrate to others. These different ways of calculating and presenting data help to illustrate some of the complexities in the picture. However, to what extent do you think that the data so far indicate which were the *poorest* households in terms of assets (labour and land)? Do you think we can assume that the non-tenant worker households were the poorest because they only had their labour to sell and no land? How would you relate this to Moser's asset-vulnerability analysis? Probably more information is needed, for example about output and income, to help us assess the relative wealth and poverty of the households, something we will come to in Section 3.5.

3.4 Inequality between households

Let us now turn more specifically to the 115 households and the inequalities between them. First let us provide a bit more background on the agrarian situation. Wendy Olsen set out to examine the effects of free-market reforms in India since 1991 on men and women in selected villages in southern Andhra Pradesh. The initial hypothesis was that cuts in subsidies in rural credit, farming inputs, health care, public transport, education, and food would have led to significant economic stress by 1995. The study intended to examine class, caste and gender differences in the effects, thus giving more nuances to the kind of national deterioration in conditions summarized by Judith Scott with respect to some African countries in *Introduction to Poverty and Inequality* (see Table 4.3 there). In India, however, the reforms of the early 1990s did not have the strong village-level effects that had been predicted. Resistance among élites, politicians, civil servants, and voters contributed to India's policy of maintaining a social safety net (see Section 2 of this Theme) and avoiding or postponing cuts that would have had a strong short-term negative effect on the poor. India devalued its currency by 100% in the 1990s but it did not reduce its government budget deficit much. By contrast, earlier structural adjustment programmes in African and Latin American countries had involved more drastic curbs on government spending.

In this context, much of the field research examined the existing uptake of, and attitudes toward, public services and those of their private-sector competitors. The research also looked at gender aspects of labouring, the use of banks, food rations, and changing intra-household relations. The findings are summarized in Olsen (2001). Here we have extracted some relevant data for you to examine from the initial household survey and some of the interviews. In reporting on this research, we use the actual village names but we have invented personal pseudonyms to protect the identities of the respondents and the people to whom they referred.

Inequality among the 115 households in the survey takes several forms. As well as the inequalities of class and caste, there is considerable gender inequality. These forms of inequality cannot always be addressed using household-level data. We have already mentioned above how gender inequality within households means that it is difficult to determine the labour relations dimension of social class of a household from the labour relations of a male household head or other individual. In addition, employing others as domestic servants is sometimes an activity overseen by women within households, not by men; and employing others as low-waged workers (with a corresponding power imbalance between the firm's owner and these employees) may be done by a particular man whose wife and other household members have little to do with the unequal relations of employment. Depending on what one wants to look at, it is not necessarily best to use household-level data and it may be desirable to examine personal or individual data.

We cannot, however, address all these dimensions in this section of the *Poverty and Inequality* Theme. So we will look here at some basic economic data to demonstrate how inequality between (rather than within) households can be measured and displayed. In doing so, we will also learn something about the relative wealth of the 115 households in this survey.

Income is often taken as a proxy for other factors that are thought to be strongly associated with inequality. Another example is inequality in access to assets. You will remember that we discussed the role of assets in livelihoods in Section 1, in particular the view that declines and increases in assets make people more or less vulnerable to further impoverishment. We cannot look at changes over time here, but in this subsection and the next, we consider the distribution of assets in land (and later in labour, and such elements as literacy).

Here we look at inequality of access to assets in land amongst the 115 households. Land in India can be held either through ownership or through rented access. We will look closely at the distribution of 'land owned' and then at the distribution of 'land operated'.

Two calculations can be made to summarize inequality using such data: the Lorenz curve, which is a diagram, and the Gini coefficient, which is a coefficient or number that summarizes the shape of the Lorenz diagram (in this case, the ratio of the degree of inequality to a hypothetical state of perfectly equal distribution).

To make a Lorenz curve for land distribution, we need to construct a table containing all the land-ownership figures for households, *ranked from lowest to highest.* After ranking the households the poorest are at the top of the list. We can then break the list up into *percentiles* and work out the sum of the land held by each percentile of the sampled households.

You came across percentiles in *Introduction to Poverty and Inequality*. Percentiles may be different in size. For example, deciles are one-tenth portions, or 10%, of the whole, and quintiles are one-fifth portions, or 20%, of the whole. In Table 3.7, we have used quintiles. For a Lorenz curve diagram based on these data, you need to plot the points corresponding to each quintile onto a graph. In this case, we are going to sum up the assets for each quintile going from the poorest to the richest. This summing up is called *cumulation*. We will then plot a graph with a horizontal axis labelled according to the *population* and a vertical axis labelled according to the *assets going to that part of the population*.

Now look at Table 3.7 which displays the data for our 115 households in the form needed to construct the Lorenz curve for the distribution of access to land. If you cumulate five quintiles of the population (i.e. the 115 households in this case), you get 100% of the households. However, the land owned is not distributed so evenly between the quintiles of households. If it were, we would have a perfect distribution of land between households – i.e. each household would own the same amount of land. (Note that a perfect distribution does not necessarily mean a fair distribution – a large household will need more assets than a small household to have the same level of wealth per capita.)

To construct this table we had to take the following steps. There were 115 households overall, and 20% of 115 is 23. Therefore the households were grouped by computer into five batches of 23, starting with the landless and moving toward the large landlord households who came last.

Table 3.7 Calculating Lorenz curves for land

Quintile	*Percentage of the households*	*Cumulative percentage of the households*	*Percentage of total land owned*	*Cumulative percentage of total land owned*
Lowest quintile	20	20	0	0
2nd quintile	20	40	2	2
3rd quintile	20	60	9	11
4th quintile	20	80	16	27
Highest quintile	20	100	73	100
Totals	100	100	100	100

Activity 3.5

Here are some interpretations of the table above. Check that you have understood them before continuing:

1. The poorest 20% of the people (in terms of access to land) own no land at all.
2. The second poorest quintile (in terms of access to land) owns just 2% of the land (meaning also that 40% of the 115 households own only 2% of the land between them).

3 Overall, the poorest 60% of the households (in terms of access to land) own just 11% of the land.

4 The quintile with the most land owns 73% of the land but is just 20% of the households in the sample.

(Spend no more than 15 minutes on this activity)

You can already see that there is a very uneven distribution of land between households and a high level of inequality. What the Lorenz curve can do is to display how unequal this distribution is.

As we said above, the Lorenz curve is the diagram giving a view of the cumulative distribution of land held against the cumulative distribution of the population. The Lorenz curve for the data in Table 3.7 is shown in Figure 3.3.

The Lorenz curve is the lower of the two lines, or the 'curve', in this diagram. In this case, the curve is approximated by line segments. If we were to rank each individual landholding, and plot 115 points showing the cumulative holding for each household, we would have a nearly smooth curve. The diagonal line is a line that shows what absolute equality of land-holdings would look like (that is, if each quintile had exactly 20% of the land, in contrast to the wide variation between the quintiles in Table 3.7). It is purely hypothetical but has an important purpose in the diagram, because it is the gap between this hypothetical line and the curve that enables us to measure the overall inequality of land distribution. The nearer the curve approaches the diagonal line, the nearer it approaches an equal distribution. Obversely, the bigger the gap between the diagonal line and the curve, the greater the inequality in land ownership. Thus having both the curve of the quintiles of the 115 households *and* the line of absolute equality of distribution helps to demonstrate the extent of inequality in land ownership in this case.

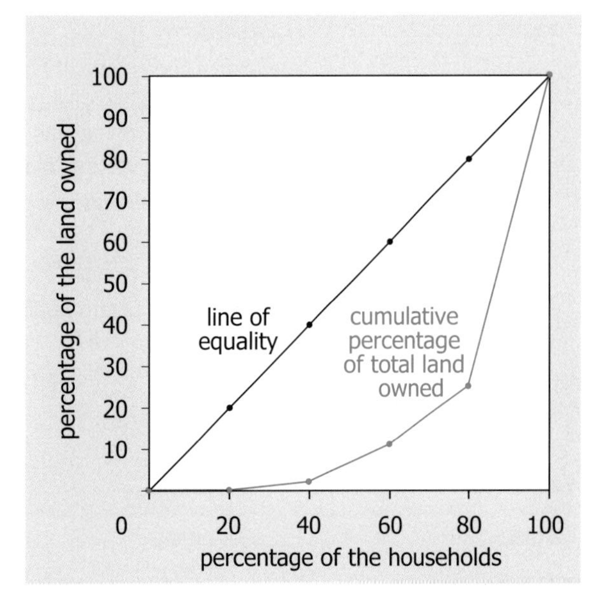

Figure 3.3 Lorenz curve and line of equality for land owned.

Activity 3.6

Write brief notes giving your own interpretation of Figure 3.3 above. Just review for yourself what you see there, referring to Table 3.7 if necessary. For example, what would you say about the data in Table 3.7 in relation to the line of absolute equality? What would you say about the curve in Figure 3.3 in relation to the line of absolute equality?

Compare your notes with ours in Appendix 2.

Finally, what do you think are the implications of lack of access, or minimal access, to land for the first 60% of households?

(Spend no more than 15 minutes on this activity)

Comment

In relation to the last question, the number of landless and near-landless rural households suggests that the people in those households do not have access to their own on-farm income and may well be working for others – with one major caveat. The landless and near-landless people, as well as the land-owning households, may rent in land. (We have seen in Table 3.6 in the previous subsection that some *kuulies* and *ryots* are tenants.)

If we allow for land rented in (adding it to a household's own land) and then subtract the land rented out, if any, we get an adjusted land-holding measure called *land operated*.*

*Land operated = land owned + land rented in – land rented out.

Let us now look at the data to find out about inequality in land operated. This time, you can construct the Lorenz curve yourself.

Activity 3.7

Use Table 3.8 below, which contains data on land operated, to sketch a Lorenz curve for land operated on Figure 3.4. First draw in the diagonal line for absolute equality between the farms. Then use the third and fifth columns of Table 3.8 to plot points on the diagram for the Lorenz curve, starting from the top. To do this, first take the cumulative percentage of households (20%) and locate the 20% marker on the horizontal axis. Then take the cumulative percentage of total land operated by that 20% (in this case 1% of the land) and plot it above the 20% marker at the 1% level according to the vertical axis. This will, of course, be approximate, as the scale does not show each percentage. Then continue down columns 3 and 5 to plot the other quintiles. Then join them up. Of course, as above, what you obtain is just a series of line segments, not a true curve.

Now look at our Lorenz curve in Appendix 2 (Figure A2.1) and compare it with the previous Lorenz curve for land owned in Figure 3.3. What do you think the differences are?

(Spend no more than 1 hour on this activity)

Table 3.8 Land operated

Quintile	*Percentage of the households*	*Cumulative percentage of the households*	*Percentage of total land operated*	*Cumulative percentage of total land operated*
Lowest quintile	20	20	1	1
2nd quintile	20	40	6	7
3rd quintile	20	60	11	18
4th quintile	20	80	17	35
Highest quintile	20	100	65	100
Totals	100	100	100	100

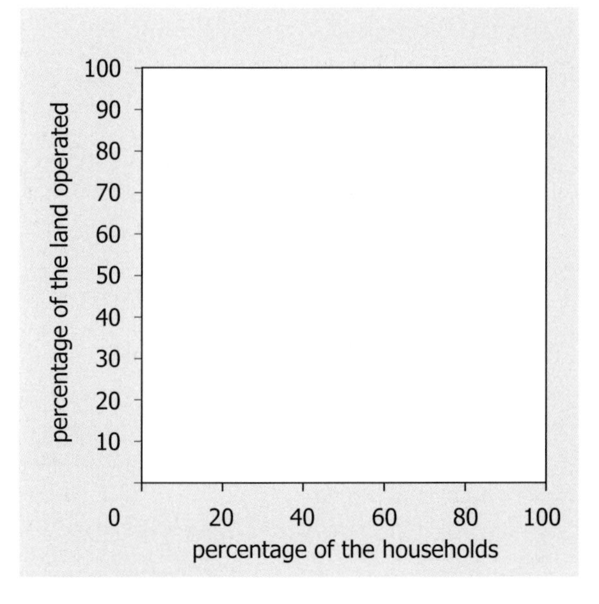

Figure 3.4 Graph for Lorenz curve.

Comment

The Lorenz curve shown in Appendix 2 is somewhat nearer to the diagonal line than the previous one. There is less 'landlessness' once tenants are counted as operating some land. There is also a concentration among the top 20% of farmers of just 65% of the land, rather than 73% as in the land-ownership Lorenz curve. (These figures are derived by subtracting 35% from 100%, giving 65%, and then subtracting 27% from 100%, giving 73%.) Thus one could say that combining ownership and renting (or tenancy) into data for land operated indicates less inequality than for ownership of land alone.

Does this mean that there is less inequality overall, or that inequality is hidden through the relations of rent – i.e. because of the fact that people rent land from landlords for their own farming? In practice, the association of land owned with land operated is very high. In Figure 3.5 you will find the scattergram relating these two variables for these two villages. Each point is one household. The scattergram shows a line that best fits the 115 points and you will see that there is a strong clustering around the line with one or two outliers. The largest landowner in the sample is at the top right-hand corner.

In relation to the issues raised by drawing a Lorenz curve for land operated in Activity 3.7 above and the data provided in Figure 3.5, let us think for a moment about the issues raised for *poverty* as well as inequality, and make an interpretation of the data we have been considering so far on these 115 households. Tenancy is a form of appropriation and control of labour by larger landowners (see Box 3.3). We saw a rather extreme example of the possible effects of this with the case of Murari's debt bondage at the beginning of this section. In other words, inequality is a representation of specific relations between landowners and those who work the land. This is a *relational* view of land poverty.

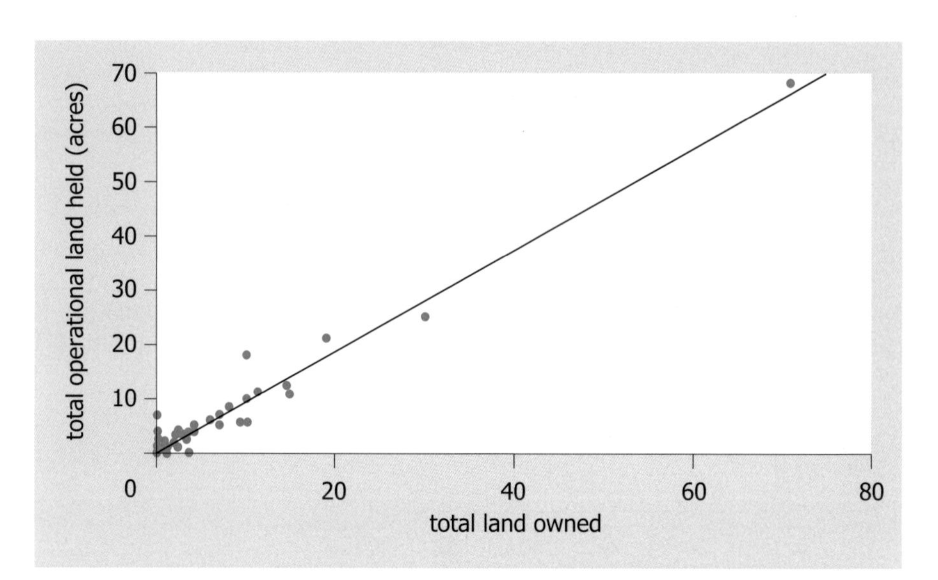

Figure 3.5 Local distribution of land owned and land operated in two Indian villages. (Data from fieldwork in 1995 by W. Olsen and U. Rani.)

Box 3.3 The social relations of tenancy

Tenancy in south India

Tenancy in south India is a labour relation which offers varying terms between landowners and the worker who manages the production of crops on a piece of land. The tenant pays a share of the crop to the landowner. In some cases the payment is a pre-arranged cash fee, but in either case the net effect is that the returns to the tenant family depend on the output of the crop and they therefore have an incentive to produce the crop with the highest physical or money return. The landowner, or landlord in local language, may supply water from a well or other inputs, and as a result there are variations in the terms of the contract such as 50:50 share or one-third share payment. In the view of labour-relations experts, tenancy relations involve a special form of exploitation of labour since the landowner does not do any physical work on the land, but still gets paid. The landlord realizes some of the proceeds of the work of the tenants. However tenancy agreements are highly popular and often run for years on end, since they are a way for both households to improve their livelihoods given the unequal initial distribution of land.

Reverse tenancy

In some other parts of India conditions are different. *Reverse tenancy* can occur. Reverse tenancy is when small landowners rent their land holdings out to larger farmers. The reasons for reverse tenancy are complex but have to do with conditions in both land and labour markets. For instance, where labour is scarce, a small farmer may be able to get a job somewhere else which offers better wages than returns from farming; in this case the farmer may want to rent out the land to another farmer. For this reason most writers about rural livelihoods are hesitant to generalize about the connection between *tenancy* and *inequality*. However, as you can see from this discussion, there is also a link, which is not straightforward either, to *poverty*. Thus renting out land to others and seeking work elsewhere may be seen as a livelihood strategy to mitigate the effects of poverty.

Finally, let us consider the Gini coefficient and what it tells us. The Gini coefficient is calculated as *the ratio of the space between the Lorenz curve and the diagonal of perfectly equal distribution, to the total space below the diagonal*. If you think of the box as having a one-unit size, and the space between the Lorenz curve and the diagonal growing with greater inequality, then clearly the Gini coefficient will increase with greater inequality. Figure 3.6 illustrates the concept of a Gini coefficient. The Gini index is the Gini coefficient expressed as a percentage (thus a coefficient of 0.45 will be an index of 45%). You will remember looking at the Gini index in *Introduction to Poverty and Inequality* (Section 6.3).

To explain the Gini coefficient in mathematical terms, look again at Figure 3.6. In mathematical terms, a square's area is calculated as height times width. A triangle like A + B has an area equal to half of that of the corresponding square. Since the scale on each axis runs from 0 to 1, the area of A + B is thus 0.5. The question is, how large is the space A, or area of A, relative to this baseline of 0.5?

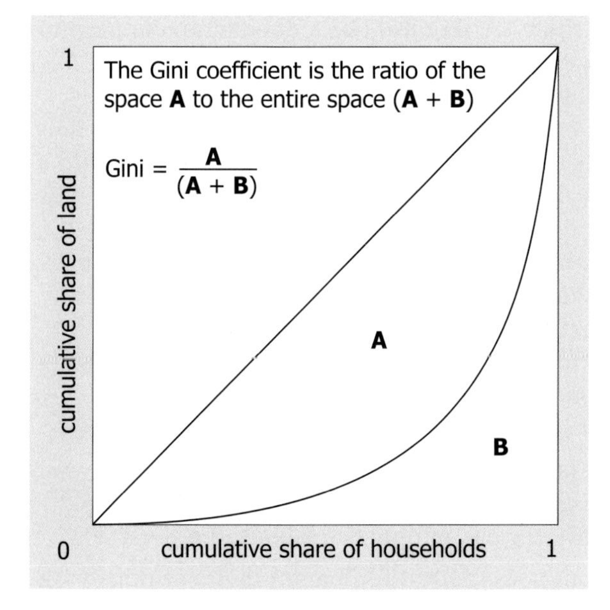

Figure 3.6 Gini coefficient formula and illustration.

If the area of A is 0.2, then the ratio is: 0.2:0.5. To work out this ratio as a fraction, you need to divide 0.2 by 0.5, which is 0.2/.5 = 0.4. This would thus be a Gini coefficient of 0.4. Expressed as a percentage, this is 40%. The Gini index would thus be 40%.

The larger A is (i.e. the more unequal the distribution), the higher will be the Gini coefficient. Obversely, the higher the Gini coefficient, e.g. 0.75 compared with 0.4, the more inequality there is.

In the case of the 115 households, we put the data into a computer spreadsheet and obtained the Gini coefficients and indexes shown below:

For land owned: Gini coefficient = 0.38; Gini index = 38%.

For land operated: Gini coefficient = 0.22; Gini index = 22%.

The best interpretation of these coefficients is to say that the inequality is less in the distribution of land operated. Notice that if there were high equality, you would have a Gini coefficient of around zero or 0.05 or 0.1, and when there is very high inequality you have a Gini coefficient around 0.8 or 0.9.

As a final reflection on the broader picture in India and our 115 households, we might note the following. The Gini coefficient for *income* inequality for India as a whole is 0.3, compared with 0.6 for Brazil or 0.48 for Malaysia or 0.4 for the United States. Thus while social inequality is great in India (as manifested in caste relations, for example) and there is rural inequality in land owned, the broader picture is one in which India's overall national *income* inequality is less than that found in, say, Brazil, Malaysia or the USA. In rural India, it is relatively hard to measure income because, as well as the diverse sources and forms of income, a proportion of what is produced is consumed directly by households rather than sold for cash. Therefore, looking at assets such as land, or particular elements of income such as wages, can help to build a picture of inequality. In the case of the 115 households, the inequality in distribution of assets in land owned was somewhat greater than the national income inequality index. (We might find that there is greater or lesser inequality in land ownership for India as a whole compared with Andhra Pradesh.) However, we also saw that the Gini coefficient for inequality in land distribution was reduced from 0.38 to 0.22 for these households when land operated was calculated. *Thus inequality in landholdings may be offset by other livelihood practices.* For example:

- Poor people may rent in land for production or may rent it out to others, thus tenancy can have an equalizing effect as well as being part of the ways that landlords can exploit the labour of others.
- Land-poor households can potentially supplement their earnings with diverse sources of non-farm income, as we shall see in Table 3.12 in the next subsection.

3.5 Livelihood practices and lived experience

We are now going to look in more detail at livelihood practices of a few of the 115 households. This will help us gain a richer picture of their lived experience than broad statistical data on land distribution, although the land data for all the households is an important part of the socio-economic context overall. We will look at livelihood practices and lived experience from the following perspectives:

1. We will take some of the survey data on the households and look at their assets, exchange entitlements and sources of vulnerability. We will also look at data on the relative time spent in farm work by men and women and how they were remunerated.
2. We will then analyse some extracts of interviews with women to see what they tell us about their lived experiences.

In carrying out these analyses and activities you will see that there are multiple ways of trying to understand and interpret the lived experience of poverty and inequality, and that we need these multiple approaches to develop a picture that can inform policy and action.

Assets, exchange entitlements and vulnerability

You will remember from Section 1 of this Theme that assets comprise a range of endowments that individuals and households have at their disposal, such as land, livestock, jewellery, housing, education (or literacy – often called human capital), etc. You will also remember how the concept of exchange entitlements has been used in this course: as the goods and services that people can exchange for income, whether in cash or kind. For many poor people, their main asset is also their main exchange entitlement,* namely their labour (you will see that we discuss both dimensions below). Other exchange entitlements include output from own production (Figure 3.7) or sale of assets (which usually only happens when an individual or household is in crisis).

*A definition and discussion is in the Course Book, Chapter 3, p.60.

Consideration of assets and exchange entitlements tells us quite a bit about the lived experiences of poor people. It can also tell us about their potential vulnerability to changes in circumstances, whether resulting from their own actions or from changes in the wider social and economic environment in which they try to make a living. It can also help us think through the implications of policy decisions in a given locality and the likely effects of different types of action on poverty.

Figure 3.7 Women harvesting rice in Maharashtra. Labour is poor people's main asset. It may also be their main exchange entitlement, in that many poor people work as wage labour for others, even if they have other sources of income from crop production, artesanal activity or informal sector work.

We should note that the concepts of assets and entitlements are imposed from the outside to help us analyse and understand the livelihood practices and lived experiences of these households. Moreover, we are going to use these concepts to see what some of the statistical data from the household survey can tell us. This is different from a process of living and working with the households, talking to their occupants over a period of time, and seeing what understandings emerge about people's lives, as an ethnographer might do. In practice, both approaches require concepts to create meaning and to enable us to convey our understandings to other people. So although there is always an outsider element in analysing and translating the worlds of others, the starting point might be different.

In the case of the eight households, we have isolated the following assets and exchange entitlements (Table 3.9), and we have also included a potential area of vulnerability, debt. (The households might be vulnerable on the other areas too, but debt can be a seriously undermining factor in people's livelihoods, not just in rural India but in many urban environments in developed countries.)

Table 3.9

Assets	*Exchange entitlements*	*Potential immediate sources of vulnerability*
Land	Labour	Debt
Labour	Crop outputs	
Literacy	Income from wages and crops (with which other goods and services can be bought)	

These data are laid out in Table 3.10 below. We are now going to interrogate them and see what they tell us about the lived experience of the eight households (in the process learning some further data skills). There are some notes below the table to explain the different categories.

Table 3.10 Livelihood variables of eight households

Household	*Land operated (acres)*	*Land owned (acres)*	*Household wage earnings (rupees, 1994)*	*Household size (number of people)*	*Number of adults in the household*	*% of household members literate*	*Sugar output (kg)*	*Groundnut output (kg)*	*Paddy output (kg)*	*Gross farm income from three crops (estimated in rupees)*	*Total gross cash income (wages and crops) (rupees, 1994)*	*Total debt outstanding (rupees)*
1	2.3	3.3	0	5	3	100	0	520	0	1 768	1 768	1 000
2	25	30	0	6	4	100	4200	4 712	3 800	42 171	42 171	30 000
3	18	10	0	4	4	75	0	11 400	23 940	44 745	44 745	8 000
4	0.5	0.5	4 300	4	2	25	0	700	0	2 380	6 680	1 000
5	2.5	0	3 350	4	2	50	0	1 750	1 140	6 235	9 585	6 000
6	0	0	4 550	3	2	33.33	0	0	0	0	4 550	6 000
7	2.5	2.5	20 000	4	4	37.5	500	0	0	3 000	23 000	2 500
8	0	0	5 950	8	6	0	0	0	0	0	5 950	1 100

Notes to table

Land operated is land owned minus land rented out plus land rented in.

Household 1: further evidence from the research showed that this household was from a merchant caste with income from a small shop, wholesale trading, and dairy activities.

Debt: this included all kinds of debt, from banks and moneylenders, for production and consumption.

Crops: sugar and groundnuts are usually sold for cash. The consumption and sale of paddy may have different patterns. Wealthy farmers are likely to store paddy for their own consumption and/or to sell when they can get a good price. Poor farmers may sell their own paddy and buy cheaper, lower quality, rice for their own consumption.

Livestock: are not mentioned in this table. Households are likely to have chickens, and some have cows or bulls.

Other crops: apart from the three crops shown, other crops occasionally grown include tomato, mulberry leaves for silkworm, and vegetables such as aubergine (eggplant, *brinjal*).

Activity 3.8

First, look at the headings and down each column of Table 3.10 and at the notes at the bottom of the table. Jot down your initial impressions.

Then look across the rows, and do the same thing.

Now make notes in answer to the following specific questions on assets, exchange entitlements and vulnerability.

Assets

- Which households rented land to others? Do you think these were cases of reverse tenancy? If not, why do you think these households rented out their land?
- What was the relationship between literacy rates (human capital) and access to land owned? What do you deduce from these data if anything? Are there any comments you might want to make about these literacy data?

Exchange entitlements

- Which households sold their labour? How did selling labour relate to their access to land?
- Which households had the highest crop values?
- To what extent did income from wage labour balance out low incomes from crops and therefore reduce inequality? (Give a quick impression here.)

Debt

- Which households, if any, appeared most vulnerable to indebtedness? (If you wish, you can calculate the net cash income from farming, according to these data, whether from crops or wages, or crops and wages, and after debts have been paid.)

(Spend no more than 1 hour on this activity)

Comment

First impressions: columns

- Two households had landholdings far above average, and two operated no land at all.
- Access to land is complicated by land rental. Household 3 rented 8 acres in, while household 2 rented 5 acres out.
- All households had at least two adults and most had two children as well.
- Literacy rates vary from 0% to 100% among the households.
- Three households do not have wage earnings and five households do.
- Households 6 and 8 focus entirely on wage earnings, not crop production, for their livelihoods.

First impressions: rows

This analysis involves interpreting the household's situation across several dimensions. We provide notes on three households:

- Household 2: four adults are busy farming three crops on their own land.
- Household 5: a marginal landholding of just a half-acre is sown with groundnuts (peanuts), and the people work for others as well as for themselves.
- Household 8: a poor household for whom agricultural wage labour is the only source of earnings. A large household with a low debt.

Assets

(Land) Households 1 and 2 rented land to others. However, these were the wealthier households amongst the eight (see the note on Household 1 below Table 3.10) – i.e. it was not a case of reverse tenancy. They could have rented out the land for several reasons:

- The land was surplus to requirements.
- They could make more money from renting it out than from growing additional crops.
- They used the land to secure labour (i.e. the land was rented out to labourers).

The critical issue here is that these households had choices that the other households did not.

(Literacy) Households 1, 2 and 3 had higher literacy rates than the other five households. However, overall one needs to treat these data with care: the literacy rates would also have been affected by the composition of the household (numbers of adults to children and the ages of the adults [elderly household members might not have been to school]) as well as people's access to schooling.

Exchange entitlements

(Labour) All the other five households (4–8) sold some labour. The relationship between the amount of labour sold (taking the wages as a proxy measure) and access to land differed across these households, indicating different livelihood strategies as well as household compositions. We can look at these particular data again, this time showing the ratio of adults to overall household size (Table 3.11). We can see that these data might now explain why Household 7 was able to earn Rs.20 000 from wages while still owning and operating 2.5 acres. All the other households had a much harder time, either because they had no or little land and/or a lower proportion of adult labour in the household.

Table 3.11

Household	*Land operated (acres)*	*Land owned (acres)*	*Household wage earnings (rupees, 1994)*	*Ratio of adults to number of people in household*
4	0.5	0.5	4 300	2:4 (50%)
5	2.5	0	3 350	2:4 (50%)
6	0	0	4 550	2:3 (66%)
7	2.5	2.5	20 000	4:4 (100%)
8	0	0	5 950	6:8 (75%)

(Crops) As might be expected (and given what we know about Household 1 from the notes to Table 3.10), Households 2 and 3 had the highest crop values, although these data do not correlate precisely with the amount of land operated. Land operated might not equal area sown (especially if the household also had livestock). There may also have been crop failure. These are speculations.

(Equalization) Income from wage labour only balanced out low incomes from crops and reduced inequality in any dramatic way with Household 7. The other equalization effects seemed relatively low by comparison.

Debt

The most vulnerable household seemed to be Household 6, which had no land and whose earnings from waged labour were less than the outstanding debt. On the surface, all other households would have been able to pay their outstanding debts as far as we know from these data. We do not know what other financial commitments they had (including to relatives), nor what their consumption needs were (including healthcare and school fees as well as food, shelter and clothing).

Overall, you will have gained a partial picture of the different livelihood situations facing these households and the different possibilities for choice. The interpretation of assets can thus be extended to describe the exchange entitlements that people have from crops and labour they sell. Even if they don't actually sell their crops (for instance when they eat the rice they have produced), we note that they have the potential to sell them. Market-based estimates of exchange entitlements offer us some insight into the range of choices open to people. In this instance, however, one or two households appeared to have constrained choices, Household 6 particularly so.

Cash income: gender inequalities within households

We are now going to look again at the data on wage earnings *from farm work* and disaggregate them by gender. In this instance, we are only going to look at five of the households as three of them did not carry out waged work (Table 3.10). The data we will now look at are in Table 3.12 below. Our intention is to see whether there are major differences between men and women in these five households in terms of remunerated and non-remunerated farm work and in wage earnings. You might start with some hypotheses of your own and see whether they prove correct!

Activity 3.9

Now look at Table 3.12 below. Bear in mind your earlier analysis of the information in Table 3.10 as you carry out this activity.

First, again take a look at the columns and rows of this table to get a general impression of the data. Note what the different columns are telling you (and read the note at the bottom of the table about days employed and days worked). In terms of rows, note whether there are any immediate differences that strike you.

Now, carry out the following calculations from these data and assess what your calculations tell you:

- Days employed as a percentage of days worked for men by household
- Days employed as a percentage of days worked for women by household
- Average daily earnings for men by household
- Average daily earnings for women by household
- What observations would you make about these data?

(Spend no more than 30 minutes on this activity)

Table 3.12 Labour and earnings from farm work for five households

Household serial number	*Males days employed*	*Females days employed*	*Males days worked*	*Females days worked*	*Males labour earnings (rupees)*	*Females labour earnings (rupees)*	*Household total labour earnings (rupees)*	*Females % of labour earnings of household*
4	127	80	137	90	3 350	950	4 300	22
5	90	95	170	165	1 925	1 425	3 350	43
6	135	105	135	105	2 975	1 575	4 550	35
7	480	320	520	410	12 000	8 000	20 000	40
8	260	240	260	240	3 550	2 400	5 950	40

Days employed include wage labour and group contracts for which the worker received daily wages. Days worked include, in addition, labour on land rented in, which is not remunerated with wages. Work done on one's own land is not recorded in Table 3.12. Work done with livestock is also not counted here.

Comment

A first observation is that women form a substantial part of wage earnings in all these wage-earning households. It is interesting that the contribution was smallest (22%) in one of the most marginal land owning households in this group, Household 4, which only possesses 0.5 acre. We do not know the age of the children in this household and it is possible that both were very young, which may have prevented the woman from doing a large amount of waged work.

In terms of the calculations we asked you to do, our results are in Table 3.13 below. We have a word of caution about this table. You will notice that we asked you to calculate average daily earnings not wage rates. This is because the data are variable and do not equate to precise wage rates. They are an indication of the overall earnings, which will be based on different tasks, wage rates and hours worked.

Table 3.13 Employed work as percentage of all farm work, and average daily earnings

Household	*Males days employed as a percentage of days worked*	*Females days employed as a percentage of days worked*	*Average daily earning for males (rupees)*	*Average daily earnings for females (rupees)*
4	93	89	26	12
5	53	58	21	15
6	100	100	22	15
7	92	78	25	25
8	100	100	14	10

In overall terms, you will have seen that there are no dramatic differences between men and women in the percentage of work that is paid work (although there is considerable variation overall between households in the amount of paid work carried out, as we also noted earlier on). In two households both men's and women's farm work was 100% paid. It is interesting also that the average daily earnings for Household 7 was the same for men and women, while in general the average daily earnings for women was less than for men. There are several reasons for this difference in male and female earnings. One is that men work with cattle doing ploughing (which is higher paid than other tasks) (Figure 3.8), and women do not. Another reason lies in labour market segmentation by gender: that is, there are sexual divisions and differences in the tasks and pay rates for men and women. A third reason is that women in this area often work a shorter day of 6 hours rather than an 8- or 10-hour day when they do wage labour.

Figure 3.8 A man ploughing a field to prepare it for transplanting rice.

Interviewing rural women

In the subsections above, we gained a picture of people's livelihoods and saw that farming in the two villages in Andhra Pradesh is undertaken as a micro-enterprise or small enterprise activity. Each farmer combines resource inputs, labour inputs, technological knowledge and planning over time to create a situation in which the outputs can be used, stored or sold. Farmers realize more or less profit. For instance they may farm for subsistence and eat the produce, including eggs and vegetables, in which case profit is a distant concept; or they may produce a surplus of a food crop and sell that surplus at market prices. In the latter case profits can be calculated, but by-products such as the green fodder from the plants or the use of hulls removed from food grains during processing are also important details of the micro-enterprise activity. Farmers may benefit from their farming activities quite apart from profitability or the 'business' aspect. They may have reduced vulnerability from engaging with both livestock and arable activities; they may gain in food security by producing vegetables or root crops; they may use common land and have an interest in the structure of land ownership and control in their area. In sum, farming in this context can be interpreted in several ways because of its intrinsic complexity.

Farming in Andhra Pradesh and in other contexts is often seen as a 'household' activity, but this tends to mask the gender relations within households and compounds. Think of the word 'farmer'. What kind of person pops into your mind? Young, old, male, female? It matters mainly if there is differentiation of poverty among rural residents by gender or age-group. Sen's concept of exchange entitlements allows us to recognize that farmers may not only sell or use their farm products but also sell their labour. It is possible to apply Sen's framework of entitlements at an *individual level* within households and find out the differences between men and women, young and old. In addition, while individuals may have different sources of income, the products of joint unmonetized activities have to be somehow allocated among the members of the household.

To find out more about the internal workings of households, we are going to look at some interviews with two women from Households 1 and 5. You can look back at Table 3.10 and remind yourself that:

Household 1 did not have a lot of land (although it rented out 1 acre), but it had diverse sources of non-farm income and was one of the wealthier households in the eight we looked at. We know this from additional data that were supplied to us rather than from the data in Table 3.12.

Household 5 by contrast rented in 2.5 acres of land, the husband and wife in the household both did waged work for others and, from Table 3.10, it is even possible that both were literate (although the literacy data could have referred to other household members). The household had an outstanding debt of Rs.6000 and a total gross income from crops and wages of Rs.9585.

The two women from these households were interviewed by Wendy Olsen. In practice, it was not easy for a foreigner of American origin to be interviewing women alone in the villages. The women were nervous and often did not expand their answers to offer deeper insights into their thinking during the interview itself. Specific problems with interviewing as a research technique, particularly when it involves women and people who have subordinate social positions, have been pointed out by many researchers. So, for your own interest, note the interaction between the interviewers and interviewees and the ways of eliciting information about people's livelihoods and perceptions, as well as the difficulties in doing so. Read the interviews carefully and try to pick up the flow and significance of the answers.

Activity 3.10

Read the following extracts from two interviews with women from two of the households we looked at in the previous section. The women's comments help to illuminate the choices individual people make within households. Make notes on:

- the types of work or work roles carried out by the women;
- what difficulties faced the interviewer and interviewees in carrying out the interview.

Our rough answer to the first part of this activity is found in Appendix 2.

(Spend no more than 45 minutes on this activity)

1 Interview with Nagaratnamma (aged 32) in Household 1

W. You do household work, and what other activities?

Nagaratnamma. What else is there? We make plastic wire bags.

W. Bags?

Nagaratnamma. Plastic wire bags, embroidery.

W. That work only?

Nagaratnamma. If we have that work, we do it, otherwise, no.

W. If you make a bag, whom do you give it to?

Nagaratnamma. We get orders. We make them on orders.

W. Do you work with any contractor?

Nagaratnamma. No.

W. How much do they give for a bag?

Nagaratnamma. 20 rupees.

W. Where do you get your orders?

Nagaratnamma. From neighbouring villages. From this village also, whoever wants them, they come to us.

W. You go anywhere to work?

Nagaratnamma. No. Our men don't agree for us to go out for work. They say, why do you need to go out? Sit at home happily.

W. You like this work?

Nagaratnamma. If we get orders, we make it. Otherwise we don't ...

W. What else you do?

Nagaratnamma. We do tailoring.

W. Hmm.

Nagaratnamma. We stitch TRYSEM* clothes, dresses, etc.

*TRYSEM is a non-governmental organization that helps to link up Indian women with the technical and training opportunities they need to get good sale prices.

W. What machine do you have?

Nagaratnamma [pointing to daughter] Show it to her.

W. For whom do you stitch?

Nagaratnamma. Anyone.

W. For money?

Nagaratnamma. Hmm

W. What do you do with that money?

Nagaratnamma. We spend it on our domestic needs.

W. What else do you do? During tamarind season, do you do that work?

Nagaratnamma. We use it at home. We ourselves make tamarind for our house needs. We don't go for others' work.

Figure 3.9 Home-based, small-scale production of goods for sale is a contributor to household and women's income. Here, women are making dolls.

W. Do you have cows?

Nagaratnamma. Yes.

W. How many?

Nagaratnamma. Two cows.

W. You do that work?

Nagaratnamma. We do.

W. All of you do it?

Nagaratnamma. All of us do.

W. How much time it takes?

Nagaratnamma. About six hours, five hours

W. Five hours?

Nagaratnamma. Hmm

W. When do you do?

Nagaratnamma. From afternoon onwards. Till evening. We take them for *metha* [grazing].

W. What it means?

Nagaratnamma. We take cows to the grazing fields. After grazing, we brought them back. That is our work.

W. Hmmm.

Nagaratnamma. We bring them back home and give them water and grass. We take milk from them.

W. How many of you do that work?

Nagaratnamma. My husband goes for grazing; if he is not there, we go ...

W. Only two cows? Sheep ...

Nagaratnamma. No. If it is Kapus [a caste of farmers], they raise sheep, goats, chickens etc ... We are Vaisyas. We don't raise them.

W. Do Vaisyas raise cows?

Nagaratnamma. Yes.

W. Do you sell milk?

Nagaratnamma. We sell it in dairy.

W. Do you have lands?

Nagaratnamma. We have.

W. Do you have own lands, is it not?

Nagaratnamma. Hmmm.

W. What work you do in that?

Nagaratnamma. We hire people to work.

W. Hire people to work? What do you do?

Nagaratnamma. We don't go to lands. We don't know those works.

W. During groundnut season, do you do those works?

Nagaratnamma. We don't do those field works at all.

W. Next, do you prepare meals for labourers?

Nagaratnamma. No. They bring their food. We pay them wages ...

W. You give works on contract basis?

Nagaratnamma. For contract also. Whatever we give, either daily wage or contract, they come and do the work.

W. But you don't serve food to them.

2 Interview with Narayanamma (aged 35) in Household 5

There were two interviewers, S. and W.

Narayanamma. Two cows.

W. Two bullocks, too?

Narayanamma. They are not bulls, they're cows!

W. Can you plough with cows?

Narayanamma. Yes, one can.

W. Who does the work with the cows, in the dawn and in the evening?

Narayanamma. We do the work ourselves.

W. How many hours do you need to do that work daily?

Narayanamma. How many hours does it take, well we do two hours then again tie them up.

W. Evening?

Narayanamma. Usually in the evening we tie them up at 7 p.m. and at dawn at 6 a.m. we let them go.

W. What time do you usually get up?

Narayanamma. Usually we get up at 4 a.m. At 4 a.m. when there's fieldwork to do. We expect to get up at 6 a.m. when there is no fieldwork and we're going to be around the house.

W. Do you both get up then or do you get up alone then?

Narayanamma. I get up alone and I get my helpers, my daughters, up.

W. Do you wake up your daughter?

Narayanamma. I get my daughter up too. There is work to be done outside, isn't there? We want to do agriculture. Every person should be doing it, shouldn't they?

W. At dawn does this girl also work with the cows? [*]

*In this household nearly all the regular work grazing the cows is done by female household members.

Narayanamma. Yes, she does.

S. Where do you get a loan?

Narayanamma. Wherever it's favourable that's where we get it.

W. Well you told Uma all the details about that. In total you borrowed Rs.6000, and you told us that before, didn't you? [and, in English: I want to know whether they have any disagreements about the money.]

S. When you need money, where will you get it, from a bank outside or from somewhere else outside?

Narayanamma. The bank won't give any to us. In order for the bank to give you have to have your own fields. When you don't have your own lands the bank won't give you any money. At that time we take some money from the farmers instead. We repay it with interest. The bank won't give us any.

W. Both you and your husband borrow money sometimes, don't you?

S. Does it ever happen that your husband borrows money at too high an interest rate, or too much money, and you question why did he take that money? Do such words ever come between you?

Narayanamma. We don't ask, why should we ask? He takes it for the family, so why should we ask? We don't ask. He has taken it because of the problems, what do you expect? [This is a loose translation of what she said. She was irritated that W and S made this enquiry.]

Sb [a listening neighbour]. Suppose she has to prepare a festival in the house. Suppose she tells her husband, I need these provisions, this is what I need, she says. If he doesn't have the money, he borrows it, right? So we don't ask what has happened. Because from the first we know. She said she needed the goods for the festival.

Narayanamma. For a festival, for a marriage, for such things he borrowed money. So why should we ask why?

Comment

First let us think about the interview with Nagaratnamma in Household 1. Clearly this woman is involved in micro-enterprise. Yet the woman perceives her stitching as household work and explains how the men prefer women (from her social position) to 'sit at home happily' rather than go out. In fact no one in this household does waged work for others. In addition much of the work on their farm is done by hired labour. Nagaratnamma also tells us about outdoor work grazing cows and gives caste-based reasons for certain restrictions on her work with livestock.

Turning to the interview with Narayanamma in Household 5, let us think about Narayanamma's comments with reference to Sen's notion of entitlements. Notice the endowments of cows, strong bodies, and land of this woman's household. However they rented in land (as shown in Table 3.10) and worked as labourers. Their exchange entitlements came from the value of the produce and the wages earned through agricultural labour. The family has put their daughter to work while their son studies in school. If you examine the average wages per day of females and males in this household (Table 3.13), you saw that Narayanamma received Rs.15 per day whereas her husband earned Rs.21 per day. Whatever the reasons for this difference, in Sen's terms the two genders had a different exchange entitlement from their labour. Notice also that Nagaratnamma's understanding is that they are not eligible for bank loans since they own no land. There also seemed to be some tension about loans (at least in talking about them in an interview).

Analysing rural women

Raw data from interviews, focus groups, and policy statements can be called 'texts', and texts are thought to represent people's underlying situation and perceptions in a way that is partial but illuminating. There are several approaches to analysing interviews to try and build a picture or story from the data they provide:

- Making typologies: a way of labelling and grouping people or particular information about people according to particular characteristics, for example by the types of work they do.
- Explanatory analysis: explaining the information in the interviews in terms of concepts from outside the text of the interviews.
- Interpretation: examining interviews looking for meanings from within the speakers' own frames of reference.

Here we will look at 'explanatory analysis' and 'interpretation'.

Explanatory analysis

Analysing interviews using explanatory analysis means explaining the data in terms of concepts from outside the text or content of the interviews. The concepts we are going to use are 'capabilities' and 'empowerment'. Both have importance for the analysis of and action on poverty and inequality.

As you saw in *Introduction to Poverty and Inequality*, one extension of Sen's theory of entitlements is the *capabilities approach*. This is one of the foundations of the new human development school of thought. From within this school, one list of capabilities is as follows (abridged from Nussbaum, 1999, p.235):

1. *Life*. Being able to live to the end of a human life of normal length ...
2. *Bodily health*. Being able to have good health, including reproductive health ...
3. *Bodily integrity*. Being able to move freely from place to place; to be secure against violent assault, including sexual assault and domestic violence ...
4. *Senses, imagination and thought*. Being able to ... use one's mind in ways protected by guarantees of freedom of expression ...
5. *Emotions*. Being able to have attachments to things and people outside ourselves ...
6. *Practical reason*. Being able to form a conception of the good and to engage in critical reflection about the planning of one's life ...
7. *Affiliation*.

   A. Being able to live with and toward others, to ... engage in various forms of social interaction ...

   B. Having the social basis of self-respect and non-humiliation ... this entails protection against discrimination on the basis of race, sex, sexual orientation, religion, caste ...
8. *Other species*. Being able to live with concern for and in relation to animals, plants and the world of nature.
9. *Play*. Being able to laugh, to play, to enjoy recreational activities.
10. *Control over one's environment*.

    A. Political ...

    B. Material. Being able to hold property ...

Activity 3.11

Quickly review the above interview extracts with Nagaratnamma and Narayanamma. Identify any of Nussbaum's human capabilities that appear there under the headings of 'capability', 'lacking in capability', and 'having capability but not using it'.

Check your answer against ours in Appendix 2.

(Take about 30 minutes making notes on this activity)

Comment

Several of the capability headings are not mentioned in the extracts, for example emotions, senses, affiliation and play. Nagaratnamma and Narayanamma may not have been asked about these areas of their lives (that is, the interviewers may not have carried out the interview with these categories in mind beforehand). It may also be because they do not have these capabilities. Which do you think is the more likely? A perennial problem in interpreting interview data with respect to outsiders' frameworks is that the true situation may not be expressed in the interview. In addition, areas of life such as emotions, senses, affiliation and play may not be expressed in ways that the interviewer expects, particularly if the interviewer is from another cultural context, or they might not be expressed in words. (This, of course, relates to some of the issues raised in Section 3.2 about epistemology, or how we know things. We return to this shortly when we consider interpretation.) A final problem is that the frameworks may simply not fit well to the situation.

Nevertheless, several of the headings in Nussbaum's list of capabilities link up with the empowerment approach, which you initially came across in *Introduction to Poverty and Inequality*. You will also remember the discussion of types of power in *Study Guide 1* (power over, power to and power with). Here we extend those discussions so that you can see how they might be used to explain how people make sense of their lived experience.

Another writer, Linda Mayoux, has presented the empowerment approach as it applies to the difficult negotiations around micro-credit development projects, particularly in relation to women's participation (1998a,b). Mayoux argues that we need to pay attention to:

- *Power within.* Empowerment can include increasing confidence of individual women; assertiveness; autonomy. It might also involve changes in aspirations and consciousness (Mayoux, 1998c).
- *Power to.* Empowerment may, in many cases, mean gaining potential but unrealized capabilities and thus the power to do things which are not within one's current functionings. (Amartya Sen used the concept of 'functionings' to mean being able to do things in practice not just in potential.) According to Mayoux, in order to widen her power to do things, a woman requires changes in her relations with others, including men, rather than merely changes within herself.
- *Power with.* Mayoux adds that many micro-credit schemes have their origin in grassroots action and collective agency. *Collective agency* is

the action of a group on behalf of its members. This action may be empowering in itself, and indeed simply being a member of a group can have powerful effects on one's self-identity and one's presentation of self to others outside the group. There are many examples in the development literature.

- *Freedom from.* Finally, an important aspect of empowerment is the process of liberation from structural relations or personal dependence relationships that result in 'power over'.

These four processes are important for thinking about development projects and other interventions. Here we might also use this approach analytically to understand how individuals and groups experience poverty and inequality and the extent to which they are able to act on their poverty and inequality.

Activity 3.12

There are common elements between Nussbaum's list of 'central human capabilities' and Mayoux's forms of empowerment. Make brief notes comparing and contrasting Nussbaum's elements of human capabilities with Mayoux's four forms of empowerment.

Our notes are in Appendix 2.

(Spend no more than 30 minutes on this activity)

Now let us apply the capabilities and empowerment approaches in the context of a different interview extract, this time from Reddamma, a woman from Household 2. You can remind yourself by looking back at Table 3.10 that Household 2 owned and operated the most land amongst the eight households (and also rented land out), and had one of the largest incomes from farming (as well as one the largest outstanding debts!). There are four adults and two children in Reddamma's household and 100% literacy among the adults. No one in this household needs to do waged work for others. If you were to do an asset/endowment and exchange entitlement analysis of this household, it compares very favourably with others we have looked at. However, what does the interview with Reddamma show with respect to capabilities and empowerment?

Activity 3.13

Read the extract below from an interview with Reddamma, and make notes on the following questions:

(a) How would you describe Reddamma's sense of personal autonomy (part of the empowerment approach)?

(b) What personal capabilities does Reddamma mention? Are they all being utilized?

(c) What capabilities do you notice that she has as *part of* her household and family, rather than in her own individual right?

(d) Is this list of capabilities temporally specific (i.e. specific to a moment in time), regionally specific, gender-specific, culture-specific?

(e) Finally, take into account the different data about Reddamma and comment on whether you think she is poor or not. To answer this question, you should make brief notes *on either side*. For each set of notes remind yourself of the *evidence that supports the position.* You can structure your answer using a table similar to the one below.

In what ways could Reddamma be called poor?	*Evidence:*
A	
B	
C	
D	
E	
F	
G	

In what ways could Reddamma be called non-poor?	*Evidence:*
A	
B	
C	
D	
E	
F	
G	

Compare your notes in this table with our answer in Appendix 2.

(Spend no more than 1 hour on this activity)

Extract from an interview with Reddamma (aged 24) in Household 2

W. You didn't try for any job?

Reddamma. No.

W. Why?

Reddamma. I don't need.

W. Why you don't need?

Reddamma. Our people don't send us for job. I am the only daughter to my parents. I have one young and one elder brother. I got married.

W. At what age you got married?

Reddamma. I was 20 when I got married.

W. How old are you now?

Reddamma. 27.

W. How old is your child?

Reddamma. 8 years.

W. If your child is 8 years and your marriage was at 20 years, how can you be 27 now?

Reddamma. When I was married I was 20 or 18 years old.

W. Tell me in Telugu. [We switch from English to Telugu.]

Reddamma. Eighteen.

W. Intermediate means, how many years' course?

Reddamma. Two years.

W. How old were you when you were in Intermediate?

Reddamma. Around 17 years.

W. You got married then.

Reddamma. Yes.

W. Do you like this place or your native place Chittoor [a town]?

Reddamma. Two are same for me. I don't go out of the house here or there. I am the only one at home here and there also.

W. Your children are studying at Chittoor, isn't it?

Reddamma. Yes, they are studying in hostel.

W. Which hostel?

Reddamma. Aasha [*sic*; like all names here, this is a pseudonym] hostel.

W. [points to the younger son] Is Venkatesh is also going to school?

Reddamma. No, he stays here only.

W. Why?

Reddamma. We don't have any other children here, it is difficult for us if we send this boy also to hostel. We would like to keep one child with us.

W. So, you three stay here.

Reddamma. Yes. ... [The talk turns to the elder son sent away to school.]

W. Baby class!

Reddamma. At the age of 4 children are admitted into the baby class.

W. Since 4th year your child is there only?

Reddamma. Yes. He has been studying there only. We don't have school here.

W. For the last 3 years he is studying there only, isn't it?

Reddamma. 4 years.

W. Why he was admitted into hostel?

Reddamma. My mother is unable to look after him. That's why we admitted him in the hostel.

W. What do you expect your child to become?

Reddamma. Doctor.

W. How many years he needs to study to become a doctor? Now he is studying in English medium is it?

Reddamma. Yes, he is studying in English medium.

W. Next ...

Reddamma. After 10th, comes Intermediate; after Intermediate, he has to write an entrance exam. If he is qualified in that, he needs to study three years for doctor.

W. Don't need to do B.A.?

Reddamma. No need of B.A., one needs B.Sc. degree for doctor course.

W. So, he needs to write the entrance exam.

Reddamma. Yes. ... [Later she says:] I get up at 6.30 a.m.

W. What work do you do then?

Reddamma. I prepare coffee and tiffin.

W. Do you do cooking?

Reddamma. Yes, only I do it. After preparing breakfast I clean house and then prepare meals [referring to cooking the lunch and evening meal].

W. What time does your child go to school?

Reddamma. 8.30 a.m.

W. Do you wash clothes?

Reddamma. Yes, I do.

W. Do you go outside to wash clothes?

Reddamma. No, I don't go. At home only I wash.

W. Do you wash for all in your family?

Reddamma. My clothes and my son's clothes. The remaining we give to washer man.

W. What time does your child return from the school?

Reddamma. 12.30 p.m.

W. Do you give him food?

Reddamma. Yes.

Figure 3.10 One of the schools in Chittoor District, Andhra Pradesh.

W. He will go back to school again?

Reddamma. Hmm.

W. What you do then?

Reddamma. He will come back at 3.30 p.m. I give him tiffin [hot snack]. After tiffin he will study till 6 p.m. ...

W. Does your sister do any job?

Reddamma. No ... no one does jobs here.

W. Is it?

Reddamma. Komatis, Brahmins do the jobs.

W. You Reddy women?

Reddamma. They don't.

W. I don't know this.

Reddamma. They are not allowed.

W. Why?

Reddamma. They are not allowed by their parents or husbands. They also don't study much.

W. Men study well, isn't it?

Reddamma. Yes.

W. What about women?

Reddamma. Some people do study well for instance my cousin studied up to M.A. ...

W. What is she doing? [meaning what job does she have]

Reddamma. She did M.A. She is staying at home only [meaning no job].

W. Telugu or English medium M.A.?

Reddamma. Telugu medium ... [The topic changes to mobility.]

W. Do you know cycling?

Reddamma. Bicycle? ... I know it.

W. Do you use cycle here?

Reddamma. No. I don't use. In villages if women travel by cycle people will laugh at us.

W. Do people laugh?

Reddamma. Yes.

W. You don't like it?

Reddamma. I don't like it. These people also don't accept.

W. If they wouldn't laugh, would you like it?

Reddamma. I like it.

Comment

You might have noticed three things whilst studying this extract. Firstly, there is a mixed result regarding poverty. Reddamma lives in a land-rich household and she has many advantages. However, she has little personal autonomy. Our interpretation thus diverges from her own feelings. She might not agree with us that she is less empowered than a woman who has high physical mobility and perhaps a job. Thus we find that there are two subjectivities involved in the 'poverty' assessment: her views, and our views.

Secondly, both the empowerment and the capabilities approaches lead us to look closely at her housewife and mother roles. She spends a lot of time developing her son's human capital. Whilst being a devoted wife and mother this could be questioned in terms of Reddamma's ability to participate in wider social and economic development in the village, or with other women. The empowerment viewpoint would argue that for her to use her own education simply to educate her sons may not be good for her. The capabilities viewpoint would note that her own daily 'functionings' (doings) do not utilize her education much.

Thirdly, our application of the two approaches is likely to be culture-specific and even time-specific. Therefore, although each approach is powerful and can be applied anywhere, the results will be different in different contexts.

Interpretation

Our second approach to analysing the lived experience of these three women is 'interpretation': examining the text of the interviews looking for meanings from within the speakers' own frames of reference. In the social sciences, there is a debate over whether direct accounts are to be treated as fact, as stories, or as potentially false. The factual approach is rarely found now, although we all recognize that what people say is important even if it is not necessarily an accurate or complete picture of reality. The second approach treats direct accounts as stories: in other words they are seen as narratives, tales, or scripts couched in discourses or idioms familiar to the speaker. The social character of narratives is stressed, yet their personal meaning (the feelings attached, as well as the intended meaning that a speaker tries to convey) is also important. Seeing narratives as socially situated, and letting meanings have both personal and social aspects, are two major challenges for qualitative data analysis. The third approach is the other side of the coin to the factual approach. In any interview, or recording of a direct account, there is always the possibility that false information is given or that the interviewee deliberately misleads the interviewer. In research, this problem is usually addressed by a process called 'triangulation'. Often, triangulation can mean that data is cross-checked from multiple sources to try to obtain a 'truth'. However, in this instance, triangulation is based on a different approach with a different purpose. It means that several viewpoints are obtained whilst recognizing that they might offer irreconcilable interpretations. Such an approach allows for different subjective positions to be expressed by the informants, which is extremely important if you want to try and understand how people perceive their realities.

There is thus another dimension, which is the extent to which interview data, particularly if the interviews are open rather than highly structured, can provide hard or scientific evidence. This brings us back to the point that we have made several times: different sources of data are needed to provide an understanding of poverty and inequality. Data on lived experience from direct accounts are part of the picture. The important issue is how they are collected, interpreted, and used for policy and action.

You have already read one interpretative account in this section: the extract from James C. Scott in Section 3.2. Scott's interpretation is a highly subtle one because it allows for the spoken word to mask important truths. Unlike the distinctions above, this approach to interpreting people's voices allows for a rich tapestry of truth, half-truth, avoidance and falsehood. The interpreter's job is to look behind some of the obvious, routine, and sometimes contradictory observations to see deeper truths behind them. Scott is an expert in this anthropological approach to data – we will not be attempting such an ambitious task here! We just want you to have an appreciation of what insider interpretation is about. Insider interpretation can only really be done by living and working in the context of the lived experience. However, you can adopt a critical approach to the assumptions made by those who do interpret data on lived experience, particularly where interpretations are informed by the interpreter's own standpoint and socio-cultural experience, rather than that of the speaker. So to gain a brief appreciation, we are going to ask you to reflect on some of the implicit and explicit interpretations already made by the authors of this section.

Activity 3.14

We would now like you to review the extracts from the three interviews above and consider critically the following interpretations that were made by us. Notice the language we have used. To what extent do you think our understandings have been imposed or not? Are there data or statements in the interviews that you would want to explore more with the interviewee to establish a more inside view?

'*Nagaratnamma in Household 1.* Clearly this woman is involved in micro-enterprise ... Yet the woman perceives her stitching as household work and explains how the men prefer women (from her social position) to 'sit at home happily' rather than go out ... Nagaratnamma also tells us about outdoor work grazing cows and gives caste-based reasons for certain restrictions on her work with livestock.'

'*Narayanamma in Household 5.* Let us think about Narayanamma's comments with reference to Sen's notion of entitlements. Notice the endowments of cows, strong bodies, and land of this woman's household ...The family has put their daughter to work while their son studies in school ... Notice also that Nagaratnamma's understanding is that they are not eligible for bank loans since they own no land. There also seemed to be some tension about loans (at least in talking about them in an interview!).'

'*Reddamma in Household 2.* Reddamma lives in a land-rich household and she has many advantages. However she has little personal autonomy. Our interpretation thus diverges from her own feelings. She might not agree with us that she is less empowered than a woman who has high physical mobility and perhaps a job. Thus we find that there are two subjectivities involved in the 'poverty' assessment: her views, and our views ... She spends a lot of time developing her son's human capital. Whilst being a devoted wife and mother this could be questioned in terms of Reddamma's ability to participate in wider social and economic development in the village, or with other women.'

You can check your thoughts with our own 'self-critique' in Appendix 2.

(Spend no more than 1 hour on this activity)

Comment

There is plenty of scope for misunderstanding since each person's past experience affects how they describe a situation or interpret an account. The possibility of multiple interpretations does not necessarily imply that there is no truth underlying the accounts, only that the reality is complex. Reality is continually being socially reinterpreted, as well. Each form of qualitative analysis comes up against two basic truths. Firstly, social reality has competing representations and interpretations. Secondly, the writer analysing and presenting her or his representation to others is also a non-neutral social actor with her or his own history (Holstein and Gubrium, 1995). Representations of lived experience are powerful forms of evidence which need to be taken into account in policy and action, even if they are not exactly 'true'.

3.6 Summary and conclusions

Summary

In this section of the Theme, we have introduced various types of data and helped you begin to analyse and interpret them. At the same time we have introduced case material on people's livelihoods and lived experience from rural Maharashtra (Murari) and Andhra Pradesh (our main case study source in this section) in India, and from Malaysia (J.C. Scott's accounts).

In Section 3.1, we saw how analysing data on people's livelihoods and lived experience can help build up *explanations* of poverty and inequality. We also saw that *concepts* and *theory* are needed to assist explanation, and that *alternative hypotheses* could be constructed for further investigation. These are some of the approaches that investigators of livelihoods and lived experience will use to try and understand why poverty and inequality occur. In addition we looked at how investigation might inform policy development and types of intervention to reduce or eliminate poverty and inequality.

Section 3.2 examined different *approaches to gathering and analysing* data on poverty and inequality. We described '*survey data*' as a particular way of collecting and organizing information, and contrasted this approach with *qualitative*, especially 'textual', data. We also contrasted the survey method and qualitative data collection with *participatory methods* so that you will be clear that these are different, and can see what some of the advantages and disadvantages are of using each approach. In Section 3.2, we reviewed three approaches to establishing the *validity of data*. These were an *empiricist* approach, a *standpoint* approach, and a *pluralist* approach. These are summarized in Table 3.14 below and can be seen as '*thinking habits*'.

If you quickly look at Table 3.14 now, you might notice that it plays down the roles of *power* and *values* in the construction of knowledge (an issue that also arises in the *Technology and Knowledge* Theme). As you can see from the empowerment debate, there are some major issues here. J.C. Scott's interpretations of poor people's resistance to non-poor people's power, for instance, might be contested by the non-poor. We know it was a value judgement for him to prioritize listening to the poor rather than the non-poor. Feminists have also challenged the existence of any absolute truths since all claims are embedded in existing power relations. So one other aspect that Section 3.2 addressed is that data are '*representations*' rather than *facts*, which is rather different from how empiricists usually see data. Data tend to be seen as representations rather than facts largely by those who work within the standpoint and pluralist positions.

The discussion in Section 3.2 should have made you more aware of how data on poverty and inequality are gathered and analysed, and some of the difficulties that investigators have in carrying out this task, whichever method they use and whether they are working for governments, NGOs or universities.

Table 3.14 Epistemological stances of three types of data interpreter

Epistemological stance of the person creating and interpreting data	*Types of claim he or she is primarily interested in*	*Types of data which usually provide the basis for such claims*
Empiricist	Facts	Detailed measurements, records of actual events; generalizations
Standpoint	Meanings	Experiences (personal and collective); sharing of interpretations of experiences
Pluralist	Claims perceived to be facts and 'facts' perceived to be claims; and meanings	Various types of data, disputed and re-assessed with a view to multiple possible interpretations

In Section 3.3, we explained how the data on poverty and inequality in our main case, villages in Chittoor District in Andhra Pradesh, were gathered and some of the *methodological* and *practical difficulties* which that involved. (Additional difficulties were mentioned later in Section 3.5, particularly in being a foreigner carrying out interviews with rural women.) In particular, in Section 3.3, we touched on the concept of *'stratified' random sampling* of households, a technique often used in carrying out surveys. In this instance the households were stratified by a key denominator of wealth (and poverty) in the countryside, their *access to land*. However, when the households in the sample were identified, the investigators stratified their households further by how they *used their labour* and whether or not they *employed other people's labour*. Identifying access to land and labour use is quite a common way to categorize social classes in the countryside. In this section, you had the opportunity to practise some data skills by calculating percentages.

Section 3.4 looked at the *inequality between the households* in Olsen and Rani's sample. There were two key dimensions here. One was the difference in households' *access to land owned*. The other was access to *land operated*, which you will remember was '*land owned + land rented in – land rented out*'. We saw that inequality in access to land was slightly reduced when land operated was taken into account. However, we also looked at the *nature of tenancy* in the countryside and saw that it can have some exploitative sides to it as well as enhancing livelihoods. We also pointed out that inequality in land may be offset by other dimensions of people's livelihoods such as access to waged income (and noted that inequality of income in India was less than in some other parts of the world such as Brazil or the USA). In this section, you learned some additional data skills: how *Lorenz curves*, *Gini coefficients* and *Gini indexes* are constructed and you practised plotting a Lorenz curve.

Section 3.5 took a much closer look at the livelihoods of particular households and at the accounts of lived experience provided by some of the women in those households. This was quite a long section because we looked at both *quantitative* and *qualitative* data and at different ways of *using* and *interpreting* qualitative data on poverty and inequality. We also considered how *capabilities and empowerment frameworks* can help explain women's perceptions of their own lives.

In Section 3.5 we first looked at some quantitative survey data to analyse the nature of a *household's assets and exchange entitlements*, and noticed an important area of *vulnerability*, namely debt. From these data we could see both the ways that people make a living and the risks they run. As we analysed in Sections 1 and 2 of this Theme, *risk mitigation* is an important dimension of poverty policy. We then analysed some data on *wage earnings* for men and women in some of these households, and saw that there was some difference in male and female earnings. We thought about some explanations for this phenomenon. Thus, by analysing primary survey data, you found substantial differences in the way people construct livelihoods from a variety of activities, even within one household. You also saw how economic inequalities are manifested in the daily lives and livelihoods of these households. *Literacy*, the only non-economic factor for which data were given, also showed a high degree of inequality (although we urged caution in the interpretation of these data). This in-depth glimpse of poverty and inequality fleshes out the overview provided by the Lorenz curve analysis of Section 3.4.

After looking at some survey data on livelihoods, we then turned to some qualitative data on women's lives. We worked through two ways of analysing these data. The first was learning how to apply *external frameworks* such as the capabilities and empowerment approaches. The second was *insider interpretation*. These interview extracts illustrated that qualitative data can provide *multiple interpretations* of poverty and inequality in ways that survey data cannot. Through these different approaches, we have tried to unpeel the layers of people's realities and gain a greater understanding of livelihoods and lived experiences.

Thus in Section 3.5, we showed that poverty and inequality are *multi-dimensional* whether approached through the lens of survey data or that of the analysis of narratives (personal accounts). Qualitative data tend to enable various *substantive issues and viewpoints* to show themselves, whilst survey data tend to force the details to conform to a single *prior conceptual framework* or *set of categories* such as 'land owned' and 'earnings from waged work'. However, we also saw that the quantitative data and the ways they could be analysed were a key element of our understanding of the lived experience of poverty and inequality in the two villages. In addition, some *broad comparisons* can be made, for example by using techniques such as the Lorenz curve to analyse data on income or other types of inequality.

As we have tried to show in Section 3.5, a full explanation of poverty and inequality would have to bring in *several types of data* – historical, socio-political, quantitative, and qualitative. Throughout Section 3.5, we underlined the role played by *gender and class relations* and *diversity* in people's livelihoods and lived experiences. In recognizing the *complexity of social relations*, we showed our preference for the '*relational*' rather than the '*residual*' approach to the analysis of poverty and inequality.

Finally, we should give a warning about the *worth of evidence*, both qualitative and quantitative. Sometimes evidence is not given because it is not asked for. In other cases, evidence is forthcoming on important issues, yet this evidence can still be wrong. One might need different types of information (and to cross-check what they say) before being able to construct explanations.

Conclusions

Looking at data on the livelihoods and lived experiences of households and individuals helps to provide both a richer and a deeper understanding of the nature of poverty (and wealth) and inequality in the two villages in Andhra Pradesh. Having such data and carrying out such an analysis would be extremely important (if not essential) for thinking about development policy and interventions in these villages. We would know more about the dynamics of poverty, the different concerns and interests of the villagers, who might resist change, and who might welcome it. We might have a sense not only of what specific interventions might be appropriate, but also what processes policy-makers might have to engage with to bring them about. However, we would need to know more about the wider context in Andhra Pradesh, for example, about markets for rural finance, for production, for labour and for crops, about access to services in health and education, about existing policy interventions and their effects, and so on. Knowing about these wider issues alone would not be sufficient for policy development that is also going to take the needs and interests of poor people into account in a differentiated way. It might also be an uncertain predictor of the specific effects of interventions on poverty and inequality on different types of household and individual.

We hope the section has helped you widen your data skills whilst encouraging a sensitivity to different representations of people's livelihoods. While we have focused on the developing world in this section of the Theme, the skills and approaches you have been learning are applicable to many contexts including poverty and inequality in developed or transitional countries. The data analysis activities that we have focused on are thus not confined to analysing lives and livelihoods of poor people in the rural areas of developing countries. The kinds of questions, issues raised and skills can be used in many contexts. Of course, there are many specific characteristics of village life in India (and in the state of Andhra Pradesh). The precise questions asked elsewhere would have to take context and history into account. As a final reflection, you might note down any thoughts you have about investigating lived experiences in situations you are particularly familiar with.

4 Action on poverty and inequality

4.1 Studying this section

Sections 2 and 3 have addressed different dimensions of poverty and inequality. In this section, we bring together these different dimensions by looking more closely at the nature and effects of action on poverty and inequality, from the macro to the micro levels. We will consider a range of types of action and use different approaches to evaluating them. This process will enable you to gain a sense of how to assess different types of action, and of what else you might need to know to judge their potential for reducing poverty and inequality. The section is organized as follows:

Section 4.2 The scope of action (about 3–4 hours' study, including Activity 4.1)

Section 4.3 Analysing action (about 4 hours' study)

Section 4.4 Evaluating action on poverty and inequality (about 8 hours' study)

Section 4.5 Summary and conclusions (about half an hour)

The total indicative study time is about 16 hours, however, we have allowed 1.5 weeks' study time for this section, as studying it thoroughly is likely to take you a bit longer than the indicative study time. As with Section 3, you are advised to break up your study of this section.

Activity 4.1

Before you read further in this section, please listen again to Band 1 of the *Poverty and Inequality* audiocassette (or review your notes on this programme), and listen to Band 2 if you have not already done so. You will remember that the first band focuses on changes in thinking and approaches to action on poverty. The second band discusses some types of community economic initiative in reducing poverty and inequality, and the role of partnership in public action. Just listen to the cassette all the way through and add to your notes, focusing on the key points of debate, as we will be referring to both bands in different sections below.

(Spend no more than 30 minutes on this activity)

4.2 The scope of action

To begin with, we will look at the scope of action on poverty and inequality. In particular we look at three aspects: conceptual or theoretical perspectives, the levels and spaces in which actors act on poverty and inequality, and the linkages between actors and actions.

Perspectives: rights, capabilities and markets

In Section 2 of this Theme, you became familiar with how some of the major institutional players, such as the World Bank and IMF, have been changing and developing their policy agendas on poverty. The World Bank and IMF are, however, not the only global players. There is considerable debate about action on poverty amongst international institutions, including United Nations organizations and bilateral donors from many countries – debates which are often influenced by NGO campaigns.

The United Nations Development Programme (UNDP), for example, has put forward a strong case for linking poverty and human rights in its *Human Development Report 2000*. It states:

> Human development focuses on expanding capabilities important for all people, capabilities so basic that their lack forecloses other choices. Human poverty focuses on the lack of these same capabilities – to live a long, healthy and creative life, to be knowledgeable, to enjoy a decent standard of living, dignity, self-respect and the respect of others.
>
> (UNDP, 2000, p.73)

You will recognize the influence of Amartya Sen in these words. The UNDP continues:

> How does a person escape poverty? The links between different dimensions of poverty – different capabilities or different rights – can be mutually reinforcing in a downward spiral or entrapment. But they can also be mobilized to create a virtuous circle and an upward spiral of escape. Expanding human capabilities and securing human rights can thus empower poor people to escape poverty.
>
> (UNDP, 2000, p.73)

Rights-based approaches have also been promoted by donors, such as the UK Department for International Development (DfID). However, this does not mean that economic growth and the role of markets are no longer seen as important amongst major aid donors. For example, both the World Bank and DfID state that markets should be made to 'work better for the poor'. What does this mean? For the DfID (2000a, pp.37–38), suggested measures include:

- Developing specific policies and interventions that influence poor people's, particularly women's, access to markets, assets and income-earning opportunities.
- Addressing labour, finance and land markets as well as those for products.
- Improving access, infrastructure and information.
- Enabling poor people to exert their rights in markets.
- Developing legal, physical and financial infrastructure, and business support services).

The World Bank (2000a, pp.72–73) has similar concerns, but adds policy areas such as:

- Reducing the regulatory burden on small firms, enabling small and medium firms to enter service provision (e.g. water, solid waste management); by contrast ensuring that there is an appropriate regulatory framework to control prices in privatized monopolies.
- Promoting labour standards supported by the International Labour Organization: freedom of association, collective bargaining, abolition of child labour, elimination of discrimination.

The overall framework for the range of economic and other policies to reduce poverty is thus on the one hand market-led growth and on the other creating opportunities for poor people to improve their livelihoods, in order to provide them with security, to enable empowerment and to support measures for equity within markets.

There is still a big question about whether forces that have helped to create poverty and inequality (see *Introduction to Poverty and Inequality*) can be controlled and steered in such a way that poverty will be reduced. Is economic growth still the key means to reduce poverty? Is the market still the appropriate arena to reduce poverty, given the right regulatory frameworks, incentives for poor people to invest and produce, and supported by measures to mitigate risk? Can empowerment and equity be achieved?

Thinking critically about such questions is not simply a process of applying particular conceptual frameworks and analysing data – essential though this is. Reducing poverty is not just a technical exercise. It is also a highly political exercise that involves challenges to major economic and political interests in the world, and changes in the thinking, policies and other practical actions of governments, corporations, donors and other international organizations.

Levels and spaces for action

One of the key dimensions of action on poverty and inequality is that it involves interests and values, and therefore conflict. For example, the World Bank may now be addressing security and empowerment to attack poverty, but it has been suggested that their earlier approaches to structural adjustment both helped create or reinforce poverty, as well as reduce it in some cases. Thus protests at international events such as gatherings of the World Trade Organization, the World Economic Forum or other intergovernmental gatherings are based on the view that governments, donors and corporations are part of the problem as well as the solution. You will also have picked up on the point made by Moser on the audiocassette that structural adjustment is still present in the World Bank's thinking, although framed very differently.

These dimensions are macro or global. One of the biggest challenges is how macro level policies and other interventions translate into positive effects for the daily lives of poor people. This suggests the need for multiple types of initiative taking place in different spaces and levels.* For example, if you were to read the *World Development Report 2000/2001* (World Bank, 2000a), you would see many types of action outlined in it. It is not easy to link such a complex array of policies, projects and mechanisms to reduce poverty with (a) what governments and other organizations might do in practice, (b) what policy and institutional infrastructure is needed to support action, (c) what resources are required and how they will be generated. Table 2.3 in Section 2 and Paul Mosley's analysis in that section, outlines different types of intervention at micro, meso and macro levels, as a way of distinguishing their scope and potential effects, as well as the type of actors that might be involved.

*'Levels' refers, for example, to macro, meso, micro or global, national, local. 'Spaces' refers to the potential for action within or across different levels.

There are important linkages between the influence of international institutions and global debates and national strategies for action. In the UK, for example, the European Union and different types of European legislation have influenced action on social issues. You saw a different type of example in the Course Book, Chapter 20, 'Life in the cities', Box 20.3, which described discussions in the United Nations Conference on Human Settlements and the kinds of policy ideas on housing and shelter that it tries to promote with governments. Another example is the recent initiative of the World Bank to persuade governments in the developing world to elaborate Poverty Reduction Strategy Papers (PRSPs). PRSPs are seen as a way of encouraging governments to put poverty centrally on their agendas by elaborating home-grown strategies for poverty reduction in consultation with the private sector and civil society organizations. Such a move could be seen as a new form of conditionality for aid, albeit one that is poverty focused.

In spite of the changing perspectives on the role of the state in development and poverty reduction, states are still seen as key actors. In the UK, for example, there have been initiatives to promote urban regeneration (see Box 4.3 below), which have included local investment and 'New Deals' for neighbourhood renewal. Such initiatives involve partnerships between the state, local organizations and private sector. (Some of the thinking behind national strategies on poverty reduction in the UK at the beginning of the twenty-first century was outlined in the article by Maxwell and Kenway that you read in Section 1.)

At a different level, the activities of development organizations, such as NGOs,* pose a different set of dilemmas. Although there is a rapidly growing number of NGOs in the world, there are limits to what such organizations can achieve. 'Scaling-up' activities and interventions have been an ongoing issue for NGOs, and is one of the reasons that many NGOs are now engaged in advocacy – trying to influence those institutions that have more power and resources to bring about change. For example, NGOs have tried to influence specific and approaches and

*The role of NGOs in development was introduced in Chapter 9 of the Course Book, and in Section 2 above.

policies, such as around the Heavily Indebted Poor Countries (HIPC), and have contributed to international gatherings focusing on the global economy or environmental issues.

NGOs have also been seen as a mechanism for donor and government policies to reach poor people, via the 'civil society' provision of much needed services, such as healthcare or micro-finance. Civil society organizations, which encompass many other types of organization, such as community groups, charitable organizations and trade unions, as well as development NGOs, have been seen as an increasingly important dimension in development as well as poverty reduction. Such engagement has been independent from, as well as in partnership with, the state (which is expected to provide an enabling framework) and the private sector. Trust and co-operation (social capital*) within and across communities and organizations are seen to play a key role in the success of such partnerships.

*See Course Book, p.37, to remind yourself of the concept of social capital. We also discussed the concept of social capital briefly in Sections 1 and 2 of this Theme.

All the levels of action mentioned so far are based on 'trusteeship',* or one agency developing the capacities of another. However, another level of action on poverty and inequality involves the daily life activities of poor people. Action on poverty and inequality is embodied in daily life strategies. In Section 3, for example, we studied data on the assets and entitlements of village households in Andhra Pradesh and the views of some of the women in those households. The actions of such individuals generally focus on survival and livelihood. The possibilities for individuals from poor households to negotiate and change the terms and conditions on which their livelihoods are gained are very constrained. However, organizations of poor and socially excluded people may well be able to exert wider influence. As the end of Chapter 9 in the Course Book suggests: 'Individuals and groups must have expectations and make demands in order for structures to be challenged. Services provided out of goodwill have to become a right' (p.215).

*See Course Book, p.41, to remind yourself of the concept of trusteeship.

Finally, what about the private sector? You will have noticed that Chapter 9 in the Course Book did not consider the private sector as an agent of development (nor, for that matter, individuals' survival strategies or social movements trying to bring about wider change). The Course Book chapter was concerned with those formal organizations whose declared purpose (or one of them) was development, much in line with the idea that development is what development agencies do. Private sector companies rarely state that their main purpose, or one of their purposes, is social and economic development. Their purpose is usually to make profits, reinvest surplus and expand business. It is evident that the private sector can help both to create poverty and to reduce it – not as a direct intention but as an outcome of its investments, disinvestments, technology changes and so on. The private sector can, however, also have a direct role in poverty reduction through social entrepreneurship* and the deliberate use of profits to enable others to invest in employment creation and income generation.

*Social entrepreneurship: producing and trading to meet social goals rather simply to maximize profits. In addition, some profit-maximizing entrepreneurs make contributions to funds for unemployed to start up businesses – see the example from the UK city of Sheffield in Section 4.3 below.

Linkages between actors and actions

None of the above actors on poverty and inequality act in isolation from each other and the wider context of power relations, different values and interests. Activity 4.2 provides a useful example of these linkages.

Activity 4.2

Read the short article 'Spilling the beans' by Kevin Watkins in Appendix 1 (Reading 5).

Identify the main actors, the levels (e.g. global, national, local) in which they act, the kinds of action in which they are engaged, and the links between them.

Notes:

- You could use the above variables as headings and make a grid. (When you have done it, compare it with ours below.)
- You could draw a multiple cause diagram with the 'declining incomes of coffee farmers' as the central issue. You can remind yourself how to draw a multiple cause diagram in *Introduction to Sustainability*, Section 3 and Box 3.5).
- You could draw an influence diagram (see Box 4.1).
- Our diagrams are in Appendix 2 (Figures A2.2 and A2.3). Note that, in our case, we did the grid first and then used the grid to draw the diagrams. You could, however, draw your diagrams straight from the information in the article.

(Take 30 minutes to read the article and do either a grid or a diagram; 1 hour to do more than one type of diagram)

Box 4.1 Influence diagrams

An influence diagram is a systems diagram or map. It presents the structural features – the main components – in a set of relationships and provides a general overview. The components may have boundaries round them. The diagram also indicates the direction of influence of the relationships with arrows. Arrows may be double-headed to indicate a two-way relationship. The different thickness of arrows can indicate the strength of influence. The space between components may also indicate the nature of the relationship.

(Adapted and abbreviated from Open University course TU872 *Institutional Development: conflicts, values and meanings*, Part 3, Section 2.5.)

Comment

We have filled out a grid below (Table 4.1) on the basis of the information in the article. Our multiple cause diagram in Appendix 2 took as the central issue the decline in income of the coffee farmers. This was because our interest is in poverty and inequality and in showing the processes that lead to it. If we had been interested in how and why consumers benefit from low prices for coffee, we might have taken the 'low coffee prices to consumers' as our central issue and drawn a diagram about the processes that led to that. The diagram might have had some very similar aspects. (However, you will notice that we put a question mark against whether consumers benefit from a low price for coffee: this will depend on whether low prices are passed on to consumers, or whether the coffee shops and coffee retailing chains keep the extra profit by maintaining retail prices.)

Table 4.1

Actors	*Levels of action*	*Kinds of actions*	*Links between actors and actions*
Individual coffee consumer	Local purchase and consumption		Difference between prices paid to retailers, processors, wholesalers and producers
Coffee farmers [Figure 4.1]	Own farms and local markets – local economy	Increase productivity and output; inter-cropping and other survival strategies	Low world coffee prices undermine livelihoods
Coffee-trading barons (TNCs)	Global	Take advantage of low wholesale prices	'Never mind the poverty, count the profit'
Government representatives from exporting countries	National and world market; global arena and commodity agreements	Increase exports; beggar-your-neighbour policies	Export more for less revenue because of drop in wholesale prices
Government representatives from importing countries	Global arena and commodity agreements	Demolished commodity agreements in 1980s	'profits for the few ... mass poverty and social instability' for coffee producers
Oxfam	Global and local	Investigation and advocacy	Create publicity about reasons for poverty of farmers and exert pressure on coffee TNCs and governments
Coffee shops and chains	National and local	Profits from retailing	Benefits from low wholesale prices
World Bank	Global, national and local	Promotion of cash crop production	Promotion of over-production of coffee
Latin American coffee exporters	Local and national levels	Withhold 20% of production to push up prices; return to international coffee agreements	
World Coffee Conference	Global	Negotiation	Could potentially improve prices to producers but unlikely to achieve this

Figure 4.1 Small coffee producers, such as these in Uganda, are in danger of losing out from low world prices for coffee.

The important thing to remember is that multiple cause diagrams encapsulate a sequence of events or processes – they are dynamic. By contrast, the influence diagram shows a snapshot in time. In drawing the influence diagram, we took Oxfam as its central component. It maps the spheres of influence of particular actors, but does not map the actual processes between actors and their outcomes, as multiple cause diagrams do.

Even reading only one article such as this reveals the complexity of the relationships between actors and their scope for action (and the spaces/levels at which they can act). Tools such as grids, multiple cause diagrams and influence diagrams can help analyse these aspects. In the article, Watkins also outlines the *structural* obstacles to action: how the coffee market works, the role of profit in driving the activities of the major players, the role of importing governments in maintaining the status quo, the lack of power of exporters (let alone small producers), etc. The relationship between structure and agency is an important dimension of the scope of action, in terms of possibilities as well as constraints. In this instance, the relative power of the different actors is a significant factor in any attempts to change the situation.

As a final note on this activity, if you ever had to make a presentation on this subject or any other subject and wanted to use diagrams as an aid, you could use the influence diagram to discuss the key actors and their spheres of influence and then use a multiple cause diagram to demonstrate the process of poverty creation for coffee farmers. In doing this, you would be using structure, agency and process in your analysis. We return to the relationship between actors (or agency), structures and processes in Section 4.3.

You can see that the scope of action on poverty and inequality is potentially complex. There are different types of organization (multilateral, bilateral, state, private, non-governmental and other civil society organizations), as well as the multiple actions of many poor individuals on their own livelihoods. There are the different levels in which such entities act – from global and transnational to regional, national and local – and the linkages between them. There are the purposes of the actions taken: some are deliberately directed at reducing poverty and inequality (whether successfully or not); others may be directed to wealth creation (such as commercial activity) but not necessarily to the reduction of poverty and inequality (although these may also be outcomes). Although not discounting the role of wealth creation, we will later consider the actions of those who are deliberately trying to reduce poverty and inequality, including individuals acting on their own livelihoods. In the next subsection, we will look more analytically at the nature of action.

4.3 Analysing action

In considering the scope of action, we have already touched on several different types of action: action on behalf of others (trusteeship), action for private commercial gain, individual and collective action, etc. Here we take a more systematic look at types of action and make the following distinctions:

1 Individual action for private needs or ends.

2 Collective action for private needs or ends.

3 Collective action for collective needs or ends.

Individual action for private needs or ends is purposive action that is carried out by the individual for the individual's own benefit. The concept 'individual' can be used to mean a firm or a unit such as a household (particularly in economics) as well an individual person. In our discussion, we will be referring to individual people and households. Both 'collective action for private needs or ends' and 'collective action for collective needs or ends' are usually termed *public action*: 'purposive collective action, whether for collective private ends or for public ends' (Mackintosh, 1992, p.5). Public action was discussed in *Study Guide 1*, Section 10, where it was defined as: 'action to meet collective private or public need while simultaneously contesting how it is framed as a public need'. We will return to the concept of public action shortly.

Action works on and within structures. By that, we mean that actors or agents and agencies, whether individual or collective, may influence or be constrained by the structures of a particular society or context. In the Course Book, Chapter 9, *agency* was defined as: 'the actions of individuals and groups, and their capacities to influence events', while *structure* was defined as 'the pattern or framework of relationships between social institutions', for example markets, families, political systems and rules of behaviour. Structures tend to be discussed as though they are mainly constraining. However, it is important not to ignore the enabling dimensions of structures (for example, *Study Guide 1* mentioned the role of law enforcement; other examples might be education or healthcare systems). Structures are also often discussed as though they exist outside or separately from agency, but we need to remember that it is human action that creates structures.

In this Theme, we are concerned with how individuals and groups can influence and change the actions of other individuals and groups as well as the structures that create or reinforce poverty. Such a process may also mean creating new structures that enable or support poverty reduction, or using other existing structures to reduce poverty. It may also mean that individuals and groups come into conflict with each other as some seek to maintain existing structures while others wish to change them.

There is thus a third concept, which we have just used: that of *process.* By process, we refer to the dynamic relationship between structure and agency, which indicates that neither is static. For example, *Study Guide 1* suggests that a structural approach to poverty would look at pre-existing patterns that have created or reinforced poverty, and an agency approach would focus on finding out why individuals and groups made the choices and decisions they did. A processual approach to structure and agency would look at the dynamics of the relationship between them and how change occurs (or might occur).

Individual action for private needs or ends

Individual action for private need or ends includes the actions of poor households and individuals in terms of their own survival. By itself, such action is unlikely to influence structures, although it may potentially influence the actions of other households and individuals in a very bounded locality. In particular, the actions of individuals within households might affect outcomes for the whole household (for example if one person decided to migrate to better paid work and is able to send remittances, or if another regularly drinks away her or his wages as a desperate response to poverty). Understanding individual survival strategies is necessary for two main reasons:

- the poor are not simply victims of their own situation – they can act on it;
- knowing more about how poverty affects people and how they act on it can assist policy development.

Without having some understanding of how people make their living, the strategies they use, the choices they make, and what influences them and determines the outcomes, it is difficult to develop appropriate approaches and interventions that might be applied more widely.

As an example, let us return to the Indian households in Section 3. You will remember that we looked at data that indicated the assets, exchange entitlements and potential vulnerability in debt of eight households. Let us just look at the households from which the three women who were interviewed came: Nagaratnamma (Household 1), Reddamma (Household 2) and Narayanamma (Household 5). Their household data is reproduced in Table 4.2.

If you look at each column in the table, you can immediately see the contrasts in livelihoods between these households:

- the assets in land available to them
- crop diversity
- the income from crops
- the income from wages
- likely income after debt repayments
- the levels of literacy (to be treated with caution, as we said in Section 3).

Table 4.2 Livelihood variables of Households 1, 2 and 5

Household	*Land operated (acres)*	*Land owned (acres)*	*Household wage earnings (rupees, 1994)*	*Household size (number of people)*	*Number of adults in the household*	*% of household members literate*	*Sugar output (kg)*	*Groundnut output (kg)*	*Paddy output (kg)*	*Gross farm income from three crops (estimated in rupees)*	*Total gross cash income (wages and crops) (rupees, 1994)*	*Total debt outstanding (rupees)*
1	2.3	3.3	0	5	3	100	0	520	0	1 768	1 768	1 000
2	25	30	0	6	4	100	4 200	4 712	3 800	42 171	42 171	30 000
5	2.5	0	3 350	4	2	50	0	1 750	1 140	6 235	9 585	6 000

In fact these households represent three quite different sets of constraints and strategies in terms of livelihoods. Household 1, you will remember from the discussion in Section 3, was a relatively wealthy household that engaged in trade and dairy processing as well as a limited amount of farming. Household 2 was relatively land rich and had a substantial income from farming, growing three different crops, and also rented land out to others. Household 5 only rented in land, grew two main crops on it (paddy and groundnuts) and household members carried out waged work.

These data also suggest some of the constraints on livelihoods, in particular for Household 5 where both adults carried out waged work. On top of this, the woman would have had an additional load of domestic or reproductive work. In her interview, Narayanamma from Household 5 states:

> *Narayanamma.* Usually we get up at 4 a.m. At 4 a.m. when there's field work to do. We expect to get up at 6 a.m. when there is no field work and we're going to be around the house.
>
> *W.* Do you both get up then or do you get up alone then?
>
> *Narayanamma.* I get up alone and I get my helpers, my daughters, up.
>
> *W.* Do you wake up your daughter?
>
> *Narayanamma.* I get my daughter up too. There is work to be done outside, isn't there? We want to do agriculture. Every person should be doing it, shouldn't they?

Narayanamma's statement conveys a view of (a) what Narayanamma thinks their main productive activity is, and (b) that everyone needs to pull their weight to ensure that they make a living. Thus one could conclude (from this extract only though) that this is a key livelihood strategy for Narayanamma and is the main arena of action to reduce or control the relative poverty of her household. Development organizations and policy-makers might also use this information to think about possible strategies for action that might enable households in similar situations to improve their livelihoods.

Developing coherent and appropriate policy interventions thus requires knowing more about the areas of vulnerability facing poor people, and the actions poor people take to mitigate risk and protect themselves. A different example from an urban context that illustrates this comes from the study by Caroline Moser of vulnerability and asset management strategies, which we touched on in Section 1 and which she discusses on the audiocassette (Moser, 1998). This example shows even more clearly the types of action taken by individuals and households to mitigate further risk of impoverishment.

Moser's study focused on four locations in the early 1990s, three in developing countries and the fourth in a transitional economy. The four locations were: Chawama in Lusaka, Zambia; Cisne Dos in Guayaquil, Ecuador; Commonwealth in Metro Manila, Philippines; and Angyalföld in Budapest, Hungary. Moser chose these locations to provide contrasting contexts and experiences of economic difficulty, although they had different histories, resource bases, incomes and paths of development. However, all the countries had experienced high inflation and declining per capita income in the 1980s, with increasing rates of urbanization and more than 40% of people living in urban areas. With the exception of Angyalföld in Hungary, the communities studied had the following characteristics:

- They were marginal areas originally settled through invasions and squatting (Figure 4.2).
- They experienced consolidation in the 1970s and 1980s with permanent housing and services.
- There was increasing socio-economic differentiation between households.

Note that these are the *structural* dimensions of the context.

Moser suggested that urban populations have somewhat different responses to poverty and impoverishment from rural populations, linked to differences in the socio-economic and physical environment. The main differences were the importance of commodities and the market in the lives of the urban poor, compared with those in rural areas, and the role of housing and the use of buildings in livelihood and asset management strategies. The comparison between urban and rural areas with respect to markets is mainly in developing countries. However, even in developing countries, the situation is changing rapidly and people's relations to commodities and markets are growing in importance. However, in times of hardship poor people in rural areas can rely more on their own production and can withdraw from markets more easily than the urban poor.

Figure 4.2 Marginal areas settled through invasions and squatting: this photograph shows such an area in Manila, Philippines.

There are two useful tables in Moser's study that provide a picture of households' asset management strategies. As you will remember, Moser was particularly concerned with the concepts of vulnerability, capacities/capabilities, assets and asset management, and with developing a framework for analysing people's vulnerabilities and the strategies they use to mitigate them. This is her 'asset vulnerability framework'. However, to operationalize this framework (i.e. to enable her to investigate it), she looked at particular assets and the extent to which people's vulnerability might be increased by threats to them. The assets she looked at were:

- labour
- human capital (health, skills, education)
- productive assets (especially housing which can be rented out or used for small enterprises)
- household relations (between men, women and children, for gaining and pooling income, sustaining consumption)
- social capital (relations of trust and networks within and between households and communities).

Moser thus collected data about people's assets in these five areas, how people managed those assets and what they did in times of crisis or economic pressure.

Activity 4.3

First look at Table 4.3 below, which has been taken from Moser's study. This table shows how households in each community have reduced their expenditures in the face of the economic pressures and impoverishment outlined above. You will notice that the data has been arranged in a *typology** (i.e. food substitutions, changes in eating habits, changes in buying habits, non-food items targeted for cuts).

Which areas of assets do you think might be threatened by these actions?

*Typology: a means of labelling and grouping people or particular information about people according to particular characteristics.

Table 4.3 Household strategies for reducing spending 1991–92

Community	*Percentage of households reducing their spending*	*Food substitutions*	*Changes in eating habits*	*Changes in buying habits*	*Non-food items targeted for cuts*
Chawama	56	Vegetables for meat	Switching to main meals consisting only of vegetables and *nshima*		
Commonwealth	30	*Am* for children (water from boiled rice) rather than milk	Cutting down from 3 to 2 meals a day	Skipping afternoon snack and purchases of cooked food (half do this)	Medicine, education, transportation, clothing, gifts, recreation
		Generic brands rather than quality processed food		Purchasing small quantities	
Cisne Dos	45	Water for milk in morning drinks	Cutting down on the number of meals – first with supper, then breakfast – or eating less at midday to allow for evening meal	Cutting purchases of cooked and fast food	Medicine, books, clothing, house repairs
				Reducing food allowance for children in school and working adults	
Angyalföld		Eggs for meat		Using cheaper cuts of meat	Semi-automatic washing machines, black and white TVs
		Low-quality substitutes		Shopping in discount food stores	
				Freezing and processing foods	
				Buying less food in bulk	

Source: Moser, C. (1998) 'The asset vulnerability framework: reassessing urban poverty reduction strategies', *World Development*, vol.26, no.1, pp.1–19 (table 2).

Now look at Table 4.4. This time, Moser has aggregated (added up or pulled together) her data across the five communities and analysed them according to the five areas of assets and potential vulnerability.

To what extent do you think that these responses make households more or less vulnerable? For example, would their capabilities be reduced?

(Spend no more than 30 minutes on this activity)

Table 4.4 Household strategies for mobilizing assets in response to changes in economic circumstances

Type of asset	*Households' response*
Labour	Increase the number of women working, mainly in the formal sector. Allocate a disproportionate share of women's time to meet increasing responsibilities. Allocate more time to obtaining services in response to the declining quality of infrastructure.
Human capital (in this case, referring to use of social and economic infrastructure to support human capital)	Substitute private good and services for public ones (water, electricity, healthcare).
Productive assets (i.e. housing and infrastructure)	Diversify income through home-based enterprises and renting out. Accommodate children's households.
Household relations	Increase reliance on extended family support networks. Increase labour migration and remittances.
Social capital	Increase reliance on informal credit arrangements (neighbours, relatives, friends, informal moneylenders). Increase informal support networks among households (e.g. sharing childcare). Increase community-level activity (e.g. school repairs and equipment from local organizations and NGOs).

Source: Adapted from Moser, C. (1998) 'The asset vulnerability framework: reassessing urban poverty reduction strategies', *World Development*, vol.26, no.1, pp.1–19 (table 3, p.8).

Comment

You will see from these data that there are many things that individuals do in response to economic hardship and impoverishment. It is difficult to see whether people's capabilities would be reduced or not: much would depend on whether their health was affected by diet changes and lack of access to medical care. However, as pointed out on the first band of the *Poverty and Inequality* audiocassette, poverty is about a range of 'denials', which poor people manage in different ways. As Table 4.4 shows, poor people also have many ways of managing their assets. Observing these actions is not accepting the conditions of poverty that drive people to take them, but it does help to contest the idea that poor people are passive victims of circumstances.

In her study, Moser also points out some of the unexpected ways in which households' strategies can contribute to benefits and losses in the longer term. For example, sending children to school may make households poorer in the short term, but may possibly increase or develop human capital in the longer term. Another example is dealing with violence in the household (an issue that Moser also mentions on the audiocassette): expulsion of troublesome members might resolve problems of domestic violence but might also reduce the amount of income coming into the household.

It is important to note that these actions are not attempts to change the conditions or structures of impoverishment but ways of managing them. It is hard for individuals and households to change the effects of conditions that may have resulted from forces outside their control. While individuals may improve their lot, the underlying causes and conditions of poverty and the processes that reinforce them require different types of action.

Finally, there are other forms of individual action not addressed so directly by the kinds of study carried out by Moser. They consist of forms of protest and resistance to processes that threaten the lives and livelihoods of poor people. We have seen that poverty can be conceptualized as multiple deprivations and as social exclusion. Often deprivation and exclusion can take the form of oppression, domination, lack of social status, discrimination, and so on. Reactions to such deprivations have been analysed by J.C. Scott, whose work you met briefly in Section 3, and are called everyday forms of resistance or 'weapons of the weak' (1985). Scott has documented actions such as poaching, squatting, desertion (from the army), evasion (of payments), fraud (for example, social security), jokes against – and tales about – dominating individuals or forces. There may also be collective forms of weapons of the weak, such as forms of subculture, millennial cults, myths and legends of resistance (for example, bandits). An important characteristic of such actions is their link to deep deprivation and powerlessness. For example, one of the critical readers for this Theme commented: 'It would be interesting to highlight what sort of circumstances drive the poor into resorting to this form of action. Usually, this is when most of their individual, group, market-based and publicly provided options fail to bring about the desired poverty reduction, i.e. it is an expression of frustration with the ineffectiveness or failure of current actions to address poverty' (Chipika, 2001). Chipika also asks whether the empowerment processes resulting from current participatory development techniques can trigger 'weapons of the weak'. We return to this point below.

Collective action for private ends, and collective action for collective ends

As we noted at the beginning of Section 4.3, both 'collective action for private needs or ends' and 'collective action for collective needs or ends' are usually termed 'public action'. Private ends may refer to the interests of members of a given group (such as a trade union) while public ends may be 'to promote the public good or assist the disadvantaged' (Mackintosh, 1992, p.5). An example of collective action for private needs or ends might thus be a strike carried out by a trade union to increase the wages of its members. An example of collective action for collective ends might be the campaign of Jubilee 2000 in relation to the situation of the indebtedness in many developing countries. Public action may comprise many types of agency, purposes and interests, from the actions of grassroots organizations such as community associations and labour unions to those of non-governmental organizations, political parties, the state and multilateral institutions. *Study Guide 1* explained how individual concerns may result in collective action for private needs or ends and, later, public needs or ends around which collective action is taken at the level of institutions such as the state (the example was given of the growth of sanitation in major European cities in the nineteenth century which started out as a form of collective action for private ends). There may also be a coincidence of private interests between different groups of people, for example between Western consumers and developing country producers over fair trade (see the case of Ghanaian cocoa in Box 7.5 in the Course Book).

What is the importance of collective action on poverty and inequality, whether for private or public ends? In considering individual action, we recognized that it could have limited effect beyond the lives of the individual person or households, key though it might be for the individual person's and household's own survival. Collective action can potentially have a much wider effect, both positively and negatively for poverty and inequality.

Activity 4.4

Note down some examples of the following, either from your own experience, or from your reading in this course or elsewhere:

(a) Collective action for private ends that has had a beneficial effect for poverty or inequality.

(b) Collective action for public ends that has had a beneficial effect for poverty or inequality.

(c) Collective action for private ends that has had a negative effect for poverty or inequality.

(d) Collective action for public ends that has had a negative effect for poverty or inequality.

(Spend no more than 15 minutes on this activity)

Comment

Examples we thought of were:

(a) The role of credit unions or other micro-finance schemes in enabling their members to take out small loans for productive and other purposes, thereby increasing incomes of members.

(b) The role of partnerships between state, private sector and civil society organizations in promoting and supporting regeneration of run-down urban areas in the UK.

(c) The example of the coffee importers and the World Coffee Conference discussed above.

(d) This is a much harder one to identify, as collective action for collective ends is by definition meant to be beneficial to a wider public. Here we might be talking about something that has had unintended or contested effects, such as the role of the minimum wage in the UK. The minimum wage was the object of campaigns or advocacy as well as of state action, but there was debate about whether one of the effects would be to reduce employment in certain low paid industries rather than ensuring people received the minimum wage.

The discussion of public action in *Study Guide 1* suggested that it is a *contested arena*. That is, collectivities (whether one or more groups of people) may debate or dispute different courses of action as well as arriving at an accommodation of interests or an agreement to act in a given way. Thus, to take the example in *Study Guide 1*, the need for sanitation might be voiced and acted on by individual well-to-do households (individual action for individual ends), which may then be taken up on a voluntary basis by a neighbourhood of well-to-do households (collective action for private ends), and then eventually seen as a municipal responsibility for the whole town or city (collective action for collective ends). There may, however, be debate about what type of sanitation is needed, how it should be financed and who should have access, particularly when it enters the arena of collective action for collective ends.* An example nearer to the concerns of this Theme is the public debate and action over the roles of organizations such as the World Trade Organization and the perceived effects of its policies and actions on the livelihoods of poor people in developing countries.

*The Johannesburg case study in the *Sustainability* Theme provides a good illustration of the debates over types of sanitation in a city, its finance and who should have access.

One potentially important arena of collective action for collective ends is policy* development and implementation. You will remember from *Study Guide 1* that policy was viewed in two ways:

*Policies: 'purposive actions undertaken by the state ... or by other institutions, with an avowedly public purpose' (Mackintosh, 1992, p.2).

1 as a *prescription* (the 'logical fit' between the analysis of the problem and a proposed solution);

2 as a *process* (the outcome of interactions and power relations between different agents or actors with different interests).

These distinctions are not always so clear in practice, as policy often involves aspects of both dimensions (you could even say that establishing the 'logical fit' between the analysis of the problem and a proposed solution is a process, as not everyone analysing problems and proposing solutions would necessarily agree). An example that we have already mentioned is the Poverty Reduction Strategy Papers of the World Bank. Listening to the first band on the *Poverty and Inequality* audiocassette, you will have gathered from Caroline Moser that PRSPs arose out of the World Bank's concern that initiatives to reduce national indebtedness did not seem to be working. Some of the reasons were internal to the indebted countries, and it was also thought that having a way of ensuring a government's commitment to poverty reduction would be a good basis (or condition) for further aid. On the one hand, persuading governments to take actions in this way could be seen as logical fit of a solution to a problem. On the other hand, there were (and are) various processes involved. First, as Moser points out, the drive to act on indebtedness has resulted from successful international campaigns and lobbying. Second, the outline of the PRSP initiative in the *World Development Report 2000/2001* expects governments to engage with the following processes:

> As important as the recipient country strategy is the process leading up to it. A broad, participatory dialogue with representatives of civil society and the private sector is expected to:
>
> - help national authorities develop a better understanding of the obstacles to poverty reduction and growth ...
> - deepen a shared vision of desired poverty reduction goals across society
> - lead to a formulation of priorities for public actions to achieve the desired poverty reduction outcomes
> - encourage the development of participatory processes for setting poverty reduction goals and monitoring implementation and progress.
>
> The results will be periodically reported in poverty reduction strategy papers expected to reflect a broadly owned development strategy.
>
> (World Bank, 2000a, p.195)

Thus, looking more closely at PRSPs shows that this policy development by the World Bank has both resulted from a process and is expected to generate a process. In Band 1 of the *Poverty and Inequality* audiocassette, Dan Murrow, from the PRSP programme in the World Bank, hopes that the outcome will achieve:

- more control by countries over their own strategies
- more involvement of civil society and those who represent the poor in the strategies
- a stronger poverty focus.

One could analyse this process as a set of different collective actions over time – or public action – intended to benefit poor people. However, the participants in this public action are not necessarily equal players. International campaigns have been able to influence powerful institutions such as the World Bank, but powerful institutions are also able to impose policy conditions on developing country governments to a certain extent. There are pros and cons in relation to this form of 'soft' conditionality (as there are, for example, around using human rights criteria for aid).

The idea of policy as process is linked to our view of the relationship between agency and structure: the interactions (including the conflicts) that bring about changes over time. This is not to say that there is no role for prescription. However, there is, at least in rhetoric, an increasing tendency to assume that policies which affect people's lives and livelihoods should be subject to consultation and negotiation.

Activity 4.5

Now look again at the article by Maxwell and Kenway in Appendix 1 (Reading 4), which you first read in Section 1, and look at your notes on the audiocassette, in particular on the points made by Marjorie Mayo on changes in thinking about poverty in the UK.

To what extent would you identify the targeting approach of anti-poverty policy in the UK as the result of prescription or of collective or public action?

(Spend no more than 30 minutes on this activity)

Comment

In fact this question is quite difficult to answer from the Maxwell and Kenway article. Anti-poverty policy in the UK is primarily directed from government initiatives in the public sector (Figure 4.3). Maxwell and Kenway suggest that it is increasingly based on a multi-dimensional view of poverty, resulting in targeting various dimensions of poverty. However, as Mayo points out, this thinking is not always as 'joined up' as it should be, suggesting that prescription in particular areas is more important than process and consultation with those whom the policies are intended to benefit. However, Maxwell and Kenway claim that targeting gives opportunities for anti-poverty campaigners to put pressure on government and promote further reform of the public sector.

Figure 4.3 Anti-poverty programme in the UK: West London Mission drop-in centre for the homeless.

This discussion has focused on two types of institution that have (or can have) a major impact on policy development on poverty and inequality: globally, the case of the World Bank; nationally, the case of the government in the UK. Neither the World Bank nor the government in the UK is constituted in a vacuum nor do they act in a vacuum. Increasingly their policies are developed, resourced and implemented with other actors in both non-governmental and private sectors, through different processes of consultation, negotiation and contestation. (One example of such action is in the first programme on the *Poverty and Inequality* video: *Small Change for a Better World*, about the Wellpark Enterprise Centre in Glasgow, Scotland, which has strong links to local regeneration initiatives.)

As indicated on the audiocassette for this Theme, there is an important role for campaigning and advocacy with respect to influencing the actions of major institutions. Thus another important arena of public action is grassroots and other types of local organization and social movement that either attempt to benefit those they represent (private ends) or the cause of others (collective ends). We have mentioned Jubilee 2000 on several occasions as a global campaign that has tackled the issue of debt. The second programme on the *Poverty and Inequality* video, *Funny Money*, provides an example of a social movement in an urban conurbation near Buenos Aires in Argentina, which is attempting to improve the livelihoods of both chronically poor and new poor* through 'community' or 'social' currencies and a barter system of exchange. This movement has spread to other parts of Argentina and exists in other Latin American countries and other parts of the world. At present, the movement works in parallel to formal markets and other systems of social support for poor people, but as the programme indicates, there is increasing interest from government in the scheme and its links to the market economy.

*To remind yourself of the concepts of 'chronically', or 'old', poor and 'new' poor, look at Section 2.2 again.

These grassroots activities and social movements are highly organized processes. Returning to the 'weapons of the weak' mentioned earlier, there may be other, more spontaneous, collective actions (for private and collective ends), particularly amongst those who sense that their actions may have some effect. Chipika has suggested that:

> ...the more socially empowered the poor are, particularly in circumstances of poor endowments and entitlements, the more they will resort to forms of resistance to press for faster action. On the other hand, the more socially empowered poor people are in circumstances of relatively fair access to assets and resources, the less likely they are to resort to resistance, and instead concentrate more on beneficial resource use activities.
>
> (Chipika, 2001)

Activity 4.6

This would be a good moment to view both programmes in the *Poverty and Inequality* video again. Add to the notes you made in Section 1 in relation to collective action on poverty and inequality portrayed in the video. You can use the following headings:

- The main actors
- Their perceptions of the problems of poverty and inequality
- The interests of the different actors
- The extent to which the action is directed to poverty
- The extent to which the action is directed to inequality
- What other benefits the action appears to have.

Keep these notes as they will be useful for later activities.

(Spend no more than 1 hour on this activity)

Links between types of action

There are obviously many types of collective action for collective as well as private ends on poverty and inequality, and we shall be considering further examples in this section. How do they intersect with the types of individual action considered in the last subsection?

In Activity 4.2 on the 'Spilling the beans' article, you saw some of the linkages between structure and agency and between different actors and actions in the impoverishment of small coffee producers. Here we look at links between types of action to reduce poverty and vulnerability.

First look at Table 4.5, which shows some of the outcomes of vulnerability in the face of economic hardship in the different communities studied by Moser. Moser again groups them in accordance with her five areas of asset management and vulnerability, and combines this analysis with a list of potential policy options or solutions. These potential solutions arise from research and consultation in the communities. Take a few moments to look at this table and see how policy proposals and interventions map on to the areas of vulnerability experienced by individual households. You will see that households' vulnerabilities are linked to a range of actions or solutions, all of which are based on public action of both informal (voluntary or community-based) and formal (private or public sector provision) kinds. If you now look back at Table 4.4 above, you can compare these 'solutions' with the households' own actions. With the exception of social capital, the actions are quite different from each other. The actions outlined in Table 4.5 are designed to provide structures that enable households to increase their capabilities and means of livelihood, while the individual actions of the households in Table 4.4 above are designed to cope with individual impoverishment in the absence of such support frameworks.

Table 4.5 Asset vulnerability: outcomes and potential solutions

Type of vulnerability	*Outcome*	*Potential solution*
Labour	Loss of income Provision of adequate non-traditional skills-training appropriate to the community	Develop NGO credit schemes for home-based enterprises
Human capital	Inability to maintain investment levels in education and preventive healthcare	Provide resources for primary education (teachers, textbooks, classrooms) Provide credit for education expenditures such as uniforms
	Inability to provide safe, clean water	Repair and maintain water supply Provide safe, easily accessible standpipes
Housing and infrastructure	Inability to use housing as a productive asset	Facilitate plot ownership or subdivision Review regulatory framework for land Provide electricity so that people can operate home-based enterprises
Household relations	Increased domestic violence	Support police stations managed by women
	Lack of adequate childcare Lack of caregivers for the elderly	Provide community based, community-supported care for children and the elderly
	Split households	Provide time-saving and labour-saving technology
Social capital	Decline in attendance of CBOs, particularly by women, or in activity of CBOs	Through social funds, provide real opportunities for CBO-organized interventions that recognize paid as well as voluntary work
	Increase in youth gangs	Give priority to community facilities, especially for youth
	Increase in crime and homicide	Support community-based solutions to crime Enhance policing capacity
	Lack of physical mobility, especially at night and for women	Provide a water supply close to residential neighbourhoods Provide safe transport Provide technologically appropriate lighting Provide wide, open thoroughfares for vendors
	Decline in night school attendance	Locate night schools close to residential neighbourhoods

Source: Moser, C. (1998) 'The asset vulnerability framework: reassessing urban poverty reduction strategies', *World Development*, vol.26, no.1, pp.1–19 (table 7, p.15).

Comparing these tables shows how important public provision of different kinds is for poor people in order to go beyond short-term responses to poverty. You can therefore also see how difficult the situation is when public resources are scarce. There was some discussion of these issues in the *Poverty and Inequality* audiocassette. Moser, for example, says the responsibilities of the state should not be ignored, while recognizing that states do not have the capacity to cover all public provision. Mayo outlines the contradictions in the UK of encouraging people to go back to work, while not making sufficient provision in terms of childcare and other benefits to enable them to do so. In addition, she points out the wider difficulties in the benefits system for those who are unable to work, as well as the problems of low wages and casualization of labour which reinforce people's vulnerability to poverty.

The first band of the audiocassette also outlined how action on poverty focuses much more on issues of risk and social protection than previously, becoming an arena for policy development (as outlined in Section 2 of this Theme) as well as individual action. Table 4.6 below illustrates a World Bank analysis of individual and collective action, in this instance primarily from rural settings in developing countries. There are three types of action listed: risk reduction, risk mitigation and ways of coping with sudden shocks. Then there are two main categories of action – informal and formal, the first involving households and communities (individual and group actions) and the second involving market and public provision. A closer look at the individual informal action will reveal that some of the actions may have short-term benefits but in the long-term they could make people even more vulnerable. Examples are the sale of assets, if these are not recovered at a later date, or putting children into work, particularly if it undermines the development of human capital.

If you read the table horizontally, you can develop a picture of options for action by both formal and informal means (individual and collective, for both private and public ends) which may potentially be mutually reinforcing. However, notice the gap in formal market-based options for action in response to risk reduction. Market activity can be a source of risk as well as an opportunity for poor people (for example, in the case of small coffee producers in the Watkins article in Activity 4.2). Also notice that the market mechanisms listed against risk mitigation and coping with shocks are based on the existence of private financial and savings provision. Such provision may well be unavailable to many poor or impoverished people (as you will have gathered from listening to the audiocassette for this Theme and from the case of women in Glasgow on the video).

Table 4.6 Mechanisms for managing risk

Objective	*Informal mechanisms*		*Formal mechanisms*	
	Individual and household	*Group based*	*Market based*	*Publicly provided*
Reducing risk	Preventive health practices Migration More secure income sources	Collective action for infrastructure, dikes, terraces Common property resource management		Sound macro-economic policy Environmental policy Education and training policy Public health policy Infrastructure (dams, roads) Active labour market policies
Mitigating risk				
Diversification	Crop and plot diversification Income source diversification Investment in physical and human capital	Occupational associations Rotating savings and credit associations	Savings accounts in financial institutions Micro-finance	Agricultural extension Liberalized trade Protection of property rights
Insurance	Marriage and extended family Sharecropper tenancy Buffer stocks	Investment in social capital (networks, associations, rituals, reciprocal gift giving)	Old age annuities Accident, disability and other insurance	Pension systems Mandated insurance for unemployment, illness, disability, and other risks
Coping with shocks	Sale of assets Loans from moneylenders Child labour Reduced food consumption Seasonal or temporary migration	Transfer from networks of mutual support	Sale of financial assets Loans from financial institutions	Social assistance Workfare Subsidies Social funds Cash transfers

Source: World Bank (2000a) *World Development Report 2000/2001: Attacking Poverty*, Oxford University Press, New York (table 8.3, p.141).

Activity 4.7

To what extent do you think that Table 4.6 is specific to developing countries?

How would you fill in the empty grid in Table 4.7 below for a context that you are familiar with, whether in the developed or developing world?

If you find this difficult, you could use the 'Potential solution' column from Table 4.5 above.

See Appendix 2 for our notes on a possible answer for the UK.

(Spend no more than 30 minutes on this activity)

Table 4.7 Mechanisms for managing risk of impoverishment

Objective	*Informal mechanisms*		*Formal mechanisms*	
	Individual and household	*Group based*	*Market based*	*Publicly provided*
Reducing risk				
Mitigating risk				
Coping with shocks				

As you can see, the examples above include both individual and collective action. As we have suggested above, the individual actions of poor people are likely to lead to risk mitigation and coping with shocks but not to more lasting forms of poverty alleviation and reduction that have a wider impact. On the other hand, collective practices (even collective forms of resistance and protest) have a greater chance of bringing longer-term reduction of vulnerability and risk. However, their effectiveness may depend on other supporting actions such as the openness of governments to new policy development, and the mobilization of other organizations, such as NGOs, as well as the extent to which existing policies and provisioning provide an enabling environment for reducing poverty and inequality.

Finally, reducing poverty may require people to take risks. Chapter 19 of the Course Book argues that risk averse strategies can mitigate against positive innovation. Certainly, innovation usually requires people to take risks (for example, to take out credit to use new varieties of seeds in crop production, or, as in the case of the Wellpark initiative in Glasgow, to take out loans to invest in small enterprises). However, as we will see in the discussion of micro-credit below, those who are prepared or able to take risks (for example, by taking out loans) are not necessarily the poorest people.*

*This point is reinforced in the case study on irrigation in the Peruvian Andes in the *Sustainability* Theme.

4.4 Evaluating action on poverty and inequality

An issue that our discussion raises so far is how one puts a value on all these possible types of action, or how one evaluates them. How effective are they in reducing poverty and inequality? What conditions need to be in place for them to be successful? How important is the role of partnership and collaboration between different types of organization and policy (the 'joined-up' approach critically appraised by Marjorie Mayo on the audiocassette for this Theme)? What about scale and whether different types of action can be replicated in different contexts? And what about the structural obstacles to the reduction of poverty and inequality – what is the potential for different types of action to change them? We cannot answer all these questions, but we can provide you with some tools to help evaluate action.

Having some means of assessing proposals for reducing poverty is a useful skill for participating in debates on poverty. It enables you to articulate a critical and questioning perspective, whether in discussion with other people or in writing documents of your own. When reading accounts or analyses of action on poverty, for example in the press, or those provided by development organizations and NGOs, you are likely to be making a quick mental assessment – or evaluation – of their content. This is an 'everyday form of evaluation' that we consciously or unconsciously carry out all the time. What we will do in this section is to make the process more conscious and analytical.

We obviously cannot address all the facets of evaluation that a practitioner or development professional would. This is a course in development studies, not in planning and project management.* Moreover, we will have quite limited information within the confines of this Theme – the data we have available are based entirely on written and audiovisual accounts of a partial nature, not on first-hand investigation. Thus the evaluative process we engage in here is intended to sharpen your critical faculties and enable you to articulate your thoughts. However, for your interest, we have outlined in Box 4.2 some of the initial steps you might undertake if you ever were involved in a practical evaluation of action.

*The Open University's postgraduate programme in Development Management addresses evaluation from the perspective of practitioners. If you would like to know more about evaluation for practitioners, you could also refer to Marsden *et al.* (1994) in the bibliography in Appendix 3.

Box 4.2 Some initial steps in evaluating action

First we would need some guidelines. Our starting point might be to try and answer the following questions:

- What do we want to evaluate and why?
- Who is the evaluation for?
- What are the criteria we are going to use?
- What methodology and methods are we going to use?
- Who are you/we in this process?

What do we want to evaluate and why?

We may wish to evaluate whether a given course of action is being, or will be, effective in reducing poverty. A more limited focus in a course of study such as this might ask the question 'what are the assumptions behind the action?' (What are the claims? Is there any implied theory or explanation of poverty?). In addition we may wish to know whether a given action is directed to the causes or the symptoms of poverty, what the proposed action is trying to achieve, and who looks likely to benefit (or is benefiting). These aspects are what we will focus on below.

Who is the evaluation for?

Is the evaluation for poor people themselves, other participants in the action, for a funding agency or a policy-maker, or for academic interest and the pursuit of knowledge? The answer to this question may or may not affect the approach to the evaluation, but it is likely to affect the way the results are presented. In this case, we will look at how different interests might view a given action and try to gain a sense of 'stakeholder' interests. The tutor-marked assignment may ask you to address a particular audience.

What are the criteria we are going to use?

If the evaluation were concerned with the effectiveness of a given course of action, the criteria might relate to the aims, goals and processes expected to achieve them. For example, if the aim were to increase incomes of a given population of people by 50% in two years, the criteria for evaluation would probably relate to the actions expected to achieve this outcome. In this case, we will not have the kind of information required; however, we can make a preliminary assessment of intent and the assumptions behind the intent.

What methodology and methods are we going to use?

If we were doing an evaluation as development professionals, a typical process might involve such elements as:

- scrutiny of internal documents (known as grey literature) and any baseline information;
- identification of stakeholders, including funding agencies, implementers, beneficiaries or other participants;

- collection of data on key variables;
- interviews, meetings, focus groups, observation of processes.

It might also involve a choice of methodology such as cost–benefit analysis and rates of return on investment or inputs; or participatory approaches in which the process and outcomes of evaluation are shared as a learning experience by all stakeholders. The relative merits of these approaches are much debated issues.

Who are you/we in this process?

We raise this question because we always bring our own values and perspectives (our standpoints) into any process of reflection, and it is therefore important to make them explicit and recognize that, while trying to be as objective as possible, we are making a personal interpretation of a process or situation.

Our own focus on evaluation will be on public action: collective action for private and public needs and ends. We focus on public action for two main reasons:

1 In practice, action for development (including on poverty) involves multiple groups, organizations and interests, which are often conflicting or have different beliefs, values and standpoints and values; moreover, no single actor or agency has complete control, either of the processes or of the outcomes (Thomas, 1996).

2 Through public action, different groups and organizations can potentially have their interests represented, even though there may be struggles to do so; by these means, there is a chance for organizations and associations of poor people to have some influence over processes and outcomes.

Focusing on public action also underlines that action on poverty and inequality is a political process and that interests, values and goals have to be negotiated and accommodated for action to be effective. These issues will be taken up in the following sections.

We will look at three different ways of evaluating action. The first is an *interpretative* approach that involves reviewing the claims and assumptions of different actors, examining their 'concerns', and looking at what 'issues' have been raised about the course of action. The second is an *explanatory* approach, to see how the concepts used to analyse poverty and inequality in *Introduction to Poverty and Inequality* can help evaluate action. The third is to make a *political assessment* of action, an approach that was initially introduced in Section 10 of *Study Guide 1*. Although there are areas of overlap, it is important to be able to make analytical distinctions between the approaches and to see their usefulness in evaluating action on poverty and inequality.

Evaluation 1: interpretation through claims, concerns and issues

Our first approach to evaluation tries to get at and interpret the inside views of the actors. In other words, it is an *interpretative analysis*, which you first met in Section 2. In this case, we use an approach derived from something called 'fourth generation evaluation', which was developed by two educationalists, Guba and Lincoln (1989). Fourth generation evaluation is an approach used to evaluate educational practice by involving stakeholder participation in the process. In other words, Guba and Lincoln were concerned to obtain an inside view by enabling people involved in education to evaluate their own situation. Guba and Lincoln used a framework that focuses on the *claims*, *concerns* and *issues* expressed by participants or stakeholders. For our purposes in this Theme, we can only interpret stakeholder views from the texts and any audiovisual material that we have available. Unfortunately, we cannot go through a more extended and shared process of evaluation with them. We are thus using the approach in the manner of trying to understand people's perceptions from the inside – or interpretative analysis. Such an approach enables us to think about the interests and agendas of policy-makers, practitioners and poor people themselves, as well as the assumptions behind given courses of action.

Thus the main focus is to try to understand the claims, concerns and issues raised by the different actors in any arena of public action; that is, to:

- review the claims and assumptions of different actors;
- examine their 'concerns';
- look at what 'issues' have been raised about the course of action.

Claims are assertions and assumptions. An example might be:

> Micro-credit programmes can reduce poverty even amongst the poorest people.

Concerns are possible, unintended or negative outcomes of a given course of action. An example on the same theme might be:

> The suggestion that the success of the Grameen Bank micro-credit programme in Bangladesh has led to replication of models in other countries rather than innovation (Hulme and Mosley, 1996, p.135).

Issues are possible areas of contention, for example:

> Whether micro-credit schemes can reduce inequality as well as poverty – or whether they are empowering to participants or not.

We are going to start with an example of public action that you might easily come across in your daily context because it is on the website of an NGO and is the kind of information that an NGO might make available to its supporters. It concerns action around the protection of girls from poor families who are in domestic service in the African country of Mali. At the time of writing, the case study was on the website of Save the Children UK (SC UK)* and was therefore public information that illustrates the kinds of action supported by SC UK.

*Save the Children website: http://www.scfuk.org.uk

Activity 4.8

In Appendix 1, there are two short articles from the SC UK web pages 'Protection and promotion of girl domestic workers' rights in Mali, West Africa' (Reading 6) and 'Women's organizations supporting the rights of girl domestic workers' (Reading 7).

Before you read them, first pause to check your own views about young girls doing domestic work. Just make a note of them and think how they might influence your analysis of the information.

Now read the articles and make notes on the following questions. (We suggest you use a grid such as that below for your answers. Where you think there is no evidence from these articles, leave the space blank.)

- Who are the main actors in this case?
- How do each of them identify the problems faced by the young girls?
- What are the claims made by each set of actors about the actions being taken?
- What are the expressed or apparent concerns of each set of actors?
- What are the issues raised by the actors?

You can check your answers against our grid in Appendix 2.

(Spend no more than 1 hour on this activity)

	Actor 1	*Actor 2*	*Actor 3*
Problems faced by girls			
Claims about the action being taken			
Expressed or apparent concerns			
Issues raised			

Comment

In terms of your own reaction to the content of the articles, and where you stand on the issues, you may have found that the information and personal accounts were quite emotive. You may also have thought about debates on the role and use of child labour. There are also different cultural perspectives on what a child is and what is expected of children. In addition, these girls have reached puberty and might be considered young adults. Thus you and other readers are likely to have different personal and cultural histories influencing reactions to these accounts, and to the kinds of action being taken.

In terms of how the problems faced by the girls were perceived, and the claims, concerns and interests held by the main actors, we might make the following observations:

- There are considerable differences in the ways the problems are perceived: SC UK located them in their broader context of poverty and family and gender issues in the villages, while the support organization, the Women's Association for Action (WAA), was more concerned with the direct effects on the girls of being domestic workers. For the girls themselves, the problems were more to do with their future prospects if they stayed in the villages (Figure 4.4).

Figure 4.4 The prospects for young girls in poor villages in Mali are limited. There are many reasons why they might wish to migrate.

- The ways the problems were conceptualized were reflected in the claims the three actors made about the action being taken, in which SC UK was supporting activities in both the villages and in the WAA, while the WAA concentrated on how best to improve the situation for the girls (expressed more vaguely by the girls themselves).
- The only apparent concern about negative consequences of the action (in this account) was raised in relation to the profile being given to the action in the publicity of SC UK and how this might create further problems for the girls (i.e. with their employers).

- With respect to any issues raised (i.e. areas of contention), the only one in this account was the hypothesis that the publicity given to the girls' situation would in fact act to protect them. Overall, the results of the actions taken in the whole programme of activities were still to be seen.

What does carrying out such as analysis enable you to see? First, both articles contain valuable information about the situation faced by the girls and the types of intervention. They also have gaps in information (which might suggest questions you would want to answer if you were to take this evaluative activity any further). Second, the perceptions and focus of SC UK and the support organization, the WAA, are rather different. SC UK articulated a range of interlinked activities that would help improve incomes in the rural communities as well as help the situation of the girls who had migrated or might migrate. The view articulated by the WAA was much more immediate in terms of how the girls could be helped once they arrived in the town. From this account, we have no information about the views of other organizations, such as local NGOs or local authorities in the villages and towns.

There are some further evaluative lessons that can be drawn from these short readings.

1 Could you identify any relationship between the intervention and an implicit conceptual analysis of poverty? Which of the concepts introduced in *Introduction to Poverty and Inequality* seem to support the action being taken (low income, multiple deprivations, capabilities, social exclusion, relational/residual notions)? Possibly poverty as low income and poverty as multiple deprivations seem to provide the underlying analysis in the articles.

2 Did you link the action being taken to the discussion of poverty agendas in Section 2 or in other sections of this Theme? Agendas that may spring to mind are those currently part of the *World Development Report 2000/2001*: opportunity, security and empowerment. On the audiocassette for this Theme. Moser was keen to highlight security as a key issue for action on poverty, while Mayo underlined the significance of the terms and conditions of employment. However, both were concerned to underline the multiple facets of deprivation in terms of building future policy agendas on poverty and inequality.

3 Were there any lessons from Section 3 that you could use in evaluating action? Did you notice which data were selected to support the case study, or how the 'voices' were used to support the story? To what extent do you think it is possible to interpret insider views from the accounts you have read (given that the accounts combined SC UK's analysis as well as the voices of some of the participants in the project)?

4 We might want to ask further contextual questions, for example, about the wider socio-economic and policy context (the structural possibilities and constraints) and whether specific initiatives in the villages are likely to increase incomes and reduce the need for migration. We might also want to investigate the significance of other factors influencing the migration process for young girls – for example, the desire to learn the Bambara language, and the desire to become 'modern'. Economic factors might not be the only issue, so that even if incomes improved, girls might still migrate for other reasons.

You can probably see that it is useful to try to interpret the standpoints of different actors to see where conflicts might lie as well as to assess the potential for a given route of collective action. However, in any course of action, the wider context in which it is located is also key for evaluating its immediate and longer-term (and wider) effects.

Evaluation 2: assessment by using explanatory concepts

Our second approach to evaluation looks at action analytically from the outside by using concepts against which to assess processes and their outcomes. In other words, we are using an *explanatory analysis* approach that you first met in Section 3. Here we use some of the concepts introduced by Judith Scott in *Introduction to Poverty and Inequality*. In addition to the common conception of poverty as low income, the main concepts were:

- poverty as multiple deprivations
- poverty as failure of capabilities
- poverty as social exclusion
- relational and residual poverty.

If you need to review these concepts, please do it now.

As was discussed in *Introduction to Poverty and Inequality*, these concepts include assumptions about the kind of action that might be taken to reduce poverty and inequality. For example:

1 Conceptualizing poverty as multiple deprivations might indicate that multiple forms of social provision are required to meet poor people's needs (as in post-Second World War Britain, as you will have gathered from the audiocassette).

2 Poverty as failure of capabilities also picks up on the multi-dimensional nature of poverty; however, action from this perspective might indicate steps to enhance human capital and freedoms. (In the terms of the audiocassette – and again thinking about the UK – this might suggest 'joined up' thinking in providing education and training to get people into work along with proper childcare support and a benefits system to enable people to take advantage of the education and training.)

3 The multi-dimensional nature of poverty is currently at the forefront of poverty agendas – at least in rhetoric – with a greater appreciation that poverty involves exclusion from many of the opportunities, services and sides of life open to the relatively wealthy, leaving poor people particularly vulnerable to risk and shocks. The concept of social exclusion tries to encapsulate these different dimensions and suggests a range of different types of action to make poor people less vulnerable, including means of enhancing participation and empowerment, as well as different means of economic provision and incentives.

4 The concepts of poverty as relational and residual suggest opposing routes of action. The first might be to change the structural creation and reinforcement of poverty, for example with measures such as land reform in developing rural economies; the second might focus on the promotion of economic growth and wealth creation more generally on the basis that the poor will benefit through increased employment opportunities and so on.

Just as these analytical concepts imply types of action that might be taken, they can also be used to assess action that is actually taken. For example, one might want to know whether a particular course of action is addressing multiple deprivations that have been identified, whether it is enhancing capabilities or reducing social exclusion. Thus one would need to find ways of evaluating action against these concepts. Evaluating public action on poverty and inequality in this way requires us to do two key things. First, we need to think about the different concepts beforehand, particularly:

- their usefulness in analysing poverty and inequality
- the kinds of actions that they imply.

Second, we need to have some way of operationalizing the concepts to be able to use them to evaluate action.

From Table 3.1 in *Introduction to Poverty and Inequality*, we have decided to select three concepts that seem to have particular strengths for evaluating the effects of public action: the capability, social exclusion and relational approaches. These approaches all focus on:

- the complexity of poverty
- the mechanisms of impoverishment
- the importance of structural causes.

They also all embody an underlying relationship between poverty and inequality.

To operationalize these concepts, we might build a matrix of possible indicators, such as those in Table 4.8 below.

Table 4.8 Possible indicators to evaluate public action on poverty and inequality

Conceptual approach	*Possible indicators to show that action is being effective*
Capabilities	Acquisition of new skills, education and training
	Improvements in health and personal well-being
	An increase in options and opportunities
	An increase in assets or endowments
	An increase in exchange entitlements
	Able to manage risk
	Growth in confidence
Social exclusion	Increase in civic and democratic rights
	Greater access to labour, finance and product markets
	Greater access to services: social, educational, health
	Increase in social participation (networks, community, etc.)
Relational	Better terms and conditions of work
	Changes in unequal relations of gender and other power relations
	Access to services from which previously excluded by virtue of social position
	Increase in social organization of poor people
	Increase in participation and voice in local decision-making structures

Our next step is to see how we might apply such indicators to an example of public action. We should emphasize that we are not carrying out a research project and are not setting up precise ways of measuring the above indicators! We are just using them to gain a picture of the potential and actual effects of public action from data available in this Theme. (If you ever do research in this area, or work as an evaluator, you might want more precise measures.)

Community economic initiatives

The example we are going to look at is the role of micro-finance in poverty reduction. This example is one of two in this section that focus on community economic initiatives. By these, we mean interventions that are directed at improving the economic and resource base and livelihoods of poor or deprived or socially excluded people in given localities. Thus such initiatives may include ways of generating work and income; they may also include protecting or reinforcing the assets of poor people and reducing vulnerabilities, as well as building capacities and giving people a voice in policy development..

Community economic initiatives could be seen in two ways:

(a) as attempts to address 'market failure'; or

(b) as addressing the ways that particular market institutions have developed in capitalist economies and how they include and/or exclude poor people (or reinforce poverty).

In the second instance we are referring specifically to poor people's relations to financial and commodity markets: access to bank credit for investment in economic activity, and access to basic goods and services (particularly food, housing, services such as sanitation and clean water, healthcare and education). Poor people's relations to these markets (or to forms of provision of services which may or may not be through the market) are, of course, influenced by their relations to other markets, in particular those for labour or employment. Consider the following commentaries on facets of poor people's access to these markets:

> Rather than people being unemployed, a major issue is that many work extremely hard but at levels of low productivity, receiving low financial recompense, and thus remaining in relative poverty. They require opportunities for better quality and better remunerated work.
>
> (Course Book, Chapter 5, p.123).

> A very large part of [capital] ... investment that has taken place in the poorer countries has been financed by public-sector authorities, often heavily buttressed by international aid, and by multinational corporations, with small farms and businesses playing only an insignificant part. The further one proceeds down the income spectrum, the harder it becomes to finance investment by borrowing from private banks, and the enterprises of the poor – both in rural areas and in the shanty towns on the edge of the cities – generally have no access to them at all.
>
> It is now no mystery why the bottom end of the capital market fails in developing countries. Most institutions regard low-income households as 'too poor' to save, while potential lenders, faced with borrowers whom they do not personally know, who do not keep written accounts or 'business plans' and who want to borrow small and uneconomic sums, are exposed to very high risks every time they lend ... Worse, they are unable to shield themselves against those risks ... since borrowers ... are too poor to offer collateral, the courts too weak to repossess any collateral which is offered, and insurance against the commonest hazards which afflict small producers in developing countries ... is generally unfavourable.
>
> (Hulme and Mosley, 1996, pp.1–2)

> [P]overty analysis, and therefore poverty alleviation strategies, must take into account the multi-dimensional aspects of social exclusion. It is not sufficient just to focus on average household incomes and commodity equivalent purchasing power of basic goods and services. In this day and age we are dealing with population groups who are also facing diminishing access and participation to a whole range of economic and social activities and institutions. Not only do they have little access to formal labour markets and therefore to political and social organizations ... They are also locked into an environment which offers them little access to civil society participation leisure activities, participation in new technology and commerce activities ... [H]ousehold survival strategies tend to focus on short term opportunities for income generation in the informal and unregulated sectors.
>
> (Pearson, 2000, p.4)

The problems are posed in different ways in each quotation. But they, implicitly or explicitly, question how conditions of access to work and remuneration can be changed, to enable poor or impoverished people to improve their economic circumstances, their means of protection from further impoverishment and their participation in wider social and political processes.

Micro-finance

It has been suggested that micro-finance is one way in which poor people can both improve their incomes and reduce their social exclusion. The example we will look at focuses on micro-credit* and, to a lesser extent, small start-up grants. However, micro-finance could also include various forms of insurance, pension schemes and other forms of financial protection against impoverishment, as well as means of increasing incomes.

*You have already read some discussion of micro-credit in the Course Book. See Chapter 5, p.122, and Chapter 18, pp.396–398.

There is a considerable literature that has documented such schemes and their effects. Micro-credit schemes in less-developed countries arose out of the failures of large (often agricultural) development banks to include poor people in their portfolios as well as to recuperate loans and be viable banks in their own right. During the 1950s and 1960s, there were concessionary loans for poor people provided by such development banks, savings and loans co-operatives and unions. The approach failed because:

> it was top-down
>
> it seldom reached the poor
>
> funds were used for unintended purposes
>
> borrowers were not properly assessed
>
> low interest rates discouraged savings
>
> financial institutions became insolvent.
>
> (Marr, 1999, p.3)

During the 1970s and 1980s, the approach changed, with an increasing role given to the market in development; credit markets and interest rates were liberalized, resulting in further exclusion of poor people. However, new ideas emerged about how to provide credit for poor people while keeping financial institutions solvent. The main initiatives in the 1980s and 1990s were promoted by NGOs using group lending schemes, often based on the model of the Grameen Bank in Bangladesh (Figure 4.5). The basis of the Grameen Bank's lending programme is that loans are made to individuals in small groups in a given locality. Further loans to the group are not made if any single borrower defaults on repayments (which have to be made on a weekly basis). In addition, borrowers have to contribute a minimum amount into a savings scheme on a regular basis. This programme has had a high rate of success and had also reached large numbers of women borrowers (although note the critique in Chapter 18 of the Course Book). A description of the Grameen Bank's lending process is provided by the founder, Muhammad Yunus, in Box 4.3.

Figure 4.5 A village banking scheme in The Gambia, based on the Grameen model.

Box 4.3 Grameen Bank: group-based lending

When a person wants to borrow from Grameen Bank, we ask him or her to form a group of five persons by finding four other friends of similar economic situation. The persons of the group must not be related to one another. We lend only to those who are landless or near-landless, that is, they must own less than half an acre of land. Only one member from any family, preferably a woman, can receive loans from Grameen. The group elects a chairperson and a secretary who hold office for one year only. The same persons cannot be re-elected until other members of the group have had their chance. The chairperson is responsible for the discipline of the group and it is through her or him that the group conducts its business with the bank.

When a new group is formed, it is observed by a bank staff member for one month. If group members conform to the discipline of the Grameen Bank, the loan process starts. We do not give loans to all five persons in the group at the same time. The group chooses the two people who are neediest, and they receive loans first. The group is asked to monitor that these first two loans are used correctly and that repayments are made on time. If the first two members have repaid their instalments on time for a month or two, the next two members become eligible to receive loans. The group secretary and chairperson are usually the last in the group to get loans.

The first loans are usually small. As members develop confidence, they ask for larger amounts. A member qualifies for a second loan after he or she has fully repaid the first loan. In each case, the group has to agree on the amount of the loan. Currently we are lending the equivalent of about one and one-half million dollars every working day. The average loan size is around 100 dollars.

The group has the power to discipline individual members. If a member does not attend the weekly meeting or pay the instalments on time, the group can, by unanimous decision, impose a fine. It can also expel any member for chronic lack of discipline. A member who leaves the group must repay the full amount of any loan outstanding. If a member leaves without repaying the amount owed, the group must repay the balance. A new member may join the group if the group agrees unanimously about admitting him or her and if he or she meets the bank's eligibility criteria.

During this lending process, a kind of group support builds up. Each member is responsible to the group for her or his actions; in turn, the members help each other overcome problems. There is no need for Grameen to ask for collateral of guarantors. The groups themselves ensure that no individual borrower takes actions that prejudice the chances of any other member. Social collateral replaces material collateral. Individual greed is suppressed by collective responsibility. Each member of a group becomes a social-consciousness-driven entrepreneur.

Besides being a lending institution, Grameen also requires its borrowers to save. Each week each borrower saves at least one taka (2.5 cents), which is deposited at the weekly group meeting. In addition, 5 percent of each loan received is levied for the 'group fund', and for loans larger than 1,000 taka another 0.5 percent of the loan amount is charged for the emergency fund. The group fund is managed by the group. Members can borrow from it in times of severe need, on terms fixed by the group; they can also invest the amount in any activity of their choosing. The emergency fund is managed by the bank and is used as a life insurance program. The total savings of Grameen borrowers now exceeds $70 million.

> Several groups get together and form a centre, and in each village there may be one or two centres. A centre chief and a deputy centre chief are elected by the respective group chairpersons from among themselves. All bank business is transacted at weekly meetings, which are held on designated days of the week for each centre.
>
> (Source: Yunus, M., 1997, pp.13–15)

There have been many studies of the role and effects of micro-credit. For example, Hulme and Mosley (1996), whose study focused on schemes in less developed countries and primarily those targeting the rural poor, conclude (pp.134–135) that:

- Many schemes are not as effective as they could or might wish to be because they treat poor people as an undifferentiated group.
- There is concentration on the regimes for disbursement of loans at the expense of diverse forms of credit or other forms of protection and assistance, and savings schemes.
- The poorest people tend not to have access to the schemes because the risks are too great for them and the benefits tend to accrue to people whose incomes have already crossed a certain threshold.
- There tends to be replication (for example, of the Grameen model) rather than innovation in the schemes.

You will also have picked up other criticisms of micro-credit in a developing country context on the second band of the audiocassette for this Theme. For example, Harsh Mander from Action Aid states that poor people have to pay more for their credit than wealthier people: the interest rates are high compared with bank rates, and the informal nature of micro-credit projects means that poor people have to spend time managing their credit in ways that people taking loans from formal institutions do not. In addition, goods produced as a result of investment using micro-credit funds need markets or 'effective demand'* to bring a return and to enable people to repay their loans. Debt relations can potentially be exacerbated as well as improved by micro-credit.

*Effective demand is demand backed by purchasing power, i.e. the ability to pay for goods and services. Effective demand is a serious problem for market development when incomes are very low.

Hulme and Mosley go on to argue that:

- The successful schemes such as Grameen Bank have walked a tightrope between ineffective targeting and financial failure and that their successes should be saluted.
- Financially, 'market-determined interest rates, the availability of savings and insurance facilities, intensive loan collection and incentives for borrowers and agency staff are all positively associated with high performance' (ibid., p.200), while models of loan administration (to groups, to individuals, etc.) do not seem to affect operational success in financial terms.

- Economically and socially, the existence of such schemes has induced informal moneylenders to lower their interest rates and vary their forms of financial support. Poorer borrowers have tended not to invest additional income in technology or labour hire from outside the family (i.e. they do not necessarily stimulate other markets). However, there are more payments to people in the family, which raises and redistributes family and household income overall. The poorer borrowers still remain vulnerable to shocks such as crop failure or other disasters. The social and political leverage of such groups has not increased (ibid., pp.200–201).

This last point is important because micro-credit schemes are often attributed with mobilizing and empowering poor people, but Hulme and Mosley are not the only writers to question this outcome. There is also debate about the extent to which women are empowered within households as a result of receiving credit. Ruth Pearson outlines this debate in Chapter 18 of the Course Book: on the one hand, loans may end up with male members of households; on the other, it is suggested that women's influence over decision-making in households has increased (p.397). In another study, Marr (1999) suggests that poor people need more than access to credit to reduce their poverty; in particular more diverse financial services are needed.

Much of the focus in the literature has been on the experiences in less-developed countries. However, there is a growing number of micro-credit schemes in developed countries, often building on the models and experiences from the South. While directed at poor and socially excluded people, their role is somewhat different because of the differences in context (Pearson, 2000). Initiatives tend to be directed to low income and benefit dependent groups, and the 'new poor' (or those whose employment has been displaced or undermined by wider changes in the capitalist economy). The initiatives have the aim of developing entrepreneurial confidence and skills as well as providing finance. Projects are often neighbourhood focused but use lessons from schemes such as the Grameen Bank with respect to group collateral. In addition groups provide solidarity and promote the empowerment of their members as well as entrepreneurial success. Further innovations are in how micro-credit and other loan schemes are financed. Although finance may come from state funds, loan schemes are also funded by other entrepreneurs and bankers, such as the Sheffield Employment Bond (SEB) in the UK. Although national unemployment was only about 3–4% in the UK, in parts of Sheffield it was 20% when the SEB was established. In the SEB scheme, local entrepreneurs put in sums from their own profits to provide loans to unemployed people wanting to set up their own businesses (BBC, 2000).

Activity 4.9

Before going on to the evaluation of our case study, either listen again to or review your notes of the second band of the audiocassette. In it you will have gathered from Erica Watson, at the Full Circle project in Norwich in the UK, that the Grameen Bank was an important model for that scheme. You will also have noticed that the work of Full Circle has helped to create a virtuous circle of empowerment, social capital and partnership possibilities. The pros and cons of other initiatives in micro-finance are discussed, including the innovations in the model and the ways that they have been extended. Make notes or review your notes and reflect on them now in the light of the above discussion before continuing.

(Spend no more than 15 minutes on this activity)

Within the UK, micro-finance tends to be part of a wider process of urban regeneration (outlined in Box 4.4) in areas that have suffered impoverishment and decline, often as an outcome of restructuring and movements of capital investment linked to globalization. The case we are going to evaluate, using the conceptual approaches we have discussed above, is the micro-credit and small grant programme of the Wellpark Enterprise Centre in Glasgow.

Box 4.4 Urban regeneration under the Labour Government 2001

The collapse of Britain's industrial and manufacturing economy has left many inner city areas blighted by unemployment, riddled with poor housing and socially excluded from more prosperous districts.

Urban regeneration is the attempt to reverse that decline by both improving the physical structure, and, more importantly and elusively, the economy of those areas. In all regeneration programmes, public money is used as an attempt to pump prime private investment into an area. [...]

One important trend has emerged over the years: the earlier projects tended to focus on physical regeneration, usually housing, whereas later programmes have attempted to stimulate social and economic regeneration. More recently, much of the responsibility for regeneration initiatives, especially economic regeneration, has switched to the new regional development agencies. [...]

There are currently two main regeneration funds: the new deal for communities and the neighbourhood renewal fund. But there are also a raft of other funding streams focused on specific activities that used to help regeneration initiatives. These include: lottery funding, cash for the education, employment and health action zones; and the Housing Corporation cash for new social housing, 60% of which has to support regeneration schemes.

The New Deal for Communities is the Labour government's flagship regeneration scheme. It was launched in 1998 and so far 39 projects have been formed across the country. Over the next three years £1.2bn has been committed to the scheme.

The main goal of the programme is to reduce disadvantages in the poorest areas by focusing on four issues: unemployment, poor health, crime and education. Other issues such as improvement to the physical environment are secondary to these main priorities.

The £800m neighbourhood renewal fund, which starts in 2001–02, will be targeted at the most deprived areas, on the basis of need, as extra help to meet government targets for reducing inequality. [...]

A number of perennial questions remain about the effectiveness of regeneration schemes. How can top-down government programmes gain the backing and involvement of local people that is usually crucial to their success? Can public cash really stimulate local economies and create jobs? How can regeneration schemes prevent displacing problems from one area to another? [...]

(Source: Weaver, 2001)

The article by Maxwell and Kenway that you have already read refers to some of the aspects of regeneration mentioned here. For an interesting case study of urban regeneration in the UK, see the article 'Turning the tide' by Hilary Wainwright in Appendix 1 (Reading 8). You do not need to study this article unless it is used as a case study for the TMA.

Activity 4.10

Now read Box 4.5 on the background to the Wellpark Enterprise Centre in Glasgow and Box 4.6 on Drumchapel, and view (or re-view) the first programme on the video: *Small Change for a Better World* (Figure 4.6).

As you watch the programme, make notes on whether you think any of the indicators linked to the three conceptual approaches in Table 4.8 above have been achieved and what evidence would support your view. Our rough answer to this activity can be found in Appendix 2.

Now summarize your notes on which approaches you think have been applied in the Wellpark case and the extent to which you think they have been successful in reducing poverty and/or inequality.

To what extent do you think that any of the issues about micro-finance discussed above and on the audiocassette apply to the Wellpark case? What limits do you think there are to the Wellpark scheme?

(Spend no more than 1 hour on this activity)

Figure 4.6 Micro-credit supports women's enterprises in Glasgow.

Box 4.5 The Wellpark Enterprise Centre*

The Wellpark Enterprise Centre is the location of a micro-credit project for women who want to set themselves up in business. Funding is provided by the European Regional Development Fund and a combination of Scottish Enterprise, Scottish Enterprise Glasgow, Scottish Enterprise Ayrshire, Scottish Enterprise Lanarkshire, the Glasgow Regeneration Fund and Wellpark Enterprise Centre.

The model is based on that of the Grameen Bank in Bangladesh, but adapted to local conditions. Women form credit groups, and meet on a fortnightly basis to build up their mutual trust and support and discuss their business plans. The credit groups develop their own criteria for approving loans. If a member wishes to take out a loan, the group discusses it and agrees the terms and conditions of repayment. All groups have the same interest rate: 2% above base calculated on a decreasing balance. The Wellpark Enterprise Centre provides complementary business advice and support, including training on business start-up and pre-start-up grants.

*The website address for Wellpark Enterprise Centre is http://www.wellpark.co.uk

Box 4.6 Drumchapel

Drumchapel is a large peripheral housing estate in Glasgow, built in the 1950s and 1960s. Its population rose to 35 000 in the 1970s but declined to 18 000 in the 1990s because of the collapse of traditional industries. There are high levels of unemployment, poor housing and poor health. Fifty per cent of households are headed by single parents. Participation in further and higher education by young people is low. Drumchapel Opportunities is the local economic development company and one of a number of organizations working for social inclusion in Drumchapel. Its mission is 'to assist Drumchapel to become a sustainable community through the economic inclusion of the Drumchapel people and the economic regeneration of the area by working with the community'.

(Source: website: http://www.drumchapel.org.uk/ [October 2001])

Comment

You will notice from our rough answer to the first question in Appendix 2 that we had more things to say about capabilities than about social exclusion/inclusion and changes to social relations. Did you agree or not with our view?

In terms of 'success in reducing poverty and/or inequality', we could make the following points:

- It is possible that the terms and conditions on which the women involved were making a living were improving. The evidence for this was not quite clear. They were, however, able to realize different kinds of work, which could eventually lead them on to higher incomes and further opportunities.
- Almost as important was the issue of equality, in that the women were able to have economic opportunities and services open to many others in society but from which they had previously been excluded.
- At present only a small number of women seem to be affected by the scheme, so there is an issue of scale.

You may have other points in your notes.

Finally, in terms of general issues around micro-finance and the limits of the Wellpark case, we might note that:

- It is possible, even likely, that it is not the poorest women who participate in the credit groups.
- Interest rates are, however, much lower than bank rates for the loans.
- The participants do have to spend time building their groups and managing their loans; however, it seems that the support and role of the groups are welcome and have other benefits, even if participating in them is time-consuming.
- In fact, these credit groups might contest the anti-empowerment thesis in a small way, as the women have increasing confidence and growth in their capabilities and skills.

As suggested by the few comments about changes in social relations in the answer to the first question (see Appendix 2), schemes such as this one are likely to have only marginal effect, if any, on the structural issues confronting the economic decline in the Drumchapel area in particular. It is the combination of this type of scheme along with other regeneration initiatives in the area that may begin to change the structural causes of poverty, in this instance arising from industrial decline.

It is, however, crucial to note that there is considerable difference between this experience and that in many developing countries. There is much greater level of social provisioning for poor people and, in the UK, a set of regeneration measures being enacted by the state with the support of civil society organizations and the private sector. You will have picked up on these differences from listening to the second band of the audiocassette. However, in developing countries, there have been other initiatives that have either enhanced the outcomes of micro-credit schemes (Moser's example of linking micro-finance to healthcare) or which have attempted to provide a different kind of provision (for example, through social funds, which were also mentioned in Section 2).

One of the critical dimensions of these types of public action on poverty and inequality is the role of partnership. In the case of Wellpark, other organizations such as Drumchapel Opportunities played a crucial role, as did the support for regeneration from local authorities and sources of funding. However, Marjorie Mayo on the *Poverty and Inequality* audiocassette emphasizes that partnerships have to be learning situations, especially as partners are often in very unequal relations with each other. The participation of all stakeholders in learning from partnerships and from the actions taken is fundamental for success in the longer term.

Evaluation 3: political assessment of action

Our third way of evaluating action is again to focus on the actors (as we did in the claims, concerns and issues approach above). However, this time we are not so concerned with trying to interpret action or gain an insider view, or to use concepts as a basis for explanatory analysis, as to make some assessment of the *political nature* of the action. Why would we particularly want to do this in the case of action on poverty and inequality? We have already said that action on poverty and inequality is a political as well as a technical process. Behind action lie implicit or explicit assumptions, understandings, beliefs and values. There are also strong and competing interests (as we saw in the 'Spilling the beans' article at the beginning of this section). However, even more important is the extent to which poor or socially excluded people are able to participate in the definition of the problem and decisions about the action to be taken. Often those whose role it is to take action on poverty, such as governments, international organizations, NGOs and so on, do not have mechanisms for including poor people in decision-making. In fact, a dimension of being poor involves such forms of exclusion. Moreover, the actions of such 'trustees' of the poor do not always benefit poor people and may even exacerbate poverty and inequality. Such a situation can result in a loss of legitimacy of the 'trustees' and in different forms of grassroots action which then may contest or present new alternatives to existing policies and interventions.

Thus action on poverty is closely associated with issues such as participation, voice and governance. It is such issues that we will now be looking at by considering the 'political assessment of action', to which you were first introduced in *Study Guide 1*, Section 10. A political assessment of action involves evaluating:

- framing: how the problem is framed in terms of public need;
- representation: how those expected to benefit are represented;
- interests: the interests of the agency (or agencies) undertaking the action;
- legitimacy: the claims of the agency or agencies to act on others' behalf;
- capacity: whether the agency or agencies have the capacity to carry out the action;
- accountability: the mechanisms that will ensure the agency or agencies will do what they say they will do.

Such an assessment involves understanding the interactions and relations between actors, and the differences and commonalities between them. In addition, it fundamentally involves the issue of representation: whether agencies act on the behalf of others (trusteeship) and/or whether, in this case, poor people are acting directly on their own behalf, and, in both cases, on what basis.

Figure 4.7 Poor residents in the town of Quilmes, near Buenos Aires.

The case we are going to look at is another 'community economic initiative', this time focusing on the second programme on the video: *Funny Money*, an initiative to mitigate the effects of recession in the Argentinian economy on residents in the town of Quilmes, near Buenos Aires (Figure 4.7). The nature and effects of the recession are outlined in Box 4.7.

As you will have seen from the programme already, the initiative is the development of a barter club on a large scale: the Global Exchange Network. The Global Exchange Network began in 1995 in the face of Argentina's recession and the effects that the recession was having on people's livelihoods, both among the chronically poor and the new poor. The three ecologists who appear in the video (Carlos DeSanzo, Horacio Covas and Rubén Ravera) started a barter system through a garage sale. They belonged to an environmental organization called Programa de Autosuficiencia Regional (PAR – Regional Self-sufficiency Programme) and wanted to link their work on sustainability to social and economic issues facing people as a result of the economic crisis (DeMeulenaere, 2000, p.2). As you will have seen from the video, the Global Exchange Network now encompasses many people and a large turnover of transactions, with 500 systems or nodes nationwide in Argentina (ibid.) The principles of its operation and the role of the social currency as a medium of exchange is outlined in Box 4.8 below.

The approach of this initiative has something in common with the asset management framework of Moser, except that in practical terms it makes use of individual assets to create further assets for the individual and the community. In other words, it is turning potential vulnerability into means for realizing and developing assets for individual and social use. As DeMeulenaere states: 'Rather than focusing on what a community is lacking, they identify what the community is possessing, and build on that foundation' (ibid., p.3). Associated with the exchange network is a process of confidence building, skill sharing, gift giving and community activity and a set of explicit ethical principles that guide the network (ibid., p.4) (Figure 4.8; Box 4.9).

Now let us see what a political assessment of such action might tell us in analytical terms.

Figure 4.8 The Global Exchange Network, Argentina.

Activity 4.11

Read Boxes 4.7, 4.8 and 4.9 below and review the second programme on the video, *Funny Money.*

Make notes on:

- how the problem is framed in terms of public need (what are the issues of poverty and inequality in Argentina?);
- how those expected to benefit are represented (what role is played by the participants in the Global Exchange Network?);
- the interests of the agency (or agencies) undertaking the action (for example, the ecologists who began the network; government officials);
- the claims of the agency or agencies to act on others' behalf (do they in fact act on others' behalf – who acts for whom in this instance?);
- whether the agency or agencies have the capacity to carry out the action (who would you see as the key 'agencies' here and what are their capacities?);
- the mechanisms that will ensure the agency or agencies will do what they say they will do (how does the Global Exchange Network keep on track?).

What do you think are the limits of this scheme in terms of reducing poverty and inequality?

(Before you carry out this activity, note that the 'political assessment of action' is framed in terms of 'an agency' that is carrying out action 'on behalf of others' (i.e. trusteeship). However, in this instance, although there are 'agencies' that have acted and act on behalf of others (the three members of the PAR in particular, and the representatives of the government who also feature in the programme), the Global Exchange Network has the character of a *social movement.* So we have broadened (or adapted or 'annotated') the headings in the activity to take into account the specific context we are looking at.)

(Spend no more than 1 hour on this activity)

Box 4.7 The Argentine crisis

In the period before the Great Depression of the 1930s, Argentina was one of the richest countries in the world. In the late nineteenth and early twentieth centuries the economy grew as foreign capital and migrant workers were imported to fuel the boom in agricultural exports. Ports and railways were built to ship beef and grain to the world market and the city of Buenos Aires emerged as a European-style metropolis in the New World.

Although Argentina is best known as a producer of agricultural products, today it is a predominantly urban country with 89% of the population living in urban areas. Since the collapse of primary product prices during the 1930s, Argentina has suffered relative economic decline and it is now classed as a middle-income country. It has been characterized by slow economic growth, and both economic and political instability.

Like other Latin American countries, Argentina accumulated substantial foreign debt during the 1970s and when the debt crisis broke out in Mexico in August 1982, the knock-on effects were soon felt in Argentina. The military, which had ruled the country since 1976 and had suffered defeat in the Falklands/Malvinas War earlier in the year, were forced back to barracks. In 1983 a new civilian government led by Raul Alfonsín of the Radical Party was elected in the midst of a serious economic crisis. The government made several unsuccessful attempts to stabilize the economy, but with debt service payments accounting for 10% of GDP, it proved impossible both to meet the demands of foreign creditors and the social expectations generated by the return to democracy. The government resorted to printing money, which fuelled inflation. The result was that when Alfonsín left office, to be replaced by the Peronist Carlos Menem in 1989, the economic crisis was even more severe than when he came to power, with inflation running at 197% a month.

At first the new government was equally unsuccessful in bringing inflation under control, but in 1991 the newly appointed Finance Minister Domingo Cavallo launched his radical new Convertibility Plan. This created a new currency, the peso, with a value of US$1, and set up a Currency Board which could only issue pesos to the extent that they were backed up by dollars held by the Central Bank. Fixing the exchange rate, and being forced to limit the growth of the money supply in this way squeezed inflation out of the system. By 1994 the annual rate of inflation had come down to 4%.

However, this policy had severe deflationary effects (reducing domestic demand) and led to high levels of unemployment. Because the peso is tied to the dollar and the dollar has been strong relative to other currencies, it has also meant that the Argentine peso became overvalued relative to other currencies, which has affected its ability to compete in its other markets such as the European Union and Brazil.

At the same time, the Menem government also liberalized the economy. Trade barriers were reduced, giving rise to increased competition for domestic manufacturers. Small and medium enterprises, which account for the bulk of employment, were particularly badly hit by increased competition from imports. They found it especially difficult to obtain credit at reasonable rates which they need in order to modernize their production. This too contributed to falling levels of employment.

A second plank of the economic reform programme was the privatization of state enterprises. From a macro-economic point of view, privatization helped the government to reduce its budget deficit, and because of inflows of foreign capital to buy shares in the newly privatized companies, it helped meet the balance of payments deficit. At the micro-economic level, however, the newly privatized firms tended to lay off workers in order to reduce costs. Moreover, because of the rush to privatize, insufficient attention was paid to the need to develop a regulatory framework for the new private monopolies that were often the result of privatization.

Another element of the economic programme was to reduce government expenditure. This involved rationalization and resulting job losses, with one estimate that at least 200 000 public employees joined the unemployed between 1990 and 1994.

This economic decline is behind the emergence of the so-called 'new poor' in Argentina over the last two decades. People who in previous, more prosperous, years would have had employment over their working life in either public enterprises, the civil service or domestic firms became out of work. And with the decline in the public finances and in the economy, the once impressive welfare state which offered benefits and health care to blue and white collar workers alike has withered away. The 'new poor' are joining the already crowded informal sector workers – the poorest sectors of the population who never really shared in Argentina's former prosperity.

As a result of the economic reforms, Argentina achieved price stability, with prices even tending to fall in some cases. However, this has been at the cost of high unemployment and increased income inequality. Unemployment in Buenos Aires, which was around 5% in the mid-1980s, peaked at over 20% in the mid-1990s. Wealth has become increasingly concentrated and the gap in income between the richest 10% of the population and the poorest 10% rose significantly during the 1990s.

The economy continues to be highly vulnerable to external forces. Each new financial crisis, for example in Mexico in 1994, East Asia in 1997 and Brazil in 1998, sets alarm bells ringing in Argentina. Loss of confidence in Argentina on the part of international bankers leads to outflows of capital and increased interest rates which put pressure on the economy. Changes in the value of the dollar, to which the Argentine peso continues to be tied, affects the country's exports and imports. The threat of renewed inflation, however, means that the government cannot afford to abandon the Convertibility Plan, so that tight monetary policies have been maintained. These processes are all part of the background to the further economic collapse in 2001.

(Source: Ruth Pearson, academic consultant to the *Poverty and Inequality* video, 2001)

Box 4.8 Money, créditos and the Argentine Multi-Reciprocal Barter Club (Global Exchange Network)

Money historically has developed an array of functions. In the modern economy, money (in its various forms) fulfils the following functions:

- *As a medium of exchange.* Money is a means of overcoming the inefficiency of direct barter.

Money avoids the need for a coincidence of wants in order to effect a transaction, i.e. you don't need to find someone who has exactly what you want to buy in order to sell what you want to sell.

- *As a store of value.* The separation of purchase and sale means that money can be hoarded and used to pay for commodities at a later date. Once transactions can become either sales (with purchases deferred to a later date), or purchases (following previous sales transactions), money then becomes the means of bridging these two aspects of transactions.
- *As a unit of account.* Money establishes the equivalence between different commodities. Since money is the means by which people carry out different and indirect transactions, the monetary unit becomes a measure whereby you can compare the relative value of different goods or services
- *As a standard of deferred payment.* Money itself becomes a commodity (to be lent and borrowed). If someone does not have money (or any means of raising money by selling their goods, labour, etc), there are mechanisms for them to obtain money to carry out their transaction. This is the basis for the development of credit and interest. Credit represents access to money (for the purposes listed above), even if people have not obtained the money via market transactions. This has a cost and is charged in interest. The interest rate is the price of obtaining money through financial transactions rather than the transactions of goods and services that people want to buy or sell.

Normally the state authorities (the Treasury or Ministry of Finance, and the Central Bank) have directed monetary policy. This includes the amount of money (in the national currency) to be issued each year in the form of notes and coins in circulation. They also have a key role in setting interest rates within the economy. In addition there is a range of commercial financial institutions (banks, finance houses, building societies) which are licensed to accept deposits (savings) from the public for which they usually pay interest. They are also licensed to create credit for individuals and enterprises and charge interest to people wishing to borrow their money. They cannot issues notes but can create money in the form of purchasing power.

Historically there was tight regulation between the amount of 'real money' in an economy (gold, coins, notes, etc.) and the amount of credit financial institutions could create, but in recent decades this control has been greatly relaxed. In previous eras there was only a limited range of financial institutions and types of credit. Now there is a very wide range, giving rise not only to the rapid growth of the financial services sector, but also to a series of quasi-monetary units (such as air miles, store points, etc.) which David Boyle has called 'funny money' (Boyle, 2000).

In economies such as contemporary Argentina there are many people who are in the position of needing money in the first sense (as a medium of exchange) but they do not have any possibility of obtaining this money through the normal markets. They have little or no money income (from employment, or transfer payments such as pensions). They have no savings that would have acted as a store of value to be cashed in when they needed money to buy things. And they are not able to borrow money to buy things because they cannot afford the interest to pay it back.

The way in which the Argentine *crédito* works is to offer such people money in the form of a means of exchange so that they can make purchases. It operates as money only in very restricted form. It serves as a medium of exchange: with the *créditos* you can buy what other people are selling in the same currency or money. You can also sell goods and services to earn *créditos*. This is important since if people were able to sell their goods and services in the formal (peso) market they would already have the money purchasing power to buy in the rest of the economy. In the *crédito* market they are only selling to people like themselves who have this special form of money: i.e. people who don't have formal money to buy things but need to have some kind of money in order to obtain what they need for household survival.

It is important to remember that this alternative money, which has been called a 'social currency', cannot be used as a means of exchange in the rest of the economy. The currency has no value in the formal economy and it cannot be exchanged for pesos even though the organizers attribute to it a formal parity (i.e. 1 *crédito* = 1 peso).

Within the confines of the Multi-Reciprocal Barter Club the *crédito* also serves as a unit of account. Prices are set by buyers and sellers in the market, and measured in *créditos*. But it must be remembered that this currency, and therefore these prices or values, have no meaning outside the limits of this protected market.

One of the stated objectives of the Barter Club is that it should be a system that encourages people to be both sellers and buyers (producers and consumers: prosumers, or *prosumidores* in Spanish). The way the system works is that once people have spent their initial quota of *créditos* they cannot purchase anything else unless they sell something to earn more *créditos*. So they are encouraged to sell what goods and services they are able to offer, which reinforces the reciprocal nature of the currency. But it also means that there is pressure not to hoard the currency – not to use it as a store of value to spend later (the second meaning above). In fact, one of the founders stated that they were considering introducing a system that he called '*oxidación*'. This literally means 'rusting' (oxidation) and refers to the process in which the *créditos* lose their value or usefulness after a certain time – like goods in the supermarket which are past their sell-by date. This built-in obsolescence would reinforce the fact that the *crédito* as social currency should not be used as a store of value. On the contrary the objective is to make people trade as rapidly and extensively as possible to maximize the purchasing power that the *crédito* system gives them.

At the same time, the fact the *crédito* does not act as a store of value means that it cannot be 'lent on' – i.e. used to create credit and earn interest. It is intended only to create an alternative money or purchasing power for those who are marginalized from the formal money market. In fact, the *crédito* is money only in the sense that it is an alternative (and limited) medium of exchange and unit of accounting within the Multi-Reciprocal Barter Clubs. It operates by separating out these functions of money from the wider and more extensive roles of money in the formal peso economy. But in doing so it offers the economically and socially excluded an additional tool in seeking to achieve or improve household living standards in a difficult and hostile environment.

(Source: Ruth Pearson, academic consultant to the *Poverty and Inequality* video, 2001)

Box 4.9 Participants' principles in the Global Exchange Network

1 Our fulfillment as human beings need not be conditioned by money, and people ought not want for their needs to be met.

2 We aim not to promote products or services, but our mutual help in accomplishing a better way of life, through work, solidarity and fair trade.

3 We believe in the possibility of replacing competition, profit and speculation by reciprocity among people.

4 We assume that our actions, products and services respond to ethical and ecological standards more than to the will of the market, consumerism and short term profit.

5 The only conditions to be a member of the Global Exchange Network are: assisting and participating at the weekly group meetings for trade, being trained permanently, and being 'prosumers' (both producer and consumer) of goods, services and knowledge and to be accepting of the opinions of the Quality and Price Control circles which aim to improve the network.

6 As we are an association of individuals, each member is responsible for her/his actions, as well as goods or services offered in the Network.

7 We believe that belonging to a group means no relationship of dependence, since individual participation is free and common to every member of the Network.

8 We claim that groups are not necessarily due to be formally organized, in a permanent way, since the network model implies permanent change of roles and functions.

9 We believe it is possible to combine the autonomy of groups (Clubs or Nodes) in the management of internal affairs with all the principles of the Network.

10 We recommend not to support, as members of the Network, morally or materially any activity that might keep us apart from the main goals of our Network.

11 We believe our best example is our behavior in and out of the Network. We keep confidentiality about our private lives and prudence in the public treatment of those matters that might alter the growth of the Network.

12 We deeply believe in an idea of progress founded upon the sustainable mutual support of the great majority of people of all societies.

(Source: DeMeulenaere, 2000, p.4)

Comment

Some of our own notes on this activity included the following points:

How the problem is framed in terms of public need (what are the issues of poverty and inequality in Argentina?)

- The increase in unemployment (particularly in the public sector but also industries such as textiles) and creation of the new poor as a result of globalization and the recession.
- The growing gap between rich and poor.
- Lack of unemployment benefit.
- No one to whom the unemployed can sell their skills.
- The need for new ways to make a living.

How those expected to benefit are represented (what role is played by the participants in the Global Exchange Network?)

- Representation is through membership of a club: people are invited to join through their attendance at meetings and demonstration of commitment.
- Membership is open to anyone.

- The club (or network) seems to have leadership and training, started and continued by the three ecologists and node co-ordinators. It is unclear in what sense they could be said to represent the members of the network, although their commitment is evident.

The interests of the agency (or agencies) undertaking the action (for example, the ecologists who began the network; government officials)

- The interests of the ecologists are quite idealistic in working towards different kinds of social behaviours. For example, they initially wanted transactions to take place without currency.
- The government officials, on the other hand, were learning about the network and recognizing its potential for social provision and supporting livelihoods in the absence of adequate state benefits for poor people.
- The participants or members can also be seen as agencies or agents, as without them the network would not function. Their interests are their own livelihoods (individual needs and ends) but their role as prosumers means they also have an interest and a function in meeting a wider social need.

The claims of the agency or agencies to act on others' behalf (do they in fact act on others' behalf – who acts for whom in this instance?)

- The legitimacy of the network is established by the extent to which people participate in it.
- However, there is an area where legitimacy is in question: the role of the state. In terms of managing the economy, the state has come under heavy criticism. Current government officials say that the state is unable to provide welfare and thus people have to find their own survival strategies. Their new claim to legitimacy is to assist people organize network fairs and begin clubs across the country.

Whether the agency or agencies have the capacity to carry out the action (who would you see as the key 'agencies' here and what are their capacities?)

- In a sense the capacity to carry out action relies on the network members themselves. There are, however, support structures: the training and running of meetings; the role of co-ordinators; printing the social currency; the running of the network fairs.

The mechanisms that will ensure the agency or agencies will do what they say they will do (how does the Global Exchange Network keep on track?).

- From the evidence we have here, this is rather speculative. The success of the network is based on mass participation. A decline in participation might reflect a lack of support and motivation by leaders and co-ordinators. Possibly the main question for the future is what the role of government will be.

The final question in the activity was: what are the limits of the Global Exchange Network in reducing poverty and inequality? There are obviously some interesting issues in terms of its relationship with the formal economy and how that might develop in the longer term. One possibility is that social currencies are only transitory and only function in crisis. The other is that their use and the ethical principles behind them could lead to different ways of organizing social and economic life.

However, for all the people participating in the network, we need to remember that there are two other sectors of Argentinian society that we have not considered:

- the wealthy who are not touched by the crisis (or not with the same effects);
- the very poor and socially excluded at the bottom of the economy and society that such a network might find it hard to reach.

We also need to remember that the national economy is tied into world markets and that the future of this scheme will need to take that into account. In this respect, the future role of the state and state policies are open to speculation.

However, such schemes do not exist only in Argentina and other parts of Latin America: there are Local Exchange and Trading Systems (LETS) and time banks in developed countries too. Ruth Pearson, the academic consultant to the *Poverty and Inequality* video, states:

> New approaches to income generation need to be based on a realistic understanding of the dynamics of new poverty in a global economy and the multidimensionality of exclusion from economic, social and political activities. Whilst this approach does not challenge the structural or cyclical nature of economic growth, nor the critique of mal-distribution or the gains from rising national income, it takes a holistic approach to the subjective experience of poverty, the complexity of income generation outside the formal labour markets and the need to explore income enhancement and expenditure substitution strategies as well as the focus on income generation per se. [...]
>
> Sceptics and opponents of this socially focused approach accuse its proponents of tokenism – of supporting small scale initiatives which can only have a marginal effect on participants and in macro terms will not radically alter income distribution or real standards of living ... [E]xperience to date does indicate that such approaches are most successful where there is national government support and leadership to place social entrepreneurship and new social actors in the economy high up on the policy agenda.
>
> (Pearson, 2000, p.13)

Evaluating action: processes and models

In this subsection, you have studied (and practised) three ways of evaluating public action on poverty and inequality. In doing so, you have been carrying out two important analytical processes.

First, you have looked at the relationship between:

Structure – 'the pattern or framework of relationships between social institutions' that forms the basis of social life.

Examples from our three case studies include:

Mali: conditions of landholding and access to markets in the villages; the labour markets in local towns; the nature of the family and household; beliefs and values about proper behaviour for girls and marriage.

Glasgow: the labour market; conditions of access to bank credit; gender issues in employment and access to services; localized recession and dis-investment.

Quilmes/Buenos Aires: conditions of recession in Argentina, particularly the links to world markets; unemployment; access to markets; role of money markets and exchange in livelihoods.

Agency – 'the actions of individuals and groups, and their capacities to influence events'.

Examples in the three case studies include:

Mali: the respective roles and actions of SC UK, the Women's Association for Action, and the girls.

Glasgow: the respective roles and actions of Wellpark Enterprise Centre, the credit groups, and the individual women involved; in the background is the role of funders who have enabled action to be taken, including government or quasi-government and European bodies.

Quilmes/Buenos Aires: the respective roles and actions of the Regional Self-Sufficiency Programme, the Global Exchange Network, the local coordinators of the nodes, and the many individual participants.

Process – 'the dynamic relationship between structure and agency' and the mechanisms through which change occurs.

Examples in the three case studies include:

Mali: how the actions taken might affect the situation of the girls through building their capacities and putting pressure on their employers; how support for other kinds of interventions in the villages might improve the local economy and services, and reduce the need for migration.

Glasgow: how the formation of credit groups and training provided by Wellpark strengthens the position of women; how it enables women to have access to credit; how it creates employment (and contributes to regeneration).

Quilmes/Buenos Aires: how the barter clubs enable people to make a living outside of formal markets; how the success of the process is changing government behaviour towards such initiatives; how the process contributes to regeneration in Argentina; how it creates new structures in the formation of global information networks and forms of solidarity.

Second, whether aware of it or not, in evaluating the three cases, we were using *models*. A model can have different but related meanings (Thomas, 1998):

- It can be an attempt to construct or replicate a simplified version of an object observed in the real world (think of a model car or train).
- It can be an attempt to represent a simplified picture of social phenomena observed in the real world – 'a simplification of the messy world that surrounds us ... made for some purpose'; for example, one might model the relationship between local government and local service provision to show how it is intended to work).
- It can be an attempt to construct an imagined situation or desired outcome (think of an architect's model, or a model for health service provision that will reach socially excluded people).

From this you might be able to see that the case studies of micro-credit in Glasgow (and Full Circle in Norwich, UK) and the barter clubs in Quilmes (and more widely in Argentina) are based on the construction of models to create a desired outcome: they are models of a given type of action to achieve certain ends. In particular, you will remember that the micro-credit schemes have their foundation in the model of Grameen Bank in Bangladesh. However, this model has been adapted to different contexts and purposes. Such a process can be called 'annotation', and you may come across it again in Part 2 of the *Sustainability* Theme.

In Section 4.4 we have also been using *analytical* models to evaluate public action on poverty and inequality. Our models were:

- interpretation of claims, concerns and issues;
- explanation using concepts and indicators: in this case around capabilities, social exclusion and social relations;
- political assessment using a given framework of questions.

These were analytical models that we used as tools to help us understand the real world. In each case, we have not been using our models rigidly but have been adapting or annotating them for the context and purpose of what we wanted to evaluate.

Finally, in Section 4.3, we also looked at models of action: individual action for private needs and ends, collective action for private and public ends, and so on. In this instance, we were looking at 'ideal types': abstract models that include defining or essential characteristics observable in the real world but that may not exactly replicate reality. They are not necessarily to be tested against the real world but are to help us analyse the real world – so, again, they were analytical models.

As you can probably see from this discussion models can be used to form blueprints for action. They can also be used to analyse action and to learn from action. Finally, they can also be used to help analyse and evaluate action.

4.5 Conclusions

What may have become apparent in this section is how important it is to be able to locate actors in context (their levels and spaces). This includes the local context of social relations, the causes of poverty (whether old or new poverty) and inequality, and the extent of public provision and intervention. It also includes the macro-level of changes in the global economy, the roles and policies of international institutions and fora such as the WTO, outcomes of gatherings such as those of the Group of 8 and of regional groupings such as the European Union, ASEAN, MERCOSUR, etc. It is thus also crucial to be able to analyse the dynamic relationship between structure and agency at different levels.

It may also be clear from this discussion that action on poverty and inequality involves powerful interests and, frequently, challenges to those powerful interests. Thus the role of organization and public action has a significance in putting pressure on international institutions and governments to change and implement policies that will reduce poverty and inequality.

Above all, it should have emerged from this section that action on poverty and inequality is a learning process, not simply in whether particular actions will achieve desired results but in the social relations and partnerships that are involved. This point was made forcefully by Marjorie Mayo on the audiocassette.

A question that you might wish to reflect on more generally for your study in this course is whether the kinds of actions we have looked at here are 'transformative' or not. For example, do they address the causes as well as the manifestations of poverty and inequality? What do you think?

Summary of Section 4

In Section 4 we have studied the following dimensions of action on poverty and inequality:

1. Its scope, in which we considered differences in perspective, the different actors, the spaces or levels in which they can act, and the linkages between them;
2. How to analyse action, in which we considered individual action for private needs and ends, collective action for private and public or collective needs and ends, and the linkages between them;
3. How to evaluate action on poverty and inequality, in which we looked at an interpretative approach focusing on claims, concerns and issues of the actors, an explanatory analysis, using concepts and indicators, and a political assessment of action.

We have also reflected on the role of structure, agency and process, and considered the role of models as an aid to action and a tool for analysing action.

5 Rethinking poverty and inequality

This Theme has scrutinized three dimensions of poverty and inequality: the policy agendas of major international institutions, the analysis of poor people's livelihoods and lived experiences, and types of action on poverty, particularly public action. In this final section, we briefly comment on these dimensions in the light of the points we asked you to reflect on at the beginning of Section 1:

- Context
- Standpoint
- Power relations
- Gender
- Public action
- Transformation

Some of these points for reflection were initially introduced and flagged for further discussion in the course at the end of *Study Guide 1*. We have added *context* and *transformation* to our list. Our comments below pick up only on those that were relevant to a particular section. Finally, at the end of this section, we also ask you to check your learning outcomes for this Theme.

5.1 Questioning Section 2: international institutions and the fight against global poverty

In Section 2 we looked at how major institutions such as the World Bank, IMF and, to a certain extent, the UK DfID, have changed their approaches to the reduction of poverty, given the global poverty reduction targets set for 2015. One of the most marked periods of change was from the late 1980s' focus on labour and labour markets (combined with policies to restructure national economies and reform the public sector) to an approach in the late 1990s that identifies security, opportunity, empowerment and equity as the key agenda for poverty reduction in the twenty-first century. On the one hand, the current approach is based on a poverty focus that tries to address the multiple dimensions of poverty, including listening to the voices of poor people. On the other, as suggested by the discussion on the audiocassette, it continues to be accompanied by a wider economic programme directed to economic growth, development of markets and economic restructuring. The new poverty reduction strategies and papers to be produced by national governments connect the two policy arenas.

Context

An important question for 'the global fight against poverty' is how and whether the new approaches are applicable in all contexts and the extent to which context is being taken into account in global prescriptions. We have seen in this Theme that the causes and manifestations of poverty and inequality have many similarities, even in different locations. However, there are also important differences between societies and groups within societies (for example, poor people in urban and rural communities), and between, on the one hand, the causes of chronic poverty arising from lack of access to and control over resources and assets, and, on the other, 'new' poverty arising from social and economic restructuring. Table 2.6 in Section 2 outlined different contexts in which certain types of policy instrument had had positive effect, and from which lessons had been learnt or could be learnt for current policy. However it would be necessary to review such experiences in detail before considering replication. Replication is an important dimension of policy development but only when context is taken into account.

Standpoint

Section 2 looked at the standpoints of specific international institutions. The World Bank and the IMF are two key players, both in global efforts to reduce poverty and in influencing macro-economic policy on growth and restructuring. These two arenas are closely related and from other standpoints it has been argued that policies in macro-economic restructuring have helped to create and reinforce poverty, not reduce it. Such are the views of many protesters at the beginning of the twenty-first century. However, there are other institutional players, such as the UN organizations, bilateral agencies, and international NGOs, which also constitute part of this global context and which have all had an impact on current poverty agendas. In line with a growing awareness of the downsides of globalization, there are now many different pressures and lobbies on major institutions, including world economic fora. As Caroline Moser said when she was interviewed for the *Poverty and Inequality* audiocassette: 'I think there is an enormous global movement now associated with globalization which is monitoring very closely development impact in a way that was never the case before … I think what is also extraordinary is the increasing power of the bilaterals … If we're talking about a post-Washington consensus, I think we are talking about different consensuses …'. This is evident even from media accounts of protests and lobbies where there is a range of views about the causes of global poverty and what should be done about it. You encountered some of these in the readings in Section 1 of this Theme.

Power relations

International institutions such as the World Bank and IMF are often criticized for the power they wield in national economic policies and the subsequent results and effects of those policies for poor people. Such power relations may be being adjusted as a result of the lobbying processes and protests. Thus we need to question the extent to which major institutions do or should create global agendas; they are not monolithic (as we have seen from the discussion on the audiocassette) – contestation and advocacy have had an effect. Given that the global dynamics that create poverty and inequality also create wealth, important issues for the future are:

(a) how wealth should be generated and distributed;

(b) how different interest groups, including poor people, can be involved in rather than alienated from those decisions.

The question is what role global institutions such as the World Bank and IMF could or should play in this process. You will remember that these issues were raised by Activity 2.9.

Gender

Although our discussion in Section 2 did not address gender issues, the major international institutions have a strong gender focus in their documents and policies. For example, the UK DfID states: 'The empowerment of women is an essential precondition for the elimination of world poverty and the upholding of human rights ... A key measure for gender equality relates to education and the need to ensure that girls get the same opportunities as boys to develop their potential and become full and equal members of society' (DfID, 2000c, p.8). There is also a global development target, which is to eliminate gender disparity in primary and secondary education by 2005. As DfID, and many other bilaterals and NGOs, indicate, the relationship between poverty and inequality is particularly evident in gender relations (for example, DfID points out that women are twice as likely to live in poverty as men). The particular experiences of women, and the particular forms that gender relations take in different social contexts, are all part of the multi-dimensional nature of poverty and inequality. Making such connections between poverty and inequality underlies rights-based approaches to development which are now under much debate and which you might like to explore further in your wider reading.

5.2 Questioning Section 3: understanding livelihoods and lived experiences

In Section 3, we went to the other end of the spectrum to global poverty agendas and looked at the livelihoods and lived experiences of poverty and inequality amongst people living in rural areas in India. India is a country that comprises wealth, industry and economic growth on the one hand, and chronic and widespread poverty in both urban and rural areas on the other. We could have chosen anywhere in the world, or a range of different situations to look at livelihoods. However, we chose to focus on one location (and a small range of experiences in that location) because we wanted to look at a case study in more depth and to enable you to gain some analytical and data skills in so doing. We focused on villages in Karnataka because of the research experience of Wendy Olsen and her colleague Uma Rani in that area, providing a rich source of first-hand data. From these data, we were able to look at the means of livelihood and the vulnerabilities of households, as well as the inequalities between them in terms of their access to land and within households with respect to gender and earnings. We also gained an insight into how women experienced aspects of their lives from the interviews.

Context

In this section, we gathered some sense of the context in which the villagers made their living: the nature of landholdings, who was and was not able to employ labour, who had to sell their labour, and so on. It was also important to know that there were wider processes of market reform and restructuring taking place. We can perhaps see how government policy-makers and development organizations would need this kind of information and analysis if they wanted to assess the effects of economic changes and to develop interventions that would enable poor households to improve their livelihoods. (In practice, the researchers who generated the data we used in Section 3 were particularly interested in how wider economic changes were affecting livelihoods.) However, there are two other aspects of context raised by this section. The first is to reinforce the role of specificity in terms of analysing and understanding poverty and inequality: we might have general approaches both to analysis and to policy development, but they need to interact with and speak to the different social and historical contexts in which poor people live. The second is that, in Section 3, we have seen that there are general principles to be taken into account in investigating any experience of poverty and inequality: what approach to gathering and analysing data might be appropriate, questions about how to interpret those data, a willingness to be challenged on one's interpretation, and so on. These are the sorts of issues you should bear in mind in studying any investigation into poverty and development.

Standpoint

Acknowledging standpoint was a fundamental part of the discussion in Section 2. There were several standpoints at work.

The *first* was the position of the researchers who gathered the data used in this section, both as subjective individuals with their own histories, but also in terms of the theoretical perspectives they brought to their research. We drew some rather sharp distinctions between different approaches to investigating livelihoods and lived experiences. It should be remembered that these distinctions are often not so clear in practice, although it is important to know they exist and to know where investigators are 'coming from'. As Rachel Marcus, a critical reader for this Theme, stated: 'In my experience, people with 'empiricist' tendencies tend to draw very little by way of broader conclusions from their data, other than those which very obviously emerge from it ... most people work with a combination of approaches, and arguably it's possible to be both empiricist and pluralist at the same time' (Marcus, 2001).

The *second* standpoint was that of the women interviewed by the researchers. While these interviews can be seen as the 'insider' standpoint, in fact they represent three standpoints. They were the voices of three women with rather different aspects to their lives and livelihoods, even though they also shared the local context in which they and their households were making a living.

The *third* aspect of standpoint was the interaction between the views of the women and the interpretation of the views by the authors. From this you can see that we do not just listen to the voices of others, but that we are constantly translating the meaning in terms we can understand (which is why self-awareness is so critical). While listening to the voices of poor people is an essential part of any policy development (and of reframing development) that tries to engage wider participation, it is also easy to see how the views of others can be open to misinterpretation (or lead to wrong generalizations). This is why the negotiation and renegotiation of assumptions and understandings are so important for the development process, a point addressed in the *Sustainability* Theme. A final point about standpoint made in this section is that there is thus no single truth about poverty and inequality and how people experience it.

Gender

Gender was a key element of the analysis in Section 3 in terms of differential earnings and in hearing the perspectives of some of the women interviewees. The concepts of capabilities and empowerment also helped us to interpret the interviews. With more time and space, we might have looked at how men perceived their lived experiences and livelihoods.

5.3 Questioning Section 4: action on poverty and inequality

Action on poverty and inequality is a hugely complex area as you will have discovered. However, as Jesimen Chipika said in her comments on this Theme: 'it is important to try to link a poverty analysis situation to possible policy and action recommendations. Studying poverty should not just be an academic research exercise; the noble goal should be to enhance effective policy design and action to tackle poverty' (Chipika, 2001). To try to break down such a complex arena, Section 4 introduced different ways of thinking about action on poverty and inequality, and the different levels and spaces in which action can take place from the everyday actions of poor people to the policies of international institutions. We used three approaches to evaluate case studies of action:

(a) an interpretative approach focusing on claims, concerns and issues of the actors;

(b) an explanatory analysis, using concepts and indicators; and

(c) a political assessment of action.

We also considered the role of models in analysing, evaluating and implementing action. However, we also need to know that all action will have its limits and contradictions, no matter how participatory, and how carefully researched and designed. Again, Jesimen Chipika comments: 'In the African context, we desperately need an answer to [What can be done about poverty?] ... It is an issue of life or death which we cannot continue to postpone. We would rather make mistakes while we are trying to determine our destiny practically' (Chipika, 2001).

Context

The context of action is supremely important. In Section 4, we evaluated case studies of action in a wealthy country (UK), a middle-income country (Argentina), and a poor country (Mali). We also considered action in both rural and urban contexts, including daily life strategies as well as policy development and public action. Context includes the socio-economic conditions of action on poverty and inequality, including the extent of institutional support and public provision. It also includes the causes of poverty and inequality, of chronic and new poverty. These dimensions underline the need to look at specificities as well as general processes and outcomes, as we stated above. It also means that situations and actions are thus not directly comparable. We need to be careful about extrapolating from one situation to another.

Standpoint

We addressed standpoint directly when we carried out an interpretative evaluation of the Mali project on girls in domestic work. However, standpoint was relevant in all the case studies: the different perspectives on micro-credit, from the academic and policy debates to the direct experiences of those who participate in such schemes; and the different voices debating barter and social currencies in Argentina, again from academic perspectives to the voices of participants. Throughout the Theme, we have picked up on the issue of participation, and its role in defining problems and carrying out (and 'owning') action. But participation itself is seen differently by different people, and is thus also subject to standpoint. Finally, the process of evaluating action also requires taking standpoint into account. We first raised it when we asked to consider your own position on child labour while studying the Mali case study. However, there are wider institutional concerns about different perspectives that enter evaluations. For example: 'Most agents, whether governments, NGOs, international development agencies, or individuals, tend to overemphasize their success story ... This means that there is an inherent weakness in self-evaluation ... thus external evaluation remains probably the best option. Safeguard should be taken, though, against unnecessarily destructive criticism...out of the context in which programmes were implemented in reality' (Chipika, 2001).

Power relations and gender

Powerlessness is a dimension of poverty, and gender relations mean that men and women experience (and therefore may act on) poverty and inequality in different ways. Power relations and gender underlie the three case studies we evaluated in Section 4. In the Malian case, they were manifest in the employment conditions of the girl domestic workers, but the gender relations of village life and marriage were also part of the migration story. Action was partly directed to empowering the girls through social awareness and skills training, as well as action to improve livelihoods in the villages. In the Wellpark study, the micro-credit scheme was specifically directed at women and developing their confidence and their business skills as well as enabling them to set up in business. Power relations were more subtly described: their lack of access to formal credit through banks, and the difficulties of arguing a case from a relatively isolated position. In the Argentinian case, we saw other ways in which power and gender relations interact: for example in the predominance of women in the barter clubs (and as co-ordinators), and in the questions around the future of government support for the schemes (represented in the video by the government officials). The barter clubs presented a challenge to power and to government by questioning how the Argentinian economy might be managed differently in the future to reduce rather than create poverty.

Public action

Public action was a central theme of Section 4 and we do not need to rehearse it here. However, it is worth thinking briefly about the role of partnerships in public action. Much is made of partnerships in the current rhetoric on development. Within the UK, there is considerable debate, in particular, about the role of the private sector, especially in service provision. You will remember from the audiocassette that Marjorie Mayo made some pertinent points about partnerships for public action. We quote here:

> I think the starting point is that typically partnerships are based on very uneven power relationships. Some of the partners have far more power and they have greater access to information than other partners. It's extremely difficult for community representatives to be effective in partnership boards and in those kinds of situations. I don't think that means that they can't become more effective and I don't think that means that professionals and decision-makers can't learn to work in different ways. I think if partnerships are going to work for community and voluntary sector representatives, then they need access to information, they need access to technical advice, they need training. But they don't need training to be parachuted down to them. They need training that really relates to their learning needs.

5.4 Transformation

The issue of transformation is a central theme in the final, integrating, unit of this course. Here we will note a few comments and questions arising from the *Poverty and Inequality* Theme.

First, we hope that you will have seen from your study of this Theme that poverty and inequality are not diseases or states. They are social processes. How we analyse and act on poverty and inequality are also social processes involving different perspectives and standpoints, interests and power positions.

Second, we hope that you have been able to see some of the differences between poverty and inequality as well as the relationship between them. We have continually asked whether reducing poverty requires reducing inequality. On the whole, our answer has been: yes it does. However, Jesimen Chipika had an interesting comment to reflect on:

> The big question now is: 'Is equality in social relations between economic agents feasible in reality and is it a necessary and sufficient pre-condition for poverty eradication or development?' I think the answer is 'No'; such an ideal state is not a necessary nor a sufficient pre-condition for poverty eradication or development. Rather, what is required is *an optimum level of equality or inequality in social relations*, a level which empowers every social group, to some extent to contribute meaningfully to the development process, and to access meaningfully

> the benefits of such development. This optimum level of social relations cannot be prescribed world-wide. It will have to be determined from nation to nation depending on the nation's endowments and entitlements.
>
> (Chipika, 2001)

Third, the comment by Marjorie Mayo on partnerships above triggers an important question: It is possible to learn from action on poverty and inequality, to think about things differently and do things differently in the future? You may remember that this kind of question was put by a member of the Argentinian barter club: he saw the experience as an opportunity for reflection on the nature of social life and social and economic priorities. A multi-dimensional phenomenon needs a multi-dimensional approach: not just action on poverty and inequality in terms of schemes and projects, but social reorganization and alternatives. These philosophical issues were evident in the discussion on the video.

Finally, returning to our underlying concerns with structure and agency, we should ask to what extent reducing poverty and inequality depends on the actions of poor and socially excluded people and to what extent it depends on organizations and institutions acting on their behalf. This is not a straightforward question with an easy answer, and it is tempting to answer blandly that both are needed. Both *are* needed, but, as Thomas (2000) suggests, the political feasibility of the one needs to be as much under scrutiny as the accountability of the other.

5.5 Reviewing the learning outcomes of this Theme

As your final steps before turning to your TMA for this Theme, just take a few moments to check the learning outcomes. Please go through the list below and tick those you think you have achieved so far. Where you think you have not yet grasped something, make a note either to review the issues now (especially if you need that particular area of understanding for your TMA) or for the end-of-course examination. There may be some learning outcomes that are achieved through the TMA itself (such as writing a short piece of critical analysis).

Content

You should be able to demonstrate knowledge and awareness of:

- [ ] the multidimensionality and historical and cultural specificity of poverty
- [ ] key institutional poverty agendas and policies on poverty
- [ ] different perspectives on and types of data used to analyse and understand poverty, at macro and micro levels
- [ ] kinds of action that might be taken to reduce poverty and inequality
- [ ] how new thinking on poverty and inequality can contribute to reframing development in the twenty-first century.

Cognitive and key skills

You should be able to:

- Reflect critically on the policy agendas and proposals on poverty of some of the major institutions ☐
- Outline the arguments behind these policy agendas ☐
- Understand and apply key economic concepts used in the analysis of poverty ☐
- Outline different perspectives on investigating the lived experience of poor people ☐
- Handle quantitative data on the assets and livelihoods of rural households in a developing country context (plot Lorenz curves, analyse household data, do simple calculations, present data) ☐
- Analyse and interpret qualitative (interview) data using interpretative and explanatory approaches ☐
- Identify the linkages between actors, the levels and spaces in which they act and their perspectives on action ☐
- Differentiate different types of action on poverty and inequality ☐
- Analyse and evaluate action on poverty and inequality using three different approaches (interpretative, explanatory/conceptual and political) ☐
- Appreciate the role of models in developing courses of action ☐
- Make arguments supported by evidence about policies and actions on poverty and inequality ☐
- Write a short piece of critical analysis. ☐

Appendix 1 Readings

Reading 1

In Seattle
Katharine Ainger

Source: Ainger, K. (1999) 'Trade wars: the battle for Seattle', *Red Pepper*, November, pp.17–19.

At the end of November [1999], people power will clash head on with corporate might in what the US media has billed as the 'protest of the century'. The face-off in the US city of Seattle will be a major landmark in the battle of profit versus people. Capitalism, with all its might, would seem to be the odds-on winner, but chinks are appearing in the corporate armour.

The salvos will start on 30 November, when representatives of the World Trade Organisation's 134 member countries will plan the future of the free-trade world in a 'millennium round' of trade negotiations.

'The confrontations in Seattle will define how the bridge to the 21st century will be built and who will be crossing it – transnational corporations or civil society,' says Mike Dolan of US pressure group Public Citizen, and a key organiser of protest.

A wide and growing global grassroots network of anti-free trade protest movements is developing as people feel control over their own lives and resources slipping away. For them, the agenda of the WTO is fundamentally irreconcilable with their needs. The ideological vacuum left by governments who believe 'there is no alternative' (TINA) is being filled by movements that embody the sentiments of globalization commentator Susan George: 'To TINA, say TATA' – there are thousands of alternatives.

The 'millennium round' of negotiations, which could take three years to complete, will lay the rules for global economic activity for decades. It will impact on everyone with 'trade' related interests – through food, water, wages, cultural identities, economies, knowledge, health, environment, communities, work, choices.

At stake are the social gains won this century through hard campaigning and struggle, from public health care to environmental protection.

In the UK, education and the NHS will suffer, says David Price of Northumbria University [UK]. Although publicly owned sectors are in theory exempt from WTO rules, the UK's private finance initiative brings the NHS within the sights of the multi-million dollar US healthcare industry, which has clearly stated expansionist ambitions.

To prepare for the WTO's millennium round, US trade negotiator Charlene Barschefsky – initiator of the banana and hormone-treated beef disputes with the European Union – consulted the US Coalition of Service Industries. It lamented that: 'Health care services in many foreign countries have largely been the responsibility of the public sector – [making] it difficult for US private sector health care providers to market in foreign countries.'

Barschefsky's objectives include 'encourage more privatisation' and 'allow more foreign ownership of health care facilities'.

George believes that: 'If an agreement on health services including all these provisions is actually tabled and signed at the WTO, we can kiss goodbye to our public health care systems in Europe.'

As well as gains won through popular struggle, areas of collective life most of us would never have imagined we might have to defend are under threat.

For example, Japanese entrepreneurs recently 'discovered' that 'by adding extracted spices to ingredients like cut and processed onions, heating the mixture, adding curry powder and heating until the mixture becomes viscous,' they could make a delicious, spicy sauce for vegetables or meat.

And they are taking out a patent on it. A billion Indians may break the copyright by continuing to cook curry. But under the patent regime of the World Trade Organisation, the Japanese entrepreneurs will be the legal owners of the process.

And it is not just the curry that India has lost to foreign ownership – the accompanying rice is hotly contested too. In 1997, US corporation Rice Tec took out a patent on basmati rice grown in the Western hemisphere. Developing countries are furious critics of corporate 'recolonisation' and appropriation at the hands of the WTO, but cannot afford to fight such 'biopiracy'.

The WTO's intellectual property rights regime does not respect collectively owned indigenous knowledge, such as that which Indian farmers used to develop basmati rice over centuries.

Yet the WTO does recognise the right of pharmaceutical companies to stop developing countries producing cheap generic medicines rather than buying expensive branded drugs. The move effectively prevents South Africa from being able to afford to treat its vast numbers of Aids sufferers.

Established out of the General Agreement on Tariffs and Trade in 1995 and based in Geneva, the WTO is the 'supreme court' of international trade. Armed with the ability to impose punitive tariffs on erring members – as already seen in disputes over bananas and beef – this is one global body with enforcement powers that bite. For the first time in history, there is effectively a world government: but its constitution acts as an instrument of corporate rule.

Time and time again, the WTO's Disputes Settlement Committee – in effect its courtroom – has swept aside environmental, social justice, health and labour considerations as 'barriers to trade'. Local and national governments have been forced to renege on their own laws. For example, the state of Massachusetts' anti-apartheid style price penalties on companies that trade with the military regime in Burma, the European ban on asbestos, and India's attempt to restrict imports while suffering a serious balance of payments problem were all challenged at the WTO.

The only policy objective that the WTO recognises is the expansion of corporate hunting grounds by opening up markets and the universal application of free-trade rules.

Its rhetoric is that of 'levelling the playing field' in world trade, presumably so the powerful can play on equal terms with the weak. Economic globalisation is creating imbalances that, in the words of the United Nations Development Programme, 'if left unchecked, will produce a world gargantuan in its excesses and grotesque in its human and economic inequalities.'

Corporate influence is endemic to the workings of the WTO, and heavyweight lobby groups such as the International Chamber of Commerce have been central to the formulation of many WTO agreements.

Take for example the Trade Related Intellectual Property Rights Agreement. James Enyart of US mega-corporation Monsanto described how: 'Industry has identified a major problem in international trade. It crafted a solution, reduced to a concrete proposal and sold it to our own and other governments.'

As Amsterdam's transnational watchdog Corporate Europe Observatory notes: 'Large corporations have been the satisfied beneficiaries of its treaties, while communities and small farmers around the world have suffered from WTO-promoted "free-trade".'

A recent sale-of-access scandal reveals how unashamed the culture of corporate influence has been.

Last April the *Financial Times* obtained a letter from the Seattle host organisation to more than 100 corporations seeking sponsorship for the November meeting. It promised 'the greatest possible interactions' and special private briefings with top US trade negotiators for the most generous givers.

Donors were divided into six classes, from 'emerald' to 'bronze'. Emerald donors (who gave more than US$250,000) earned the biggest perks. Forty companies are sponsoring the Seattle meeting, including Microsoft, Boeing, General Motors, Proctor and Gamble, and the Ford Motor Company.

Nation states are not as weak as some make out – they do have the power to seek alternatives. The rise of corporate power is a direct result of governments' actively adopting neoliberal economic policies. Although the party complexion of most Western governments has changed in the past four years, this has not, with the exception of France, shaken Western governments' belief that what is good for McDonald's, Ford, Nissan, Siemens and the rest is good for their countries.

Moreover, as is likely to be evident in Seattle, the role of the state remains strong in areas such as the protection of private wealth against states' own protesting populations. As a Seattle police spokeswoman pointed out: 'We have access to pepper spray'.

One reason for the corporate world's successful lobbying of the WTO is the remoteness of its decision-making from the people these decisions affect. For example, trade disputes are settled by three bureaucrats who meet in secret. Until the blowing open of international negotiations for the Multilateral Agreement on Investment, the WTO, like other international economic organisations, was effectively protected from popular knowledge, let alone pressure.

Officials have shown ignorance of the fact that locking their countries into trade rules can have unforeseen consequences. Ministers who rushed through the General Agreement on Trade in Services, for example, never saw the full list of 'services' the agreement affected. In fact, almost two-thirds of the industrialised world's economic activities counted as 'services', covering 160 areas including education, health, broadcasting, water services, tourism, and energy.

The WTO is keen to defend itself against charges that it is undemocratic, pointing out that ministerial meetings consist of representatives of 134 member states, each of whom has a vote. Decisions are supposed to be reached by consensus. But the powerful countries dominate, according to the World Development Movement: 'During the previous round of negotiations key decisions were taken behind closed doors with Third World representatives left in the coffee bar dependent on Western journalists for information.'

The consequences of signing up to these agreements have neither been debated in parliament, nor subjected to public gaze. The only effective scrutiny has been from the civil movement, which has gained in confidence and built up information through global campaigning networks.

They have, often using e-mailed trade and investment information, forced governments to account for their role in the WTO and other international bodies. Popular protests over the MAI had this effect on the French government, for example.

The European Union is currently pushing for an investment agreement eerily similar to the MAI to be included in the next round, while the USA and other big agricultural exporting countries are gunning for the removal of European farm subsidies. Both could stir up farmers and consumers.

Indeed, French farmers have already demonstrated their fury over US-style globalisation by carrying out several 'Big Mac attacks', dumping manure in, and dismantling, McDonald's outlets. Their anger was triggered by the punitive measures the WTO dispute settlements panel imposed on French Roquefort cheese and other quintessentially French foodstuffs after the EU refused to lift its ban on hormone treated beef. But the biggest EU–US trade war is yet to come – and all the signs indicate it will be over genetically engineered food.

America's pledge to use WTO rules to challenge the EU over genetically modified organisms is sure to fuel anti-WTO sentiment in the UK. The challenge would undermine campaigns to stop commercial planting of GM crops. If campaigners succeed in getting mandatory labelling of GMOs coming into the UK, or even getting an outright ban, these will be challenged by the main GM exporting nations.

It will then be up to a body called the Codex Alimentarius Commission, which is packed full of food industry members, to take an objective decision about whether the food ban is scientifically justified. The question of whether we want the food or not doesn't enter into the equation.

Environmental impacts will be severe in other areas. Removal of tariffs on forest products will have devastating environmental consequences on the world's remaining forests. The Global Forest Products Agreement – again, one of US trade representative Charlene Barschefsky's main negotiating objectives – will open up virgin forest to multinational logging companies. The pulp and paper industry says this agreement could increase forest product consumption by 3–4 per cent globally.

If this contribution to the rise in global warming weren't enough, environmentalists believe WTO agreements could override the Kyoto agreement to cut carbon emissions. Not to mention other Multilateral Environmental Agreements such as the Montreal Protocol to curb ozone depletion. The Biosafety Protocol on trade in GMOs has already been fatally undermined by rich countries in the name of free trade.

It was precisely because the MAI was so overreaching that international civil movements became galvanised against it.

Another key factor was disagreements between countries themselves. And there will be no shortage of arguments at the WTO, which has also been beleaguered by a long-running dispute over who to appoint as the next director-general. As the head of Pirelli said, the next round of trade liberalisation 'is going to be very difficult – resistance will be bigger than before'. In short, the credibility of the WTO as a functioning institution is facing its most serious challenge yet.

Shaken by mass protests outside the WTO headquarters in Geneva in May 1998, John Weekes, chairman of its general council, admitted that 'trade is no longer seen as an arcane subject of no interest to the public'.

The trade issues are convoluted, but the fundamentals are simple. The WTO and the agenda of economic globalisation have already provoked a massive backlash, from millions-strong peasant farmer movements in India to steel-workers in Seattle.

This backlash is an increasing concern for the WTO and for those who run the global economy. The director of global economics at finance house Morgan Stanley warns of the coming 'raw power struggle between capital and labour'. The latest environment report from the UN highlights environmental collapse in the coming decades.

As people's realities come increasingly into conflict with neoliberal economics, it will take more than the PR image consultants the WTO has hired to 'persuade the public of the benefits of free trade'.

This looks to be the crucial battle of the coming century.

Katharine Ainger is a freelance writer and researcher on globalisation.

Reading 2

Protest against the protesters
Samuel Brittan

Source: Brittan, S. (2000) 'Protest against the protesters', *Financial Times*, 28 September, p.27.

There is plenty to protest about in the behaviour of the International Monetary Fund and the World Bank.

As Jeffrey Sachs has argued (Personal View, September 26), the two institutions have become too much of a debt-collecting agency for western nations. Moreover, the World Bank directs many of its loans to creditworthy countries that could borrow in the market. It should become instead a direct grant development agency.

The Group of 24 emerging countries has a good case for saving the transparency timing of some policies – for example, whether capital account liberalisation might have come too early for some countries. But the main thrust of the opponents of globalisation is to say that the whole development has been wrong.

The clearest rebuttal can be found in some information conveniently collected together in the winter 2000 issue of the *Journal of Economic Perspectives*, published by the American Economic Association (2014 Broadway, Suite 305, Nashville, TN).

Richard Easterlin shows there growth rates since 1950. There is also a column giving the ratio of per capita gross domestic product at the end of the period to that at the beginning. This reveals that in the developed countries income per head in 1995 was three times as high as in 1950. The Prague protesters may be surprised to learn that a ratio of almost three also applies to the less developed areas, with 80 per cent of the world's population.

Sub-Saharan Africa, containing 11 per cent of world population, did not share in this prosperity. Here output per head at the end of the period was only 1.2 times as high as it had been in the beginning. This may have been due to bad luck, natural disasters or the way in which this part of the world has been governed. But it can hardly reflect on the international economic system, given what has happened elsewhere.

Of course GDP per head can be a misleading guide to welfare; but Professor Easterlin does have a close look at other indicators. Life expectancy, for instance, increased by more than 20 years in the less developed areas and even by 12 years in sub-Saharan Africa. Another index is adult literacy rates, which grew from 40 to 70 per cent in the less developed areas.

In the same issue of the Journal there is a fascinating attempt by Robert Lucas to look behind the growth numbers and speculate on what they might portend for the 21st century. He starts with the stylised fact that income per head in most of the world in about 1800 was in the neighbourhood of dollars 600 at present dollar values. This is about the level that today brings out the anti-globalisation protesters. But it is also the level at which the now advanced countries began; and if countries such as China and India are prevented from competing on the basis of their most favourable temporary asset – namely cheap labour – their whole development will be delayed.

To be precise, if a 'decent wage' could be enforced in the emerging countries, then employment in their industries would be much smaller and a higher proportion of their population would be crowded into the subsistence or primitive agricultural sectors. Parity with the industrial west, instead of being approached by the end of the present century, could be postponed for a good many generations.

But to come back to Professor Lucas: he assumes that one country takes off at a growth rate per head which averages about 2 per cent a year. This is followed by a series of further take-offs like a succession of rockets. His model cannot tell us which specific countries will take off at any particular time. But it does say that the probability of any country getting into a growth orbit depends on the distance between its own income levels and those of the leaders. Moreover, once a lagging country does get into orbit, it will temporarily grow faster than the leaders until it eventually catches up with them.

He mentions three possible reasons for this catch-up. One is that knowledge produced anywhere benefits everyone everywhere. The second is that the governments in the previously unsuccessful countries can adopt the institutions and policies of the successful ones. Third – and highly relevant to globalisation – relatively high wages in the successful economies can lead to capital flows to emerging ones.

With these few stylised facts and bits of arithmetic, Professor Lucas is able to come to some forceful conclusions. "Sooner or later everyone will join the industrial revolution, all economies will grow at a rate common to the wealthiest economies and percentage differences in income levels will disappear." As growth gets under way in the pioneering countries the income gap between leaders and laggards ("the degree of inequality", if you insist) increases, reaching a maximum around the end of the 20th century. But as more and more countries achieve developed status income gaps start to narrow. Eventually we end up with most societies being roughly equal in income levels, as they were in 1800, but of course at much higher levels.

This story does not tell us much about the policies and institutions that produced growth. And it admittedly skates over short-term reverses and fluctuations due to wars, depressions or misgovernment. But it nevertheless gives an idea of what science and technology can deliver if only human institutions will allow them to do so.

There is nothing inevitable about the process; and well-intentioned protest movements, which are radical about the wrong things, could bring this development down to a crawl. If only compassion could be combined with wisdom!

Reading 3

The IMF's agenda

Horst Köhler

Source: Köhler, H. (2001) 'The IMF's agenda for the new year', *Financial Times*, 8 January, p.23.

Much of the world began 2000 with its fingers crossed, hoping that transport, communications and power systems would not be disrupted by the Y2K bug.

Now, at the beginning of another new year, much of the world is again preoccupied with near-term threats to political and economic stability including unresolved conflicts in Africa, Asia and the Middle East and slowing economic activity and falling stock prices in the United States and other advanced industrial countries.

A natural human tendency, in the face of such personal insecurity, is to become self-absorbed. And yet it is clear that during the past year, people the world over have instead turned outward.

There is an increased awareness of the need for co-operative action. I want to assure our member governments and the broader public that the International Monetary Fund recognises the challenges ahead and intends to do its part in meeting them.

The immediate task is to safeguard growth in the world economy. In the US there is room for manoeuvre in both monetary and fiscal policy, to ensure that the current weakening of activity is transformed into a soft landing rather than a recession. Last week's reduction in US interest rates was a timely and appropriate way to strengthen US and global growth prospects.

The IMF has advised Europe and Japan to make further progress in growth-oriented structural reform and even to accelerate this process. It is also encouraging both borrowers and lenders in international capital markets to take measures to enhance their resilience at a time of economic uncertainty. With action along these lines, there is no reason to be pessimistic about the global economy.

More broadly, the international community needs to find ways to make globalisation work for the benefit of all humankind. The IMF is committed to playing an active role in this undertaking. A sampling of the activities of the IMF's executive board during the last two weeks of December [2000] give some idea of the complex and broad-based effort that is under way.

During those two weeks, the board took the final decisions necessary to begin providing debt relief to 22 heavily indebted poor countries.

It welcomed the Federal Republic of Yugoslavia – under new democratic leadership – back into the IMF and provided it with emergency financial assistance. It debated further steps to improve the IMF's capacities for crisis prevention and management, through surveillance over financial sectors in member countries and a streamlining of the IMF's policy conditions.

The fund also supported Argentina and Turkey in their efforts to overcome difficult financial situations. The continued success of those efforts now depends crucially on the implementation of the well-defined adjustment policies. Determined policy action will also be the best confidence-building signal these countries can provide to capital markets.

In many of these and other current activities, the IMF is taking risks. But I would argue strongly that it is a part of the fund's mandate to act decisively and adapt to changing circumstances.

Looking ahead, the most important area for further reform of the IMF is to develop a deeper understanding of international capital markets and greater financial sector expertise. Our objective must be to help member countries to take advantage of the opportunities of international capital markets, while minimising the associated risks and finding constructive ways to reduce capital market volatility.

In an increasingly interdependent world, prosperity will not be sustainable unless it is broadly shared. Thus, decisive action by the international community to eliminate poverty is both a moral imperative and a matter of vital self-interest. James Wolfensohn and I have pledged that the IMF and World Bank will make every effort to ensure that debt relief is provided to as many heavily indebted poor countries as possible.

But debt relief is only one part of the equation. Increasingly, developing countries recognise the need to help themselves through better governance, conflict resolution, human development and the creation of a vibrant private sector.

The international community must support these self-help efforts by providing enhanced opportunities for international trade and investment.

That is why the IMF strongly supports calls for a new round of multilateral trade negotiations, as well as steps to provide poor countries with access to markets in the advanced industrial economies.

In addition the IMF will continue to call on the wealthy countries to meet their long-standing promises to increase aid to developing countries to 0.7 per cent of gross national product – about three times the current level.

The writer is managing director of the International Monetary Fund.

Reading 4

Poverty in the UK: any lessons for the South?
Simon Maxwell and Peter Kenway

Source: Maxwell, S. and Kenway, P. (2000) 'New thinking on poverty in the UK: any lessons for the South?', *ODI Poverty Briefing*, 9, November.

The picture in brief

On a global scale, absolute poverty is concentrated in the South – but relative poverty and real deprivation also exist in the North. In the UK, over a quarter of people live in low income households, with worse health, lower life-expectancy, lower levels of social participation, and worse life chances than those above the poverty line. Children are disproportionately disadvantaged.

Current UK policy takes a cross-cutting approach to multiple deprivation and social exclusion, with over 100 separate programmes, some targeted at individuals at different stages of the life cycle, others targeted at deprived areas. There are some notable features of UK anti-poverty policy:

- The use of a social exclusion vocabulary, which draws attention to the causes of deprivation;
- The adoption of a life-cycle perspective, recognising the needs of individuals of different ages, but also the cumulative nature of deprivation;
- An emphasis on work for those who can, and social security for those who cannot, and targeting the obviously 'deserving' poor, particularly children;
- A primary focus on public expenditure and public service reform as the instruments to tackle poverty, with macro policy designed to underpin growth and stability;
- A cautious and largely covert approach to redistribution, avoiding overt redistribution through the tax system; and
- Widespread use of targets to create a culture of public service accountability – both output and input targets being embodied in Public Service Agreements and Service Delivery Agreements between the Treasury and other Government departments.

These features do not constitute a 'model' that developing countries should adopt. There is an active debate in the UK about whether the model is working and about what might be missing. There are also lessons that the UK can learn from the poverty debate in the South. However, the resurgence of debate in the UK confirms the potential for a fruitful dialogue across the boundary between developed and developing countries.

Some challenges for development co-operation

- Find ways to develop a dialogue between North and South on anti-poverty policy.
- Consider adopting the language of social exclusion, in order to highlight the causes of poverty.
- Look more closely at trajectories of exclusion and at cumulative deprivation.
- Investigate a life-cycle approach to poverty analysis, with multiple interventions for different age-groups.
- Consider whether area-based programmes help tackle multiple deprivation.
- Make redistribution a higher priority, and set targets for reductions in inequality.
- Recognise the political value of targets, use them pragmatically, and expect them to be used as rallying-points by anti-poverty campaigners.
- Remember that there are no universal models of poverty reduction.

Introduction

Rich and poor countries differ markedly in income, economic structure, administrative capacity and political configuration. But are there some lessons developing countries can learn from current thinking in developed countries? Experience in the UK suggests there are. The context is a sharp increase in the level of poverty in the UK during the 1980s, largely sustained in the 1990s. Poverty is usually defined in relative terms, for example as half mean income, but relative poverty has real consequences for such quality of life outcomes as health and life expectancy (Box 1).

Box 1 Poverty in the UK – relative deprivation, real disadvantage

- The percentage of people in households below half mean income rose from under 10% to almost 25% between 1979 and 1999.
- Children are disproportionately represented among the poor: over one-quarter of children live in low-income households.
- Poor people have inadequate diets – poor lone parents, for example, failing to meet recommended daily allowances for iron, calcium, dietary fibre, folate and vitamin C.
- Men in social classes I and II have a life expectancy at 65 which is 25% higher than men in classes IV and V.
- People in the poorest fifth of the income distribution are over one and a half times less likely to participate in social, political or community organisations than those in the richest fifth.

Poverty policy in the UK

The UK has always had substantial social security programmes, but the political salience of poverty reduction increased sharply with the election of the Labour Government in 1997. New policy work on poverty was carried out by the Treasury, a Social Exclusion Unit was created in the Cabinet Office, and the Secretary of State for Social Security was given overall responsibility for poverty reduction policy. In 1999, a new Annual Report was launched on poverty and social exclusion (Box 2).

Box 2 Opportunity for all

In 1999, the UK Government published its first Annual Report on tackling poverty and social exclusion. Entitled 'Opportunity for All', the report: reviewed the extent of poverty in the UK; reiterated targets, such as the objective of eliminating child poverty within twenty years; and summarised programmes designed to tackle poverty.

The second Annual Report was published in September 2000. The focus is on 'tackling the causes of poverty and social exclusion and helping individuals and communities to take control of their lives', in a partnership with local government, the voluntary sector, business, and others. Overall and sector specific targets are reiterated and developed. Specific strategies for different age groups are identified, for example: 'investing in the crucial early years and education to break the cycle of deprivation'; 'building a proactive welfare system which helps people into work'; 'tackling the problems of low income and social exclusion among today's pensioners'; and 'ensuring core public services address the special needs of deprived areas'. The strategies are supported by 'policy milestones', e.g. to establish 500 Sure Start programmes to support young children by 2004, or publish a strategy on fuel poverty by 2000.

(www.dss.gov.uk)

UK policy (as summarised in 'Opportunity for all' – Box 2) is characterised by a model of poverty which focuses on multiple deprivation, for example a combination of unemployment, poor skills, low income, poor housing, a high crime environment, bad health and family breakdown. A life-cycle perspective (distinguishing children, young adults, people of working age, older people) breaks the problems down by age group, and also brings out the cumulative nature of deprivation. The over-arching principle underlying policy appears to be to provide work for those who are able, and social security for those who are not.

The role of macro-policy is to underpin growth and stability; this contributes to poverty reduction by reducing unemployment and by strengthening the public exchequer. Additional and specific anti-poverty interventions then focus on public service delivery, featuring efforts to reform the public sector and improve accountability, as well as the introduction of new anti-poverty programmes.

In 1999, there were more than 120 specific interventions underway; not all new (Box 3). Some are targeted at individuals at different stages of the life-cycle, for example the New Deal (providing work experience and training for the unemployed) or the Working Families' Tax Credit (designed to increase the income of those in low-paid work). Most of these are means-tested. Others are targeted at deprived communities, for example the New Deal for Communities or the Single Regeneration Budget (investing in infrastructure, job creation, health and education in the poorest communities).

Box 3 UK anti-poverty policy – examples of key programmes

Sure Start: Integrated services for families with young children (home visiting, expanded day care, health education, other services).

Education Action Zone: Additional resources for schools in deprived areas, to encourage local partnerships.

ONE: A single gateway providing advice on work, benefits and childcare to people of working age.

New Deal for 18–24 olds: Benefits conditional on taking up training, working in the voluntary sector or with an Environmental Task Force.

Working Families' Tax Credit: Guarantees a minimum income for families in work.

Pensioners' Minimum Income Guarantee: A means-tested benefit to underpin the income of elderly people.

UK policy is target- and performance-driven. National targets include the commitment to eliminate child poverty within twenty years, and a whole series of target-group or sector-specific targets: for example, to improve educational attainment ('85% of 14-year-olds to reach the required standard in English, maths and IT by 2007'), reduce crime ('burglary down by 25%') or improve housing ('sub-standard houses reduced by 30%'). For individual ministries, targets are embodied in Public Service Agreements. These provide the basis for budget settlements through a Comprehensive Spending Review process, which sets spending in a three-year framework: the latest was announced in July 2000.

How successful is this strategy? Since 1997, favourable macro-economic conditions have delivered lower unemployment and (eventually) higher public expenditure. More specific anti-poverty interventions are mostly too new to evaluate fully: inevitably, there are both some successes and some lessons to learn. Child poverty is down by over a million.

Lessons for the South?

A social exclusion model

As the DAC poverty guidelines point out, understanding of causality is weak in most donor analyses of poverty: it has been described as the 'missing middle', between description and prescription.

The social exclusion model puts causes more firmly in the picture. Social exclusion is defined as 'the process through which individuals or groups are wholly or partially excluded from full participation in the society in which they live' (European Foundation 1995). Poverty is seen as resulting from different processes in the realms of rights, resources and relationships: the focus is on institutions.

A further strength of the social exclusion approach is that it encourages poverty analysts to look at the pathways or trajectories of disadvantage. Sometimes, these apply to individuals over a relatively short space of time – for example, an individual who loses a job, whose marriage breaks up, and who then finds themself homeless. Sometimes, trajectories into poverty may extend over years: poor education, leading to low-wage and insecure employment, leading to a poor environment for raising children, and so on.

UK anti-poverty policy responds to this in two ways: first, with its emphasis on the life-cycle, developing different measures for different stages: and second, with programmes designed to tackle multiple deprivation on an area basis, for example Action Zones, or the New Deal for Communities. In the latter, at least, it has followed the French example, which has long had programmes of this kind (by the early 1990s, there were already 400 programmes funded under the Social Development of Neighbourhoods (DSQ) initiative).

Rights and responsibilities

Some social exclusion models rest on theories of solidarity and of rights, particularly economic, social and cultural rights (see ODI Briefing Paper 1993 (3)). In the UK, rights are recognised (the European Convention on Human Rights was taken into UK law in October 2000), but are also balanced against a notion of responsibility. Those who can work are encouraged and required to do so (including those with child care responsibilities and mild disabilities). Those who cannot find a place in the labour market are expected to take up training or participate in work experience. Workers are encouraged to save for their retirement. Communities are encouraged to participate in regeneration programmes. There are financial incentives to fulfil these responsibilities; and some degree of coercion (for example, on training and job-seeking). A distinction is implicit between the deserving and undeserving poor.

A corollary of the new approach is a bias to means-tested benefits. For example, a much-debated issue has been whether additional payments to old-age pensioners should take the form of increments to the untested standard pension, or whether they should form part of the means-tested minimum income guarantee. The Labour Government has favoured the second, but many argued that the basic pension was a right, and that means-testing was demeaning. A further argument was that political support for benefits (and other public services) was stronger if they were universal: means-testing was argued to weaken middle-class support for transfers, and result in 'poor services for poor people'.

Beyond public expenditure

Public expenditure is probably the main weapon in the armoury of UK anti-poverty policy, and has been harnessed to a strongly instrumental, target-driven programme. The other important leg, however, has been reform of public services, to improve efficiency and accountability.

Sometimes couched as an assault on 'forces of conservatism' in the public services and the professions, reform has involved setting targets, publishing league tables of performance, and setting incentives to reward success, for example through performance-related pay. Thus, annual tables are now published giving exam results for every school in the country, and for the performance of every health authority. Teachers are just one group of professionals struggling with the implications of pay awards linked to these results: how can the impact of social deprivation on quality of intake be allowed for? How can the contribution of individual teachers be isolated in a team-work setting? And is it fair to do so? Can performance-related pay actually be de-motivating?

The jury is out on whether these innovations will lead to a sustainable improvement in the public services, independent of additional funding: the government does, however, claim some levelling up. Alternative models exist: for example, offering citizens more choice as consumers between alternative service providers, or setting up internal markets (as the previous Conservative Government tried to do in the National Health Service). Sometimes, better performance can be encouraged by giving the consumers of public services an exit option.

Redistribution

Redistribution is important in the UK, not least because poverty is defined in relative terms: a target of eliminating child poverty in twenty years means that no children will be living in households below half mean income (a brave, if not completely unrealistic target). Redistribution is also important because equality (of opportunity if not outcome) is valued in itself: as a spur to growth, and as an attribute of a socially cohesive society.

The gini-coefficient, which measures inequality, is relatively low in the UK by many developing country standards at 0.35 (1998-9), but still implies large differences in income: figures show the richest 20% of the population earning nearly seven times more than the poorest. Inequality has been worsening in the UK, as it has in many countries: for example, in the first two years of the Labour government, the household income of the richest 10% rose by 7.1%, that of the poorest 10% by only 1.9%.

The problem is that redistribution is a political hot potato. The Labour Government was elected on a platform designed to appeal to the centre, for example pledging not to increase income tax, and, for the first two years of its administration, not to violate spending limits imposed by its Conservative predecessor. Its subsequent strategy has been called 'redistribution by stealth', a combination of 'hidden' tax increases, for example based on technical changes to company law, and careful targeting of additional expenditure, for example using the proceeds of a windfall tax on formerly monopolistic utilities to fund the New Deal for the unemployed. The tax component of this strategy may have exhausted its potential, however. In the autumn of 2000, tax levels featured prominently in a public outcry about the rising price of fuel.

On the expenditure side, spending on education and health can also be seen as redistributive in both intent and outcome: redistributing opportunity rather than income per se. This is a long-term strategy, however. There has been no attempt to redistribute wealth, for example by introducing a wealth tax or by increasing inheritance tax.

This is a cautious philosophy, perhaps unnecessarily so – and is likely to be slow-acting. Some countries (e.g. Taiwan) have shown that it is possible to achieve significant redistribution through the tax system. Others have achieved significant redistribution of land and other assets. Should targets be set for lowering inequality, of similar weight to those set for growth and poverty reduction?

Targets

The enthusiasm for targets is one of the most debated aspects of poverty policy in the UK, as it is in developing countries. Do targets provide political momentum, focus resources, motivate staff, and provide the basis for rewarding good performance? Or alternatively, do they over-simplify complex problems, distort spending, encourage falsification of records, and conceal underlying problems? Both pro and anti positions receive support in the UK.

The UK Government has been challenged by the debate over targets, for example on hospital waiting lists (Box 4). Nevertheless, it has retained an enthusiasm for targets and indicators, as embodied in the Comprehensive Spending Review and in Public Service Agreements. As *Opportunity for All* (2000) illustrates, the multiplication of programmes is associated with the proliferation of targets and policy milestones, with consequent implications for monitoring.

Box 4 Targets in practice – the case of hospital waiting lists

The Labour Government elected in 1997 pledged itself to a reduction in waiting lists – by 100,000 by the next election. This target proved problematic, however, not least because resources remained constrained and because the country suffered a severe flu outbreak in the winter of 1998/99. More awkwardly, hospitals were found to be targeting the waiting list at the expense of other, more important medical criteria – for example, prioritising less-urgent but easy-to-treat cases at the expense of needy but costly cases. The policy was revised in October 1999, shifting the focus more squarely onto reducing waiting lists for cardiac surgery and cancer treatment. Nevertheless, waiting lists remained an area of concern. In July 2000, a new ten-year plan for the National Health Service specified cutting waiting times rather than numbers. The 100,000 target was met, however.

One consequence of a target-driven approach is that published targets provide rallying-points and pressure-points for anti-poverty campaigners in the UK. This is in part an intended outcome (see the discussion on reforming the public sector).

Conclusion

Focusing on the experience of the North does not imply that there is a 'model' on offer that can be transferred to the South. Anti-poverty solutions need to be tailored to specific circumstances; and in any case, the 'model' currently deployed in the UK is neither settled nor uncontroversial. It offers merely one attempt to grapple with familiar issues, and one opportunity to study the merits and demerits of different solutions.

Furthermore, a focus on the North does not imply that there are no lessons to transfer the other way. Quite the reverse. For example, the North can learn much from the South's experience of participation; and from its long experience of targeted interventions, such as micro-credit.

The real lesson is that there are valuable learning opportunities across the boundary between developed and developing countries. Globalisation means that the causes of poverty are increasingly common to countries in North and South. For example, social safety nets may be harder to sustain if countries are competing to attract foreign investment with low tax regimes. Developed and developing countries have many common interests in social policy' (see also ODI Briefing Paper 2000(2)).

References

European Foundation (1995) *Public Welfare Services and Social Exclusion: the development of consumer-oriented initiatives in the European Union*, European Foundation for the Improvement of Living and Working Conditions, Dublin.

de Haan, A. and S. Maxwell (eds), 1998, 'Poverty and Social Exclusion in North and South', *IDS Bulletin* 29:1, Institute of Development Studies, University of Sussex, January.

Rahman, M., G. Palmer, P. Kenway, and C. Howarth, 2000, *Monitoring Poverty and Social Exclusion 2000*, New Policy Institute, London, December.

UK, Department of Social Security, 2000, *Opportunity for All: One Year On: Making a Difference*, CM4865, December.

World Bank, 2000, *Attacking Poverty: World Development Report 2000/2001*, World Bank, Washington, September.

The authors of this paper are Simon Maxwell (ODI Director) and Peter Kenway (Director of the New Policy Institute, London).

ODI Poverty Briefing Papers are available online:
http://www.odi.org.uk/publications/poverty.html

Reading 5

Spilling the beans
Kevin Watkins

Source: Watkins, K. (2001) 'Spilling the beans', *Guardian Society*, 16 May, p.9

If you're reading this over your morning cup of Nescafé, spare a thought for Tatu Museyni, a 37-year-old widow and coffee farmer living on the slopes of Mount Kilimanjaro in Tanzania.

Last year, the coffee crop on her half-acre plot made enough money to keep two of her four children in school. Now an unprecedented slump in prices has forced her to keep them at home. "How can I pay for school fees when I can barely feed and clothe my children," she asks, adding: "The price of coffee is destroying my family and our community."

Cut from an impoverished Tanzanian farmer to one of the world's most expensive hotels. Tomorrow [17 May, 2001], the London Hilton hosts the World Coffee Conference (WCC). At a cost per head of £1000 – roughly what Tatu Museyni will earn over the next four years – government representatives from coffee importing and exporting countries will meet with barons of the coffee trading world. Faced with the deepest crises in a global commodity market since the great depression of the 30s, they can be confidently expected to do nothing.

Not that you would have noticed it when you bought your last cup of designer *latte*, but the price of coffee on world markets has fallen in recent months to its lowest ever level in real terms. Two years ago, it fetched almost $1 a pound. Today, traders are buying at less that 50 cents per pound – and prices are still falling,

Price data cannot capture the scale of human tragedy unfolding across the developing world. An estimated 20m households depend on income from coffee to pay for food, clothing and education. The livelihoods of these households are collapsing, with devastating consequences for poverty and the environment.

Over the past year, Oxfam has interviewed hundreds of coffee farmers in a global research project. The picture that emerges is uniformly bleak. In the Mexican state of Chiapas, thousands of indigenous Indian farmers are migrating to find work picking fruit on commercial farms. In the Kafe region of Ethiopia, where coffee originated, falling prices are translating into food shortages. And women farmers in the Dominican Republic report that they are unable to meet the cost of treating childhood sickness.

The collapse of the coffee economy threatens whole environmental and agricultural systems. No other crop is so well suited for cultivation on the steep hillsides of Chiapas and Kilimanjaro, where its deep roots bind soil and prevent erosion. In both areas, local communities have developed complex inter-cropping systems, where coffee is grown as a cash crop, with food crops such as maize, bananas and beans. Take away coffee and the entire system collapses.

Not that everyone involved in the coffee trade is losing out. Starbucks, the Seattle-based coffee shop chain, has posted a 40% increase in profits in the first quarter of 2001. Meanwhile, for the transnational companies that dominate the global coffee economy, the slump in coffee prices is generating windfall gains. Nestlé, the world's largest coffee roaster and, coincidentally, the sponsor of the WCC, had profits exceeding $1bn (£750m) last year from its beverage operations – and first quarter results point to a 20% profit growth this year.

The company's last report to shareholders comments: "Trading profits increased and margins improved thanks to favorable commodity prices." Taken from a different perspective, that could translate as: never mind the poverty, count the profit.

The underlying problem is simple. World production of coffee is increasing at twice the rate of consumption, leading to massive over-supply and an accumulation of stocks. Rising productivity and the emergence of East Asia as a major exporter have compounded the problem, as have World Bank programmes designed to expand cash crop production.

Coffee exporting countries have not helped their own cause. Instead of working together to restrict supply and boost prices, the major players have adopted a "beggar your neighbour" strategy of compensation for falling prices by exporting more. The upshot: they collectively export more for less revenue.

Short of praying for frost in Brazil, is there an alternative? Latin American exporters have taken the lead in pressing for a coffee retention plan, under which exporters withhold 20% of their production. The aim is to push prices back to around $1 per pound. But even if it enjoyed universal support among exporters (which it does not) the plan would probably fail. Its effect would be to add to stocks without tackling the fundamental problem of over-supply.

What is needed is a one-off programme of stock destruction in exporting countries to remove around 1m tonnes from the market – roughly equivalent to stocks in consuming countries. This would cost around $250m, part of which could be financed by a windfall tax on coffee roasters such as Nestlé and Kraft Foods.

Looking to the future, exporters and importers need to develop a credible supply management programme to stabilize prices at more remunerative levels. Colombia, the world's second largest exporter, has called for a return to the International Coffee Agreement – a system of export quotas that collapsed in 1989.

This remains anathema to northern governments – who spent most of the 80s demolishing commodity agreements – and to politically powerful transnational companies. Their "business as usual" alternative is continued toleration of a system that creates profits for the few, and mass poverty and social instability for millions.

Kevin Watkins is Oxfam's policy adviser.

Reading 6

Protection and promotion of girl domestic workers' rights in Mali, West Africa

Andrea Hizemann and Kadiatour Paté Touré

Source: SC UK web-page article (2001) 'Protection and promotion of girl domestic workers' rights in Mali', Save the Children UK, http://www.scfuk.org.uk/development/lfe/index.htm [accessed August 2001]

Save the Children UK has been involved in the Sahel in Mali for 15 years, and in the Sahel of Burkina Faso for 25 years. So we are building on a vast experience in the sub-region and relations with partner organisations have been strengthened throughout this time.

Increasing poverty, limited access to goods and services, and extremely scarce job opportunities – particularly in rural areas in Mali, and especially in the Region of Mopti (the poorest region of the country) – have driven an increasing number of young girls to larger towns in order to seek work and contribute to their families' income.

Most of these girls are 11 to 15 years old, but some are as young as 8 years, and they primarily belong to the Dogon ethnic group. In 1999, for example, 90 per cent of young people left a village called Dansa and among the 400 children, 184 were girls. A recent study in the same village revealed that only one 12-year-old girl was in school: all the other girls of the same age and older had left the village and worked in towns. When asked, the girls admit that they wanted to earn money for their marriage (girls want to buy modern items for when they get married) and thus help their parents who would otherwise have to provide the dowry. They also want to learn the Bambara language, widely spoken in Mali, in order to be able to show off and be considered modern when they come back to their villages.

The results of a study done by SC UK in April 1999 in the Mopti Region found that these girl domestic workers are often exploited (at least 12 hours of work, seven days a week); they are paid very little (on average 3.5 GBP per month)* or often not paid at all. They are at high risk of being infected with sexually transmitted diseases (STDs) and/or HIV/AIDS. They are sexually abused, beaten by their employers, and they usually sleep in crowded and unhealthy conditions.

*A 100 kg bag of millet costs about 12 GBP.

On their reason for coming to town for work:

"I come because of the difficulties at home; come to earn money for my marriage trousseau [her bottom drawer]."

"I come to town to earn money because during the dry season there is nothing in the village. When I have money, I will buy millet for my parents."

Impact on village:

"Before girls leave, they are engaged, but when they return, there are problems. They think that they are superior to their fiancés, they often break the engagement. This is not good." (Village Chief)

The study undertaken by SC UK, in April 1999, suggests a number of surprising findings which challenge previous assumptions. Most importantly, "...field results indicate that girls 'chose' and are not 'forced' by parents to work." The girls themselves are the prime decision-makers. In some cases, they may even steal money from their mothers and run away to the larger towns without the consensus of their families. But, even in these cases, they usually come back after a few months with some money in order to show their parents that their decision had been for the benefit of the whole family.

The project aims, on the one hand, to tackle the causes of migration at a village level and, on the other hand, to support local organisations that strive to help the girls legally, and improve their working conditions in town. Three strategic components are used to reach these objectives:

- base-line analysis and in-depth studies in collaboration with the children themselves, local partners such as Jigiseme and Essem, two women's organisations in the Mopti Region, UNICEF, and the Regional Social Welfare Department (see UK Fundraisers visit report below*)
- pilot interventions, based on research findings and implemented by local partner organisations and NGOs, in order to improve living conditions in the villages; working conditions in the villages; working conditions in the towns; and promote the rights of children and, in particular, girls in a very traditional environment
- advocacy towards governmental, and non-governmental, organisations and the donor community at local, national and international levels in order to incorporate issues relating to girls' rights.

*See next Reading.

The project covers four urban and rural areas in the Mopi Region: the towns of Mopti and Sévaré, and the rural villages of Dansa and Koriaberi. Pilot interventions and awareness-raising campaigns will be implemented here.

The project is being implemented within the Sahel Programme Strategy between April 1999 and March 2003. Some base-line research and feasibility studies have already taken place in rural and urban areas. These have actively involved the girl domestic workers themselves, in all stages of fact-finding and discussion through a broad consultation process together with local NGOs, donors and government agencies. In particular, the project aims to:

- reduce the number of girls migrating to the towns
- reduce the number of young girls (particularly those under 12 years of age) participating in domestic work

- improve their working conditions (limited hours per day and limited days per week) in order to allow for non-formal education and training
- secure their rights and protect them from physical and economic exploitation and sexual abuse.

SC UK works in close co-operation with its local partner NGOs by providing advice, funding, and methodological supervision on different approaches to be used, particularly in improving working conditions and the defence of girls' rights.

Pilot interventions in the villages will include income generation and work-load reduction investment, possibly combined with aspects of non-formal education or training.

Research is carried out with local or international consultants, and in close co-operation with the other three SC UK programmes within the Sahel Programme: HIV/AIDS, Livelihoods/food security, and Basic Services. The 'Protection and promotion of girl domestic workers' rights in the Mopti Region of Mali' project is one of four projects within the SC UK Children and Work Programme in the Sahel. The **goal** of this programme is:

- to ensure that no children are engaged in hazardous or exploitative work
- that children are listened to in relation to policy decisions made about their working lives
- to secure the right of all working children to adequate rest, play and education opportunities necessary for their growth and development.

The impact of the project cannot yet be measured. But we have observed that employers in the Mopti region have become more careful in how they treat girl domestic workers, knowing that a structure is effectively in place to help girls whose rights have been violated and who are seeking legal advice. Making particular cases known publicly is a powerful tool for local NGOs, as adult neglect of minors is culturally not acceptable and support is being provided by the relevant authorities.

Andrea Hizemann is the Deputy Programme Director and Kadiatour Paté Touré is a Project Officer.

Reading 7

Women's organisations supporting the rights of girl domestic workers
Janet Greaves-Socker

Source: SC UK web-page article (2001) 'Women's organizations supporting the rights of girl domestic workers', http://www.scfuk.org.uk/development/lfe/index.htm [accessed August 2001], Save the Children UK

SC UK is working with two local women's organisations in Mali, Essem and Jigiseme, which support girls in domestic service. Both organisations carry out similar work to protect migrant girls from rural areas, run literacy classes for women and girls, and raise awareness of topics such as HIV/AIDS, other STDs, childhood diseases and skills training. They also support the girls in settling disputes with their employers, for example, in the case of pregnancy, non-payment of wages, and physical violence. In February [2001], three SC UK Fundraisers from the Marketing Department visited the Sahel Programme and met some of the women and girls involved in this project. Below they write about their visit to Jigiseme.*

*Essem, the Association for job protection and the health of mother and child, was set up in 1997. Jigiseme, the Woman's Association for Action, was set up in 1995. Both Essem and Jigiseme are local NGOs with female membership who pay a fee to fund their activities.

Jigiseme visit

The village of Dansa, where the girl domestic workers we spoke to originated from, is extremely poor and very isolated. The nearest market is about five to six miles away in Douentza. When girls reach puberty they start to think of having their own home and they see that their parents and family have little to spare. As a result the girls want to find a way of gathering enough money to buy things like pots, pans, buckets, utensils, mats etc., mainly because when a young man decides to marry he looks at what his future wife can bring into the home as her dowry. The girls recognise that if they are to be attractive as wives they must somehow make some money to buy items that they can then add to their bargaining power.

The work that SC UK is supporting in Dansa is helping girls from this village who migrate to work in domestic service to be better cared for, to not suffer abuse, etc. But it is also putting in place viable economic activities for the community of Dansa so that the families can start to generate real income. In other words, SC UK is supporting the community work in providing girls with a happy, safe environment where they feel respected and secure. As a consequence they will be able to buy sufficient items to set up their own home when the time comes, without having to leave their villages to work in town.

Visit to Jigiseme, the Women's Association for Action, Sévaré

There were 11 women in the room when we started to talk. More arrived during the visit. We were welcomed to the Association's headquarters by their President. She explained that the members had asked her to speak on their behalf.

Tulaye Gariko – President of Jigiseme

"I am so happy to be greeting you today. Please accept our welcome from everybody here. The Association was created 5 years ago. We created the Association to make the children's lives better. If you cannot afford to help all the children you have to target your help. We saw the way many young girls who came to Sévaré from villages were being badly treated and decided to help these girls.

"We started to put money together to form the Association. Then we heard about Save the Children. We went to them to tell them we want to help the children in the community.

"First of all they started to train us because if you want to help someone you need to have the skills. They sent us to Bamako [the capital city] to meet women from another Association and to see their work with children. They also taught us about HIV/AIDS. It is important that we know about and understand the problems.

"Save the Children also knew there was a problem. They asked us to do a study before deciding where to start our work so that we would be helping the girls in the most vulnerable areas of the town. We started to do the study. We went from house to house talking to the girls and the employers about the problem of HIV/AIDS and of young girl domestics. Since we did the census we have a better understanding of the problem we have here in Sévaré.

"Save the Children asked us what we wanted to do about the problem to help the children. We told them that we wanted economic activities which can generate income. We told them we wanted new skills and Save the Children are helping us now so that we can help the children who come to us. They are giving us new skills."

Can you give us an example of how you have helped a young domestic worker?

"When we went to Bamako to meet with the other organisation we were asked to help a young girl who was pregnant and very poorly. Nobody could heal her in Bamako but we knew of a place here in Sévaré run by Médicine du Monde who support this sort of problem. We brought the girl back with us and put money together to look after her while she was here in the hospital. We kept her for one month and 16 days. They had to do surgery twice. When she came from the hospital she stayed with us for 10 more days to really get better. Then we put more money together to pay for her transport to return home.

"We go to see the policeman and talk with them. We ask them to tell us if any children come to see them with a problem so that we can help the child. Every single day we have someone come to us for help. Last month a 13-year-old girl, Aissa, came to us for help. She was working for a soldier. One day he was very angry because she did not water the garden. He beat her badly. Three of us went to the soldier's commanding officer and told him of the actions of the soldier. We told him that the girl had not been paid for her work and that she had been badly beaten. The Captain sorted the matter out and Aissa was paid the money she was owed, 1,500 cfa (£1.50 pounds sterling) per month. The soldier was so ashamed of his actions he did not have the courage to come here himself with the money he owed; he sent it with someone else. We found Aissa a job with another family who treat her more kindly and they pay the proper rate which is between 3,000 and 5,000 cfa per month. We always advise the girls to come here first to this office before they find a job."

What do you want for the future for Jigiseme?

"We want to do more economic activities which can generate income. With the help of Save the Children we have started to help the children. We need to give the children new skills. We have a garden so that we don't have to spend so much time and money going to the market. This allows us to develop our skills. We are learning to read and write in our own language. We want to make a centre for the girls to come to when they arrive from the rural areas. When they come they do not know how to do anything. If we had a centre we could train them before they found a job."

We then went to meet with Aissa, the little girl who had been beaten by the soldier.

Tell us about your day, Aissa.

"I go to the well to fetch water, then I wash the clothes, clean the house, cook and tend the animals."

Do you like this job?

"This one is better. My last job the lady is nice but the man is nasty."

What do you want for your future?

"I do not want to spend my life as a domestic worker. When the sun sets I want to go home. When the rainy season starts I want to go home."

How did you know that Jigiseme would help you after you were beaten by your employer?

"A long time ago I saw this lady (the president of Jigiseme) call on my employer. He hid me away so that I could not talk to her but I remembered."

About three years before the original study, the young girl had seen the president of Jigiseme call on the house where she worked. She was collecting information on where domestic workers lived and worked. This showed the girl that there were people in the community to whom she could turn. It was at this point that we left the young girl, who was very shy and frightened of all the attention she was causing.

We then spoke to one of the facilitators working in Jigiseme and to some of the other members about their work in the organisation. It was at this point that we told the women of Jigiseme just how inspiring they were to us; that their courage and energy were phenomenal.

"No we are not unusual. We are typical of African women."

Judy Marris, Wendy Bailey and Janet Greaves-Stocker are now the three newest members of Jigiseme. We paid our subscriptions for the next few months and were each given a bracelet as our badge of membership. In order to join the association the women decided that we should have African names. In the true tradition of the people of Sahel we were given a name from each of the main ethnic groups.

Dogon Janet Ina Ouloguem, which means *The name of my grandmother*

Sunrai Wendy Beba Maiga, which means *The first born girl*

Funali Judy Fanta Sidibe, which means *The little girl that I love*

Report by Janet Greaves-Socker. Many thanks to Kadiatour, Project Manager in Sévaré, for additional information on the project and local women's organisations.

Reading 8 (optional)

Turning the tide
Hilary Wainwright

Source: Wainwright, H. (2001) 'Turning the tide', *Guardian Society*, 16 May, pp.2–3

In transport terms, Barrow-in-Furness is the end of the line. Isolated on the north-west coast of England, it has suffered hugely from its dependence on a single industry and a monopoly employer. But this very vulnerability has led to the Cumbrian town becoming a hot house for large-scale community enterprise.

Many local authorities are discovering the value of homegrown enterprises which pursue social goals, in stark contrast to the approach of footloose global capital. But such projects are often dismissed as of marginal worth and divorced from economic reality. What is happening in Barrow turns this criticism on its head.

For 10 years, the town has been battling to recover from the best part of a century's dependence on a single employer – Vickers, as the ship-builder will always be known locally. In the early 1990s, it shed 9,000 jobs in a town of 70,000.

Trade unionists in the huge submarine and warship sheds on Barrow Island had long urged diversification from military production, but the cosy commercial habits of the company's arrangement with the Ministry of Defence proved too difficult to break. "In 1987, when we put forward our plans for civil production, they laughed us out of the boardroom," recalls Terry Waiting, then a shop steward and now leader of Barrow council. "In 1991, they called us into the boardroom to say we should all pull together. It was too late."

The baton of diversification in Barrow was taken up by an unlikely band of vicars and voluntary workers, whose improvised attempts to deal with the social earthquake of losing almost one in three of the town's jobs have launched a federation of community enterprises: Community Action Furness (CAF). This has created a network of social enterprises that holds out a potential alternative to rootless, profit-seeking corporations such as Motorola – currently pulling out of Scotland's Silicon Glen, with devastating consequences for the local labour market.

For the first five years, CAF grew creatively and chaotically, following through the ideas and the people who happened to come through the door and procuring funds from the European social fund (for training), the national lottery and, to a lesser extent, national and local government. But when CAF stood back to consolidate, it realised it had created a cohesive network of enterprises, united by shared workspaces, financial and administrative services, common social values and a joint strategy for fundraising to supplement their growing revenues. Crucially, it had also created a very supportive environment. It had, in effect, turned serendipity into a coherent strategy.

At the outset, CAF had employed Anne Diss, a former teacher and youth worker, to "do something about young people". The razing of the renowned, 400-place Vickers apprentice college symbolised the end of the future to which they had become accustomed. Many were homeless because unemployed parents could no longer afford to keep them.

Cue Project John: a scheme which brought together redundant skilled workers and young people in need of skills training and a home. In the past six years, it has refurbished dozens of houses, trained some 200 young people in practical skills and is expanding fast to include a maintenance team with contracts with the council, charity Age Concern and several other community organisations.

Project John is now just one of 20 or so training projects cum community enterprises under the CAF umbrella, of which Diss is director. Its latest is a cybercafe and IT centre. One enterprise often leads to another: Project John helped stimulate Sash (Safe and Sound Hearts), a company offering house security products in co-operation with the council, Age Concern and the police. Sash shares premises with two other CAF enterprises, Furness Community Recycling, which does the town's kerbside paper collections, and Growing Concerns, a gardening and landscaping co-operative providing training and taking on commercial contracts.

The same linking of needs with training and jobs inspired Cycloan, which began by training young people to recycle bikes and developed into a courier service, now doing work for the council. Together, the 20 enterprises have, over seven years, brought £4.2m into a beleaguered economy, created more than 150 jobs and trained at least 300 young people and another 50 or so volunteers.

CAF's good reputation feeds its momentum; its momentum feeds its reputation for "putting things on the ground", as Diss put it. "Once you're working with people directly on the ground, needs and opportunities constantly emerge," she says. CAF's door is always open and people come in with "problems no one else can solve" and with skills, time and energy for which there is no employment. The rationale is to use these redundant skills and teach new ones, in order to meet needs that nobody else is addressing. Training and trading simultaneously is crucial. Nicola Biggs, co-ordinator of Project John, says: "By training and making a business at the same time, people are achieving something; the positive contribution they are making is real, not hypothetical."

One of the core values is self-management. To maintain its independence, CAF decided to become more rigorous about its trading side. At present, self-generated revenue is about 20% of annual income; its aim is 60%. Will this undermine its social values? Diss says: "There could be a danger that the trading pressure leads to subordination of the training, but we've created an environment to prevent this." She describes how Jibcraft, a garden furniture company, will protect training opportunities by having three different workshops in one site: one making commercial products and two concerned with training, where time pressures will be less. "Business techniques are just a means to achieving our social goals," she insists.

Cross-company co-operation is not only about mutual support, however, as it is also a source of stimulus. Every fortnight, the project co-ordinators meet to report on progress and bounce ideas off each other. In this way, new projects are born or existing ones expanded. As with jazz, a well worked out structure makes it possible constantly to improvise.

Driven by the necessity for jobs, the co-operative principles of CAF have spread outwards. Three years ago, the main players in the town – the voluntary sector, council, and private sector (Furness Enterprise) – came together with CAF to create the Community Regeneration Company. Until recently, community enterprises would have been marginal in such an alliance, but the weakness of the town in the face of corporate decision makers – combined with the steady erosion of the powers and resources of local government – has meant they are now taken seriously.

Andrew Robinson, head of community development banking at the NatWest, recently spent two days looking at CAF's work. He says simply: "Anyone who makes the claim that full employment is within our grasp, and doesn't start to shift policy to support this way of working, ain't going to realise their dream."

But Diss is still conscious of an imbalance within the alliance of local authority, private and voluntary sectors. "If you start unequal, there's no chance of a genuine partnership," she says. "To make the best of it, we've had to do a lot of bobbing and weaving."

One reason for the relatively low status of the social economy is the absence of direct funding for community enterprise.

Government funding, through a variety of partnership agencies, is complicated and time consuming to access. Policy on the social economy is in a flux, but government agencies tend to view community enterprise as "capacity building" – in other words, "preparing" deprived communities for the mainstream economy, rather than being a viable economic sector in its own right. Their professed commitment to social enterprise may be seen to sit uneasily with their continued enthusiasm for the big private sector.

In a modest but resilient way, Barrow's experience suggests that in order to flourish, the social economy requires changes in both government funding and the behaviour of the corporate-dominated mainstream.

Appendix 2 Suggested answers to activities

Activity 1.2

	Growth and poverty	*Growth and inequality*	*Globalization*	*Debt and conditionality*
Ainger	TNCs could prevent cheap drug production in developing countries. Small farmers suffer rather than benefit from free trade.	Indigenous knowledge could be undermined by WTO's IPR regime. Level playing field which is advantageous for coming powerful struggle between capital and labour.	Private finance could adversely affect public service provision. Potential undermining of subsidies by powerful interests. Potential trade war over GMOs. Role of agreements in opening up markets and undermining natural resources.	
Brittan (Note that the argument in this article is based on analysis from Easterlin and Lucas in an issue of an American journal)	Both developed and developing countries' income per head has tripled (although on a different base level) between 1950 and 1995, except for sub-Saharan Africa. This has been accompanied by increases in life expectancy (by 12–20 years) and adult literacy rates (from 40% to 70%). There may be short-term reverses in growth because of war, calamity, etc. Science and technology have the potential to deliver the world from poverty.	Inequality between countries: although developing countries are behind developed countries in wealth and growth terms, once they take off, they can eventually reach parity (this is a hypothesis!). Income gaps between countries will narrow.	The competitive advantage of developing countries based on cheap wages would be reduced (as would employment) if 'decent wages' were paid. Knowledge benefits everyone everywhere. Governments in unsuccessful countries can adopt the institutions of successful ones. Relatively high wages in successful economies can lead to capital flows in emerging ones.	

	Growth and poverty	*Growth and inequality*	*Globalization*	*Debt and conditionality*
Köhler	Need to safeguard growth in world economy. Need action to eliminate poverty as well as growth.	International prosperity not sustainable unless broadly shared. Wealthy countries should increase aid to developing countries. Provide poor countries with access to markets in advanced industrial economies.	Need to make globalization work for humankind. Need new round of multilateral trade negotiations.	Decision of IMF to provide debt relief for 22 HIPCs. Financial assistance to several other countries in difficulties. Success depends on implementation of well-defined adjustment policies. With World Bank, ensure further debt relief. Developing countries also need to take steps: better governance, conflict resolution, human development, and creation of active private sector.

Activity 1.3

	Vulnerabilities	*Capabilities*	*Assets*	*Asset management*
Glasgow	Lack of adequate income Lack of secure income Fear of debt Lack of business skills Margins tight – e.g. vulnerable if equipment breaks down	Opportunity to take advantage of credit scheme Able to choose to become involved	Own labour Professional skills Training in business skills via Wellpark	Nancy: very careful with respect to managing income – everything carefully accounted and new expenditures carefully weighed up. Briony: had loan to help buy equipment; shares workshop space with others; works part-time in café to supplement income. Both use credit groups as form of moral support. Strategies are income raising.
Quilmes	Lack of employment and income Lack of sources of employment Lack of state provision for unemployed	Opportunity to organize Networks provided by the social currencies Educational background (in some cases) and capacities to organize Links with government for the future support of the initiatives	Labour of participants, including to produce goods to barter	How people use barter to meet their needs and manage their domestic economy – this is income raising rather than consumption modifying. Prior to the existence of the social currencies, asset management was also characterized by consumption modification.

Activity 1.4

What particular aspects of the *context* in the UK support the reduction of poverty (and inequality)?

- The existence of social security programmes.
- The existence of public services.
- The creation of a Social Exclusion Unit at the end of the 1990s.
- Macro-economic policies to promote growth and stability.
- A place for public expenditure (and the resources to back public expenditure) to support public services and welfare programmes (which also act as a means of redistributing opportunity).
- A functioning taxation system that has potential to redistribute wealth.

Activity 1.5

Policy agendas	*Voices*	*Participation*	*Policies*
Economic growth and reducing the role of the state	World Bank/IMF		Structural adjustment
Empowerment, opportunity, security	World Bank Voices of the poor	Participatory studies in over 60 countries	Risk reduction and safety nets Asset management Community-driven projects
Indebtedness	World Bank, other donors/lenders, indebted country governments, international campaigns	Participatory processes to consult civil society and private sector	Poverty reduction strategy papers
Rethinking structural adjustment and improving implementation Continued role of market in broad-based economic growth	World Bank	Developing country governments	Sectoral approaches and interventions
Structural changes in people's livelihoods	Agencies such as Action Aid, organizations of poor people	Communities	Greater control over resources by poor people

continued overleaf...

Activity 1.5 *continued*

Policy agendas	*Voices*	*Participation*	*Policies*
Global coalitions	World Bank	From the powerful to the dispossessed	For example, link poor people fighting for land with those wanting to privatize it
Rights-based approaches	Agencies such as Action Aid, organizations of poor people	Organizations of poor people	Address causes of poverty Start with poor people's rights and denials rather than service delivery
Welfare state	UK governments (for example), labour organizations, etc.		Social safety nets and social provision
Social inclusion	UK government, other agencies in the UK	Local communities and service users	Getting people into work Minimum wage New Deal Urban regeneration Health and education action zones

Activity 3.4

Column percentages of tenants and non-tenants in each social class

Class by labour relations	*Not a tenant*	*Tenant*	*Total*
Workers (*kuulies*)	19 (17%)	2 (2%)	21 (19%)
Farmer-workers (*ryots*)	28 (24%)	36 (31%)	64 (55%)
Ryots (farmers not workers)	6 (5%)	7 (6%)	13 (11%)
Supervisors only	17 (15%)	0 (0%)	17 (15%)
Totals	70 (61%)	45 (39%)	115 (100%)

The percentage of households in each social class that are tenants

Class by labour relations	*Total number in each social class*	*Number of tenants in each social class*	*Percentage of each social class that are tenants (rounded to nearest whole percentage)*
Workers (*kuulies*)	21	2	10
Farmer-workers (*ryots*)	64	36	56
Ryots (farmers not workers)	13	7	54
Supervisors only	17	0	0

The column percentage of tenant farmers in each social class

Class by labour relations	*Tenant*	*Percentage of tenants in each social class (rounded to nearest whole percentage)*
Workers (*kuulies*)	2	4
Farmer-workers (*ryots*)	36	80
Ryots (farmers not workers)	7	16
Supervisors only	0	0
Total	45	100

Activity 3.6

Our description looks like this:

The landless are at the left.

The top one-fifth of the households own the vast bulk of the land – about four-fifths. In exact terms it is 73% but this is somewhat hard to read off the graph.

According to the line of equality, the same group, the top one-fifth, would own just 20% of the land. This can be read off the graph as 100% minus 80% (where the diagonal line cuts through the imaginary vertical line representing 80% of population).

The landless have no land, obviously, but in addition the lowest 40% of the households own just a few per cent of the land held.

The middle quintile owns about 10% of the land. This can be seen as the vertical change in the Lorenz curve over the range from 40% to 60% of the households on the horizontal axis.

The inequality looks quite considerable.

Activity 3.7

See Figure A2.1.

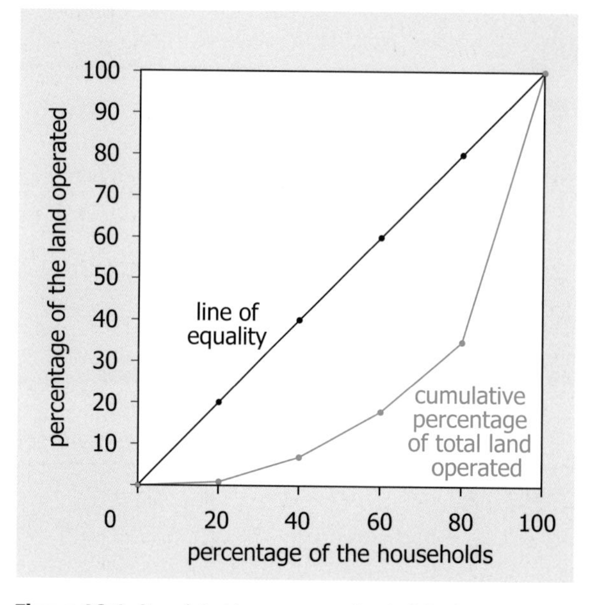

Figure A2.1 Completed Lorenz curve for Activity 3.7.

Activity 3.10

	Nagaratnamma	*Narayanamma*
Types of work	Make wire bags; embroider; sit at home; make tamarind during season at home; cow-grazing; milking cows	Cows, field work, cooking (man gets the provisions from shop and the loan from bank?)
Work roles	Doing micro-enterprise; doing domestic work; employing others	'Doing agriculture' doesn't specify the labour relations each day
Interaction of interviewer(s) with interviewee(s)	Dialogue	Respondent seems impatient (describing her routine is dull to her)
Difficulties in eliciting people's talk	Interview seems too oriented toward actions rather than viewpoints	Anger at intra-household relations question

Activity 3.11

	Nagaratnamma	*Narayanamma*
Capability	Income generation; reproduction of household. Is able to hire others to do her work; this is not in Nussbaum's list.	Knowing about farm work, including livestock and arable farming (any limits to capability here?) Planning festival provisions.
Lacking in capability	Relieved from field labour and perhaps has lost the knack of doing it.	Doesn't use bank herself. Can't get loans from bank either.
Having capability but not using it (i.e. not functioning that way)	Could manage money. Could do field labour but chooses not to.	Can influence husband, but lets him implement some decisions, e.g. to take loan from a farmer.

Activity 3.12

Shared activities probably include: increasing confidence of individual women; assertiveness; autonomy; getting the power to do things which are in one's potential capabilities but not within one's current functionings.

It is much harder to see how *collective agency* or *freedom from structural constraint* would fit into Nussbaum's framework. These two are both inherently defined at a level above that of the individual. To achieve them, social change is needed. Nussbaum's framework, in contrast, seems to be defined mainly at the level of the individual. In a sense perhaps Nussbaum has tried to widen the feminist notion of a good life for women into a notion of a good life generally. It appears to be somewhat individualistic, whereas the latter part of Mayoux's 'empowerment' analysis is non-individualistic.

Activity 3.13

Question (e)

In what ways could Reddamma be called poor?	*Evidence*
A She does not use a bicycle. Her functioning is limited.	She said so.
B She has to educate the children herself to some extent. The schools in the village are not considered good enough.	There is evidence of her high aspirations on behalf of her sons. The tutoring by her and another are aimed to offset poor local schools.
C She does work without recompense, such as clothes washing and cooking.	She is unable to eat without cooking. She lacks the capability to enjoy a luxury meal?
D She is jobless and will remain so.	Joblessness shows its subjective element here, since she doesn't want a job.

In what ways could Reddamma be called non-poor?	Evidence
A She knows how to use a bicycle. She has this particular capability.	She learnt it early in childhood.
B She can choose whether to have each son with her, or away from home in school.	She can afford to pay someone to tutor her son. Her aspirations for sons' jobs are very high.
C She has a good education.	She uses her education to further the interests of her family.
D She has a notion of collectivity, which is her household and family.	She has 'affiliation' to family.

Activity 3.14

'Self-critique': these comments are made by Wendy Olsen, who carried out and interpreted the interviews, and are therefore written in the first person. They make interesting reading!

Nagaratnamma, Household 1

Elements of my own theories have filtered into my analysis. Regarding household 1, the contrast of micro-enterprise and household work is one that I introduced. I also labelled other work as 'outdoor work'. However, the idea of restrictions is Nagaratnamma's.

Narayanamma, Household 5

My comments include a commentary on a general pattern that poor families remove their daughters from school while they keep their sons in school for several more years. My objection to this pattern of education is revealed in my analysis of Narayanamma's interview. In my view, this is the value of triangulation, because I actually observed this pattern (i.e. of behaviour around children's education) in data I collected separately in 1999. Thus my observation of Narayanamma's comment is partly reinforced by my 1999 experience rather than derived specifically from the analysis of her interview.

We could explore Narayanamma's feelings about her social exclusion from bank loan opportunities. However, we need to be open to the idea that a loan would be good for her, even though the overall situation of poverty in which one needs loans for consumption (rather than production) presents a contradiction. Is credit good or bad for people? [Note that we return to some aspects of this issue in Section 4 of this Theme.] It would be important to consider her and her husband's perceptions of their situation in this respect.

Reddamma, Household 2

My answer reveals my understanding of interviews as an interaction that is shaped by the subjectivity of both participants. It could be argued that my interpretation of her autonomy is not objective: i.e. it is hard to claim a 'truth'. My main objective in analysing qualitative data is to expand my understanding.

Overall, the three issues raised in these interpretations (household work, differential treatment of daughters, personal autonomy of housewives) deserve further study.

Activity 4.2

See Figures A2.2 and A2.3.

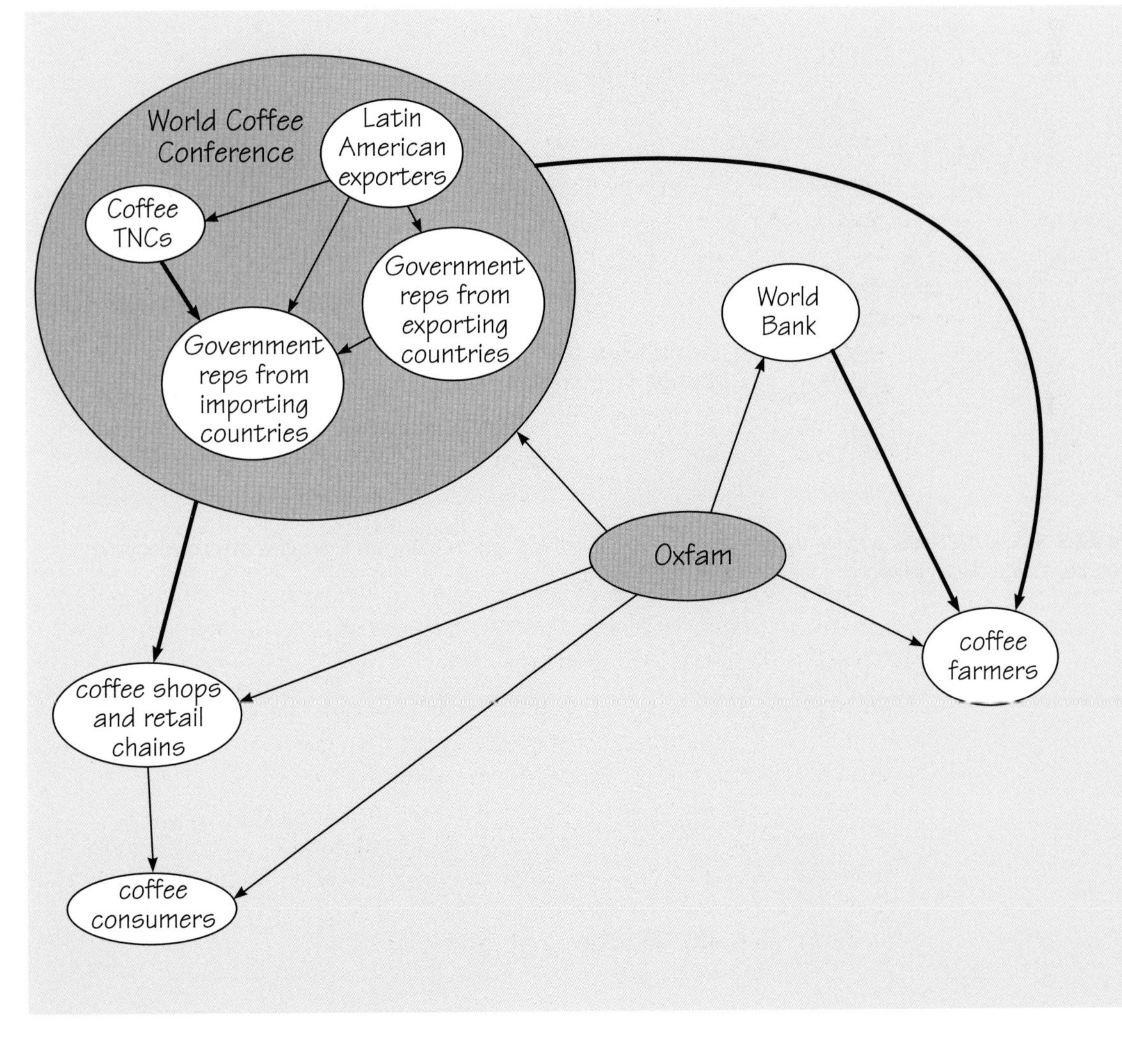

Figure A2.2 Spilling the beans: an influence diagram.

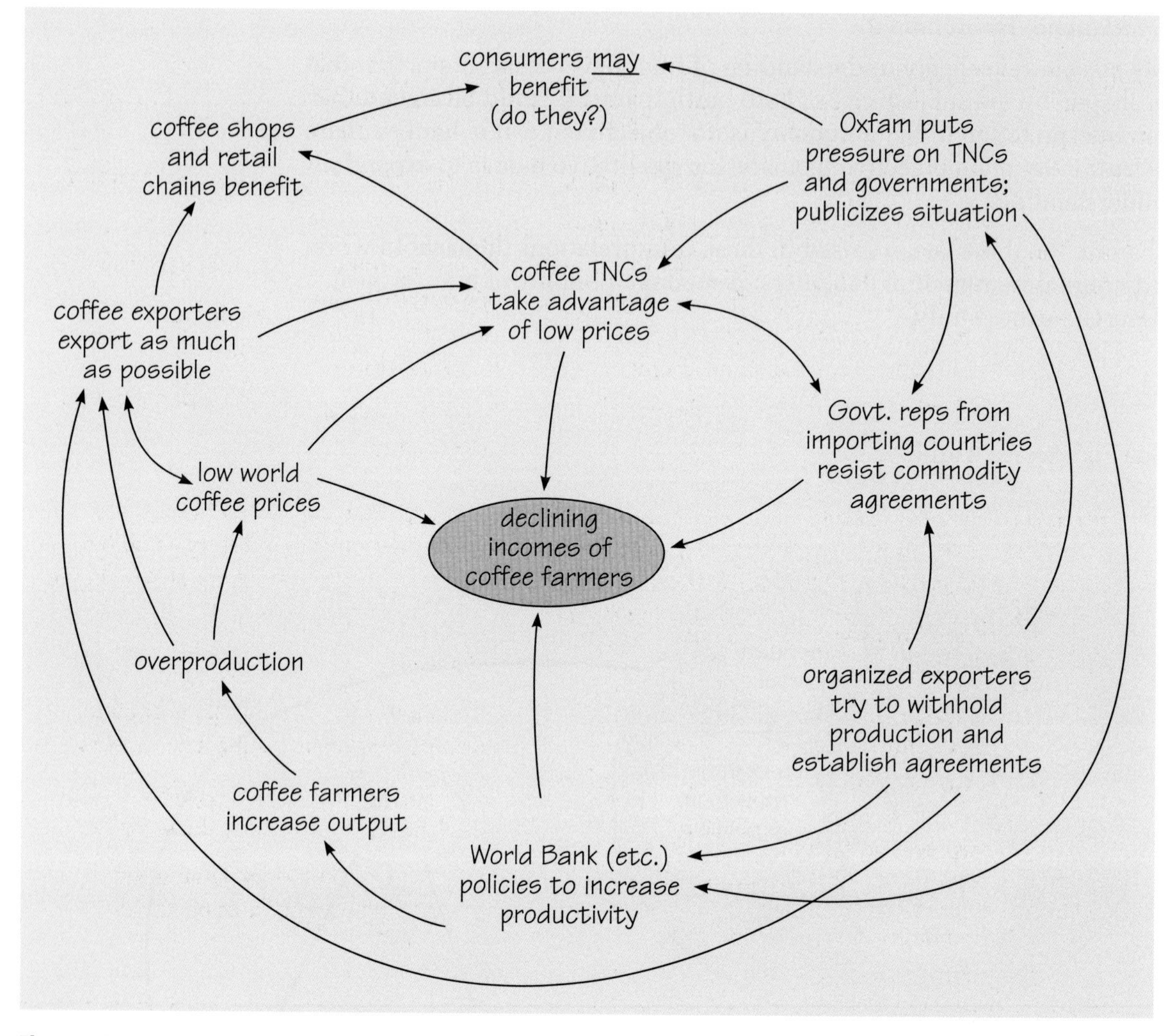

Figure A2.3 Spilling the beans: a multi-cause diagram. Note that in this diagram Oxfam has a negative effect on declining incomes, i.e. it's actually an influence to raise, not lower, incomes.

Activity 4.7

Mechanisms for managing risk of impoverishment (a UK example)

Objective	*Informal mechanisms*		*Formal mechanisms*	
	Individual and household	*Group based*	*Market based*	*Publicly provided*
Reducing risk	Change job to one that is more secure or is better paid (or has additional services attached such as child care support).	Collective action in the community to improve physical and social environment, reduce social exclusion, etc.	Public–private partnerships for urban regeneration. Private service provision.	Social services. National Health Service. Education system.
Mitigating risk	Enabling own children to get a better education. Life insurance and savings schemes.	Community savings schemes; Local Exchange and Trading Systems (LETS).	Bank savings accounts. Private pension schemes.	'New Deals' for elderly, disabled, young children, etc.
Coping with shocks	Reduce expenditure on non-essential consumption items. Borrowing from neighbours. Pawning assets.	Support from religious organizations or other voluntary or neighbourhood organizations.	Benefits from private schemes.	Range of social security benefits. Emergency healthcare. Provision for homelessness.

Activity 4.8

	SC UK	*Women's Association for Action*	*Young girls*
Problems faced by girls	Rural poverty and lack of job opportunities. Physical isolation of village(s). Long hours of work in domestic service for low pay. Sexually transmitted diseases, violence, unhealthy living conditions.	Being badly treated by employers; being made pregnant, being beaten.	Want to earn money for marriage (dowry). Enhance attractiveness as a potential wife. Want to learn Bambara. Want to be 'modern'. Want to buy food for families.
Claims about the action being taken	Research, pilot interventions and advocacy will tackle causes of migration and reduce number of girls migrating and doing domestic work (through income generation and 'work-load reduction investments); and provide support for local organizations helping the girls, leading to improving their working conditions, non-formal education, and protection from abuse. Knowing about the support organization will encourage the girls to seek help.	Developing skills amongst the staff of the organization will enable them to help the girls. Income-generation activities will assist both the organization and the girls. Implied that training the girls before they look for jobs will help them [by enabling them to gain other employment or to resist their employers?]. Being a first port of call for the girls will enable them to find better employers or employment.	A support organization can help.
Expressed or apparent concerns	None made apparent.	None made apparent.	Publicity or public attention from SC UK could create problems.
Issues raised	Too soon to measure impact. Suggested that publicity will prevent abuse but yet to be tested properly.	None made apparent.	None made apparent.

Activity 4.9

Conceptual approach and indicators	*Indicators*	*Evidence*
Capabilities	New skills, education and training	Training on business and marketing skills from Wellpark adds to personal professional skills.
	Increase in options and opportunities	Realizing new work opportunities, including being able to realize own talents.
	Increase in assets and endowments	Equipment for Nancy's sandwich bar and Briony's tools.
		Increase in business expertise.
	Increase in exchange entitlements	Products from business (although Briony suggests that they might be better off on the dole in some circumstances).
	Risk management	Having access to emergency funds.
	Increase in confidence	Getting over fear of borrowing money.
		Proud to be running own business.
Social exclusion	Increased access to services from which previously excluded	Loans via credit groups, 70% going to women from poor areas.
	Increase in social participation	Participation in credit groups provides mutual support and relieves isolation.
Relational	Better terms and conditions of work	Nancy wants a decent wage via own business.
	Changes in gender relations	Difficult to say but women's groups encourage greater confidence in dealing with others, e.g. bank managers.
	Increase in social organization	Importance of micro-credit groups in providing mutual support – almost more important than income.

Appendix 3 Further reading

Section 1

Further reading on participation

Chambers, R. (1997) *Whose Reality Counts? Putting the last first*, Intermediate Technology Publications, London.

Guijt, I. and Shah, M.K. (1998/99) *The Myth of Community: gender issues in participatory development*, Intermediate Technology Publications, London.

Nelson, N. and Wright, S. (eds) (1995) *Power and Participatory Development. Theory and Practice*, Intermediate Technology Publications, London.

Section 2

Edwards, M. and Hulme, D. (1992) *Making a Difference: NGOs and development in a changing world*, Earthscan, London.

Edwards, M. and Hulme, D. (1996) *Beyond the Magic Bullet: NGO performance and accountability in the post-cold war world*, Kumarian, London.

Hubbard, M. (ed.) (2001) 'Special issue: the 2000/01 World Development Report on poverty', *Journal of International Development*, vol.13, no.2.

Lister, S. (2001) 'NGOs in a globalizing world: further reflections', paper presented at DSA conference, *Journal of International Development*, vol.13, no.6.

Riddell, R. and Robinson, M. (1992) *The Impact of NGO Poverty-Alleviation Projects: results of the case-study evaluations*, ODI Working Paper 68, Overseas Development Institute, London.

Section 3

Further reading on lived experience

Narayan, D., Patel, R., Schafft, K., Rademacher, A. and Koch-Schulte, S. (2000) *Voices of the Poor. Can Anyone Hear Us?* New York, Oxford University Press for the World Bank.

Narayan, D., Chambers, R., Shah, M.K. and Petesch, P. (2000) *Voices of the Poor. Crying out for Change*, New York, Oxford University Press for the World Bank.

Both the above are also available at: www.worldbank.org/poverty/voices

Section 4

Marsden, P., Oakley, P. and Pratt, B. (1994) *Measuring the Process: guidelines for evaluating social development*, Intrac, Oxford.

Appendix 4 Glossary

Prepared by Seife Ayele for the Course Team

agricultural pricing In many instances the selling prices of produce will be based on market prices but in other circumstances government may intervene in the market. One common intervention in developing countries is guaranteeing minimum prices for agricultural produce. Should prices fall below this guaranteed minimum, the government must buy the produce at this price.

balance of payments problems Balance of payments data show the records of all transactions that a country undertakes with the rest of the world over a given period of time. It can be seen as the difference between a country's income and its expenditure abroad. Balance of payments problems arise when import values far exceed export values on a sustained level and when there is shortage of foreign exchange to pay for imports. One of the measures to correct balance of payments problems is devaluation (*see* devaluation) as it raises the price of exports and imports at home.

capital investment Investment made in assets like buildings, equipment, plant and machinery and tools in order to produce goods and services for future consumption. Broadly speaking capital investment could include investment in human capital (see human capital), natural resources such as forests and wildlife, social capital as in networks of institutions and social relations that form the basis for the functioning of legal and economic systems.

comparative advantage The ability to produce a particular good or service more cheaply than some other goods or services (this may be assessed at national, regional and firm levels).

concessional aid funds Aid is the transfer of resources from developed to less-developed countries (and Eastern Europe) for the purpose of encouraging economic growth and development. Aid may take different forms like finance, expertise, education and training and technology. Bilateral aid is from a donor to a recipient country, while multilateral aid is provided by a group of countries. Emergency aid is short-term aid, generally given in response to disasters, while structural aid is given to promote long-term development. While generally the purpose of aid is to promote development, donors may set conditions to the use of it: for example by requiring it to be spent on a particular purpose, or to be accompanied by policy actions such as devaluation. NGOs also provide aid but with fewer conditions.

decapitalization The opposite of constant accumulation of capital. It also means a fall in the ratio of capital per head of population due to depreciation and/or accumulation less than the growth rate of the population.

devaluation A decrease in the value of a nation's currency relative to other currencies (and/or gold) or, conversely, a rise in the price of other currencies (and/or gold) relative to a particular currency. Devaluation is generally undertaken in order to make a country's products more competitive in the world market. Devaluation is a matter for governments that maintain fixed exchange rates (*see also* exchange rate).

exchange rate The price at which one currency is bought with another currency (or with gold). In practice it is often the price at which a currency is bought with the US dollar. For example, on 26 July 2001 a unit of US dollars bought 70 pence sterling, or a unit of pound sterling bought one US dollar and forty-one cents, i.e. the pound sterling–US$ exchange rate was £1 = US$1.414.

fiscal and monetary adviser Governments (in less-developed as well as developed countries) increasingly use advisers in policy-making processes. In fiscal and monetary policy-making processes (as on tax and spending levels and bank credit and interest rates) advisers provide an 'unbiased opinion' and 'specialized competence': for example, in forecasting events. But little is known about the impact (or effectiveness) of advisers on the performance of the economies.

fiscal deficit Governments use spending and taxation instruments to achieve desirable social and economic goals. Fiscal deficit refers to a situation in the government budget where expenditure exceeds revenue.

global public goods Public goods, generally speaking, are those goods whose consumption by one person does not alter the availability of the good for the other consumer. Such a good is 'non-rival' in consumption. In the case of 'pure public good' it is also impossible, or possible only at a prohibitively high cost, to prevent people from consuming the good, hence the existing quantity of the good is consumed by all people. Clean air is an example of a global public good.

group insurance mechanisms As in 'self-insurance' but provided for a group.

headcount index The definition and measurement of poverty is a complex exercise: in its 1990 World Development Report, the World Bank defined poverty as 'the inability to attain a minimal standard of living' (World Bank, 1990, p.26). But, as acknowledged by the Bank, what was meant by 'minimal' and the measurement of 'standard of living' were not universally accepted. The Bank, however, used US$1 a day, measured in international prices, as a cut-off point to define the poor (*see* international poverty line). Then the 'headcount index' of poverty was coined to express the number of people living below this line as a proportion (usually expressed as a percentage) of the total population.

high default risks High failure rate to meet obligations such as loan repayment.

home-based and export-based industrialization Industrialization is a process by which manufactured goods increasingly become important compared with agricultural products. The market for these manufactured goods may be largely home based (hence home-based industrialization) or export based (hence export-based industrialization) or a combination of both home- and export-based industrialization.

human capital A form of capital stock that consist of human skills (general or specific) and knowledge. As in other forms of capital (like physical capital) human capital increases the productive power of the individuals who possess the skills and knowledge. Investment in human capital stock (i.e. in education and training) is necessary to maintain or increase the stock.

inflationary expenditure Often governments finance their spending programmes from taxes (also in less-developed countries from external sources like loans and aid). If a government's spending exceeds its revenue and the government finances the deficit through domestic bank borrowing, then it is likely to cause inflationary pressures. This means that, given limited goods and services, the money injected into the economy is accommodated through rises in prices.

international poverty line A measure of poverty that holds the real value of the poverty line constant between developed and developing countries (*see* headcount index). In the 1990 World Development Report, the expenditure required to buy minimum standard nutrition and necessities was set to $1 a day, measured in 1985 international prices and adjusted using the purchasing power parity (PPP) conversion factors. The PPP conversion factor allows for differences between countries of what a given sum of money will buy. International poverty line is criticized for, among other things, not accurately taking into account the differential cost of staple food in urban and rural areas.

intersectoral mix of public expenditure The allocation of public spending between sectors such as education, health and transport. (Intrasectoral expenditure refers to spending programmes and projects within a sector as in education from primary to tertiary levels.)

macro-analysis An analysis using aggregate data for large groups of persons or products, for example, as in employment, national income and price levels.

micro-analysis Analysis of a particular market, product, firm, industry, household or individual. An example of micro-analysis is studying the demand for and supply of mobile phones.

minimum social cost adjustment As part of the conditions for securing international aid, developing countries may be expected to undertake 'structural adjustment' measures like devaluation and reforming of the public sector. There is a broad agreement that structural adjustment programmes, at least in the short term, widen income inequality between the better off and poorest sections of the society. Public sector reform, for example, includes cuts in food subsidies and spending on primary health care and education services which hurt the poor most. In addition to the poverty reduction programmes aimed at the 'old' (or existing) poor, funds might be provided, therefore, for meeting the minimum social cost of victims of adjustment programmes such as to provide for labour-intensive employment schemes.

moral hazard The tendency of guaranteed assistance to encourage careless behaviour. One everyday example is that if our possessions are insured, we may be less careful in looking after them. An application to this chapter is that if countries in financial trouble (for example Turkey and Argentina in 2002) know that the IMF is always there to give them emergency loans, their governments may be less careful in restraining public spending.

physical capital Items like plant and machinery, buildings and land that can be used to produce goods and services, and thus cash income, often over a long period of time.

public enterprise reform To various degrees governments own and manage enterprises and assets (like factories, mines, railways, utility companies, banks and insurance and land). Public enterprise reform refers to changes in the ownership and management of such enterprises and assets as, for example, in the British privatization of the railways.

public expenditure programmes (and composition thereof) Government spending programmes (e.g. on health, education, transport and local governments) principally financed from taxes (supplemented, in less-developed countries, by loans and aid). A public expenditure review is a policy that considers, among other things, the composition and priority of spending programmes, and whether the programmes should be delivered by the government and/or in partnership with other agencies like the non-governmental agencies and the private sector.

secondary industries These days the term industry is used to cover any form of economic activity, such as 'the railway industry', 'the tourism industry' and 'the music industry'. More specifically, industry is divided into: primary industry – the acquisition of naturally occurring resources like coal and fish; secondary industry – the production of manufactured goods; and tertiary industry which serves the public as well as primary and secondary industry: as in transport, warehousing and retailing.

self-insurance The provision of a sum of money or a collateral arrangement to protect an individual loan from hazards to life or property (as in death or fire).

short-term capital movements Capital (money) moves between countries by agents like individuals and companies. Capital movements seek long-term gains like setting up factories abroad, or seeking short-term (less than one year) speculative gains, such as those taking advantage of temporary high interest rates in another country.

social capital The ability of people to work together for common purposes in groups and organizations.

stabilization Government action aimed at the correction of economic imbalances that are believed to be unsustainable. Typical examples of these imbalances are balance of payments deficits, government budget deficits and inflation (*see* balance of payments problems).

structure of supply The nature and composition of goods and services produced in an economy. Specifically, the structure of supply could mean the range of goods and services supplied by a particular sector (such as the private sector, or manufacturing sector) for the domestic and/or foreign markets. The key factors that influence the production of goods and services are the range of resources and capabilities such as labour force, capital investment, incentives to encourage investment and work, and physical infrastructure.

supply-side (fragile) In economic policy terms the 'supply-side' refers to measures that influence the production of goods and services. These include measures that encourage labour mobility, investment, increased infrastructure, increased supply of health and trained people. What makes less-developed economies fragile is that these countries' economies (largely agriculture) are dependent on the vagaries of nature, poor infrastructure, poorly trained labour force, etc. Also, less-developed countries' primary export earnings fluctuate due to unstable demand and protective policies of developed countries.

tariff reform Changes made by governments to import and export taxes in the interest of managing the economy. Tariff reforms affect the size and structure of revenue from duties and the production and consumption of imported as well as home-produced goods and services.

tariffs Taxes levied by governments on goods that are imported or, less often, exported across the country's boundaries. Two of the principal reasons for tariffs are raising more revenues (referred to as a revenue tariff) and discouraging imports and encouraging domestic 'infant industry' (referred to as a protective tariff).

tax reform In order to provide services like education, health and police (and sometimes goods too) governments collect a range of taxes from individuals and businesses. Tax reform refers to changes to the size and structure (composition) of taxes in the interest of generating the desired level of tax revenues as well as managing the economy.

References

Ammer, C. and Ammer, D.S. (1984) *Dictionary of Business and Economics*, revised and expanded edition, The Free Press/Macmillan, New York.

Bannock, G., Baxter, E.E and Davis, E. (eds) (1998) *The Penguin Dictionary of Economics*, Penguin, London.

Eatwell, J. *et al.* (eds) (1987) *The New Palgrave: a dictionary of economics*, vols 1–4, Macmillan, London.

Markandya, A. *et al.* (2001) *Dictionary of Environmental Economics*, Earthscan, London.

World Bank (1990) *World Development Report 1990: Poverty*, Oxford University Press, New York.

References

Abercrombie, N., Hill, S. and Turner, B.S. (1994) *The Penguin Dictionary of Sociology*, Penguin Books, London.

Agarwal, B. (1997) 'Bargaining and gender relations: within and beyond the household', *Feminist Economics*, vol.3, pp.1–51.

Allen, T. and Thomas, A. (2000) *Poverty and Development into the 21st Century*, Open University in association with Oxford University Press, Oxford. (Course Book)

Allen, T. and Weinhold, D. (2000) 'Dropping the debt for the new millennium: is it such a good idea?', *Journal of International Development*, vol.12 no.6, pp.857–876.

Appleton, S. (2001) 'Reductions in poverty in Uganda, 1992–2000', unpublished paper, University of Nottingham.

Ashley, C. and Carney, D. (1999) *Sustainable Livelihoods: lessons from early experience*, Department for International Development, London.

Ayres, R. (1983) *Banking on the Poor: the World Bank and world poverty*, MIT Press, Cambridge, Mass.

Basu, K. and Van, Pham Hoang (1998) 'The economics of child labour', *American Economic Review*, vol.88, pp.412–428.

BBC (2000) *Nice Work*, BBC Radio 4, 12 December.

Bernstein, H. (1992) 'Poverty and the poor', in Bernstein, H., Crow, B. and Johnson, H., *Rural Livelihoods: crises and responses*, Oxford University Press, Oxford, in association with The Open University.

Boyle, D. (2000) *Funny money: in search of alternative cash*, Flamingo, London.

Caines, J. (1983) Communication at meeting with Independent Group on British Aid, 11 February.

Chambers, R. (1988) 'Poverty in India: concepts, research and reality', Discussion Paper 241, Institute of Development Studies, University of Sussex.

Chambers, R. (1994) 'Participatory rural appraisal: analysis of experience', *World Development*, vol.22 no.9.

Chambers, R. (1997) *Whose Reality Counts? Putting the Last First*, Intermediate Technology, London.

Chenery, H., Bell, C., Duloy, J. and Jolly, R. (1975) *Redistribution with Growth*, Oxford University Press, Oxford.

Chipika, J.T. (2001) Critical reader comments to U213 Course Team, 4 April.

Collier, P. and Dollar, D. (1999) 'Aid allocation and poverty reduction', unpublished paper, World Bank.

Collier, P. and Gunning, J. (1999) 'The IMF's role in structural adjustment', *Economic Journal*, vol.109 (November), pp.F634–F652.

Cornia, G.A., Jolly, R. and Stewart, F. (1987) *Adjustment with a Human Face*, Oxford University Press, Oxford.

Cornia, G.A., Stewart, F. and Vayrynen, R. (2001) *War, Hunger and Displacement*, 2 vols, Oxford University Press, Oxford.

Cox, P. (1983) 'Implementing agricultural development policy in Kenya', *Food Research Institute Studies*, vol.15, pp.153–176.

Demery, L. and Squire, L. (1996) 'Macroeconomic adjustment and poverty in Africa', *World Bank Economic Research Observer*, vol.11, no.1.

DeMeulenaere, S. (2000) 'Reinventing the market: alternative currencies and community development in Argentina', *International Journal of Community Currency Research*, vol.4; online: http://www.geog.le.ac.uk/ijccr/4no./3.htm [accessed October 2001].

DfID (1997) *Eliminating World Poverty: a challenge for the 21st century*, White Paper on International Development, HMSO, London.

DfID (2000a) *Eliminating World Poverty: making globalization work for the poor*, White Paper on International Development, December.

DfID (2000b) *Halving World Poverty by 2015: economic growth, equity and security*, Department for International Development, London.

DfID (2000c) *Poverty Elimination and the Empowerment of Women*, Department for International Development, London, September.

Elson, D. (ed.) (1991) *Male Bias in the Development Process*, Manchester University Press, Manchester.

Evans, A. (2000) 'Can overseas aid be effective in reducing poverty?', talk given by Alison Evans at Overseas Development Institute, 22 November.

Ferroni, M. and Kanbur, R. (1990) 'Poverty-conscious restructuring of public expenditures', unpublished paper.

Fishlow, A. (1970) 'Size distribution of Brazilian national income', *American Economic Review*, vol.60.

Galeano, E. (1973) *Open Veins of Latin America: five centuries of the pillage of a continent*, Monthly Review Press, New York and London.

Gore, C. (2000) 'The rise and fall of the Washington consensus as a paradigm for developing countries', *World Development*, vol.28, pp.789–804.

Guba, E.G. and Lincoln, Y.S. (1989) *Fourth Generation Evaluation*, Sage Publications, Newbury Park, Calif.

Haddad, L. and Kanbur, R. (1990) 'How serious is the neglect of intra-household inequality?', *Economic Journal*, vol.100, no.404, p.866.

Hanlon, J. (2000) 'How much debt must be cancelled?', *Journal of International Development*, vol.12, no.6, pp.877–901.

Hanmer, L. and Naschold, F. (2001) 'Attaining the international development targets: will growth be enough?', Chapter 13 in Booth, A. and Mosley, P. (eds) *The New Poverty Strategies: what have we learned?*, Macmillan, London.

Hanmer, L., Healey, J. and Naschold, F. (2000) 'Will growth halve global poverty by 2015?', *ODI Poverty Briefing* No. 8, Overseas Development Institute, London.

Hirschman, A. (1970) *Exit, Voice and Loyalty*, Harvard University Press, Cambridge, Mass.

Hitchcock, G. and Hughes, D. (1995) *Research and the Teacher: a qualitative introduction to school-based research*, Routledge, London.

Holstein, J.A. and Gubrium, J.F. (1995) *The Active Interview*, Qualitative Research Methods, vol.37, Sage Publications, Thousand Oaks, Calif.

Horrell, S. (2000) 'Destined for deprivation: human capital formation and intergenerational poverty in nineteenth-century England', paper presented at DSA conference, School of Oriental and African Studies, London, 4 November.

Hulme. D. and Mosley, P. (1987) *Finance Against Poverty*, 2 vols, Routledge, London.

Iliffe, J. (1996) *The African Poor* (African Studies Series), Cambridge University Press, Cambridge.

ILO (1973) *Employment, Incomes and Equality: a study of Kenya*, International Labour Organisation, Geneva.

Lipton, M. and Longhurst, R. (1989) *New Seeds and Poor People*, George Allen & Unwin, London.

Lister, S. (2001) 'NGOs in a globalizing world: further reflections', paper presented at DSA conference, *Journal of International Development*, vol.13.

Mackintosh, M. (1992) 'Introduction' in Wuyts, M., Mackintosh, M. and Hewitt, T. (eds), *Development Policy and Public Action*, Oxford University Press, Oxford, in association with the Open University, Milton Keynes.

Marcus, R. (2001) Critical reader comments to U213 Course Team, April.

Marr, A. (1999) 'The poor and their money: what have we learned?', *ODI Poverty Briefing*, no.4, March.

Massey, D. (2000) 'The geography of power', *Red Pepper*, July, pp.18–21.

Maxwell, S. and Kenway, P. (2000) 'New thinking on poverty in the UK: any lessons for the South?' *ODI Poverty Briefing*, no.9, November.

Mayoux, L. (1998a) *Women's Empowerment and Micro-Finance Programmes: approaches, evidence, and ways forward*, DPP Working Paper No. 41, The Open University, Milton Keynes.

Mayoux, L. (1998b) 'Participatory learning for women's empowerment in micro-finance programmes: negotiating complexity, conflict, and change', *Bulletin of the Institute of Development Studies*, vol.29 no.4, pp.39–50.

Mayoux, L. (1998c) 'Women's empowerment and micro-finance programmes: strategies for increasing impact', *Development in Practice*, vol.8 no.2, pp.235–240.

Melzter, A. (2000) *Commission Hearings*, International Financial Institution Advisory Commission, Washington, DC.

Moser, C. (1998) 'The asset vulnerability framework: reassessing urban poverty reduction strategies', *World Development*, vol.26, no.1, pp.1–19.

Mosley, P. (2001) 'The IMF after the Asian crisis: merits and limitations of the 'long-term development partner' role', *The World Economy*, vol.24, no.5, pp.597–629.

Mosley, P., Harrigan, J. and Toye, J. (1995) *Aid and Power*, 2 vols, Routledge, London.

Myrdal, G. (1957) *Economic Theory and Under-Developed Regions*, G. Duckworth, London.

Narayan, D., Patel, R., Schafft, K., Rademacher, A. and Koch-Schulte, S. (2000a) *Voices of the Poor. Can Anyone Hear Us?* New York, Oxford University Press for the World Bank, 2000.

Narayan, D., Chambers, R., Shah, M.K. and Petesch, P. (2000b) *Voices of the Poor. Crying out for Change*, Oxford University Press, Oxford, for the World Bank.

Nussbaum, M. (1999). 'Women and equality: the capabilities approach', *International Labour Review*, vol.138, no.3, pp.227–246.

OECD (1986) *Twenty-Five Years of Development Co-operation*, OECD, Paris.

Olsen, W.K. (forthcoming) *The Limits to Conditionality in India: evidence from the rural grassroots*, WorldView Publishing, Oxford.

Olsen, W.K. and Rani, U. (1997) *Preparing for Rural Adjustment*, Research Monograph No. 2, Development and Project Planning Centre, University of Bradford.

Overseas Development Administration (1975) *Overseas Development: The Changing Emphasis in British Aid Policies: more help for the poorest*, Cmnd 6270, HMSO, London.

Overseas Development Institute (2000) 'Were the 'Voices of the Poor' really heard?', 6 December, http://www.odi.org.uk/speeches/booth8.html [accessed August 2001].

Pearson, R. (2000) 'Income generation strategies in a globalising world: learning from international experience', paper presented to an international seminar *Towards a more egalitarian society: strategies for the improvement of living conditions*, Ministry of Social Development and Environment, Republic of Argentina, Buenos Aires, June 2–3.

Pretty, J. *et al.* (1995) *A Trainer's Guide for Participatory Learning and Action*, International Institute for Environment and Development, London.

Ravallion, M. (1991) 'Public employment schemes as instruments for poverty reduction', *Journal of Development Economics*, vol.21.

Robson, C. (1993) *Real World Research: a resource for social scientists and practitioner–researchers*, Blackwell, Oxford.

Sahn, D. (ed.) (1996) *Economic Reform and Income Distribution in Africa*, Oxford University Press, Oxford.

Save the Children UK (2001) 'Protection and promotion of girl domestic workers' rights in Mali' and 'Women's organizations supporting the rights of girl domestic workers', online: http://www.scfuk.org.uk/development/lfe/index.htm [accessed October 2001].

Schadler, S. and Bredenkamp, H. (1997) *The ESAF at Ten Years: economic adjustment and reform in low-income countries*, International Monetary Fund, Washington, DC.

Scott, J.C. (1985). *Weapons of the Weak: everyday forms of peasant resistance*, Yale University Press, New Haven, Conn.

Sen, A.K. (1983) *Poverty and Famines*, Oxford University Press, Oxford.

Sen, A. (1999) *Development as Freedom*, Oxford University Press, Oxford.

Stiglitz, J. (1998) *More Instruments and Broader Goals: moving toward the post-Washington consensus*, WIDER, Helsinki.

Summers, L. (1999) speech at London Business School, 14 December. Website: http://www.lbs.ac.uk. news-events

Symposium (1988) 'Whatever became of integrated rural development?', *Manchester Papers on Development*, 1988.

Thomas, A. (1996) 'What is development management?', *Journal of International Development*, vol.8, no.1, p.95.

Thomas, A. (1998) 'Making institutional development happen', Part 3 of *Institutional Development: conflicts, values and meanings*, The Open University, Milton Keynes.

Thomas, A. (2000) 'Development as practice in a liberal capitalist world', *Journal of International Development*, vol.12, no.6, pp.773–788

Thomas, A., Chataway, J. and Wuyts, M. (1998) *Finding Out Fast. Investigation for policy and development*, Sage, London, in association with the Open University, Milton Keynes.

Uganda (2001) *Report of the Poverty Commission*, Government of Uganda.

UNDP (United Nations Development Programme) (2000) *Human Development Report 2000*, Oxford University Press, Oxford.

United Nations (1951) *Measures for the Economic Development of Under-Developed Countries: report by an expert team* (A.B. Cortes, D.R. Gadgil, G. Hakim, W.A. Lewis, T.W. Schultz), United Nations, New York.

Walker, B. (2000) 'A short history of the debt crisis', in Nyamugasira, W. and Walker, B. (eds) *The Poor Can't Wait: poverty and debt relief*, Working Paper No. 1, World Vision, Geneva.

Watkins, K. (2001) 'Spilling the beans', *Guardian Society*, 16 May, p.9.

Weaver, M. (2001) 'Urban regeneration: the issue explained', *Guardian Society*, 19 March, online: http://www.guardian.co.uk/Archive/Article/0,4273,4154663,00.html [accessed October 2001].

Weeks, J. (1997) 'Analysis of the Demery and Squire "Adjustment and Poverty" evidence', *Journal of International Development*, vol.9, pp.827–837.

Wiggins, S. (1986) 'Planning and management of integrated rural development in drylands: lessons from Kenya's arid and semi-arid lands programmes', *Public Administration and Development*, vol.5, pp.91–108.

Williamson, J. (1990) 'What Washington means by policy reform', in Williamson, J. (ed.) *Latin American Adjustment: how much has happened?*, Institute for International Economics, Washington, DC.

World Bank (1990) *World Development Report 1990: Poverty*, Oxford University Press, New York.

World Bank (1993a) *Poverty Reduction Handbook*, World Bank, Washington, DC.

World Bank (1993b) *World Development Report 1993: priorities and policies for the health sector*, Oxford University Press, New York.

World Bank (1994) *Adjustment in Africa*, Oxford University Press, New York.

World Bank (1999) *World Development Report 1999: the changing development landscape*, Oxford University Press, New York.

World Bank (2000a) *World Development Report 2000/2001: Attacking Poverty*, Oxford University Press, New York.

World Bank (2000b) *Evaluation and Poverty Reduction*, Proceedings, Operations Evaluation Department, Oxford University Press, New York.

World Bank (unpublished report) *Development Assistance and Poverty Reduction*, Operations Evaluation Department.

Yunus, M. (1997) 'The Grameen Bank story: rural credit in Bangladesh', in Krishna, A., Uphoff, N. and Esman, M. (eds) *Reasons for Hope: instructive experiences in rural development*, Kumarian Press, West Hartford, Conn., pp.9–24.

Acknowledgements

Grateful acknowledgement is made to the following sources for permission to reproduce material within this text.

Text

Box 1.2: Walker, B. 'A short history of the debt crisis', in Nyamugasira, W. and Walker, B. (eds) *The Poor Can't Wait: poverty and debt relief,* Working Paper No. 1, World Vision; *Box 4.3:* Yunus, M. (1997) excerpts from 'The Grameen Bank Story: rural credit in Bangladesh', in Krishna, A., Uphoff, N., and Esman, M. (eds) *Reasons for Hope: instructive experiences in rural development,* Kumarian Press, West Hartford, Conn., pp.13–15; *Reading 1:* Ainger, K. 'WTO faces biggest protest in years', *Red Pepper,* November, 1999, Red Pepper Publications. redpepper@redpepper.org.uk; *Reading 2:* Brittan, S. 'Protest against the protesters', *Financial Times,* 20 September, 2000; *Reading 3:* Köhler, H. 'The IMF's agenda for the new year', *Financial Times,* 8 January, 2001; *Reading 4:* Maxwell, S. and Kenway, P. *ODI Poverty Briefing,* No. 9, November, 2000. © Overseas Development Institute 2000; *Reading 5:* Watkins, K. 'Spilling the beans', *Guardian Society,* 16 May, 2001. © 2001 Guardian; *Reading 6:* Hizemann, A. 'Protection and promotion of girl domestic workers' rights in Mali, West Africa', in Thompson, M. *Learning From Experience: global action for girls' equality, development and peace,* May 2000, Save the Children, UK; *Reading 7:* 'Women's organizations supporting the rights of girl domestic workers', in Thompson, M. *Learning From Experience: global action for girls' equality, development and peace,* May 2000, Save the Children, UK; *Reading 8:* Wainwright, H. 'Turning the tide', *Guardian Society,* 16 May, 2001. © 2001 Guardian.

Figures

Cover photo: Panos Pictures/Sean Sprague; *Cover montage left to right*: Still Pictures/Harmut Schwarzbach; Associated Press/Ralph Radford; Panos Pictures/ Sean Sprague; Associated Press/Greg Baker; Associated Press/Kamenko Pajic; *Figure 1.1:* Associated Press/Jeronne Delay; *Figure 1.2:* Margaret Waller/Link Picture Library; *Figure 1.3:* Courtesy of Paul Mosley; *Figure 1.4:* John Harris/ Report Digital.co.uk; *Figure 1.5:* Narayan, D., Chambers, R., Shaha, M. and Petesch, P. from *Voices of the Poor: Crying out for Change*, copyright © 2000 The International Bank for Reconstruction and Development/The World Bank. Used by permission of Oxford University Press, Inc.; *Figure 2.1:* Associated Press/ Kamemko Pajic; *Figure 2.2:* Pollard, S. (1990), *Wealth and Poverty: an economic history of the twentieth century,* Equinox, Oxford; *Figure 2.3:* Popperfoto; *Figure 2.4:* Popperfoto/Kevin Lamargue; *Figure 2.5 left:* Panos Pictures/Sean Sprague, *right:* Panos Pictures/Paul Smith; *Figure 2.6:* from *World Development Report 2000/2001* by World Bank, copyright © 2001 by the International Bank for Reconstruction and Development/The World Bank. Used by permission of Oxford University Press, Inc.; *Figure 2.7:* Popperfoto; *Figure 2.8:* Popperfoto/Rafiqur Rahman; *Figure 2.9:* Associated Press/Ralph Radford; *Figure 3(a):* Associated

Press/Sherwin Crastow, *(b):* Associated Press/Desikan Krishnan; *Figure 3.7:* Panos Pictures/Piers Benatar; *Figure 3.8:* Panos Pictures/Tom Learmonth; *Figure 3.9:* Panos Pictures/Neil Cooper; *Figure 3.10:* Wendy Olsen; *Figure 4.1:* Panos Pictures/J. Hartley; *Figure 4.2:* Panos Pictures/Martin Flitman; *Figure 4.3:* Panos Pictures/Philip Wulmoth; *Figure 4.4:* Panos Pictures/Betty Press; *Figure 4.5:* Panos Pictures/Sean Sprague.

Tables

Tables 2.1, 2.3 and 4.6: from *World Development Report 1999/2000* by World Bank, copyright © 2000 by the International Bank for Reconstruction and Development/The World Bank. Used by permission of Oxford University Press, Inc.; *Table 2.6:* from World Bank, copyright © 2000 by the International Bank for Reconstruction and Development/The World Bank. Used by permission of Oxford University Press, Inc.; *Tables 4.3–4.5:* reprinted from World Development, vol.26, Moser, C. 'The asset vulnerability framework: reassessing urban poverty reduction strategies', pp.1–19, Copyright 1998, with permission from Elsevier Science.

Every effort has been made to contact copyright owners. If any have been inadvertently overlooked, the publishers will be pleased to make the necessary arrangements at the first opportunity.

The Course Team

ACADEMIC STAFF

Joanna Chataway, *Co-Chair and author, Technology and Knowledge*
Jenny Robinson, *Co-Chair, co-ordinator and author, Displacement*
Gordon Wilson, *Co-Chair, co-ordinator and author, Sustainability*
Simon Bromley, *co-ordinator and author, Transitions*
Will Brown, *co-ordinator and author, Transitions*
Pam Furniss, *author, Sustainability*
Tom Hewitt, *co-ordinator and author, Technology and Knowledge*
Hazel Johnson, *co-ordinator and author, Poverty and Inequality*
Bob Kelly, *assessment strategy and author, Study Guide to the Course Book*
Maureen Mackintosh, *author, Transitions*
Judith Mehta, *author, Transitions*
Stephen Peake, *author, Sustainability*
Sandrine Simon, *author, Sustainability*
Alan Thomas, *author and co-editor of the Course Book*
Richard Treves, *author, Sustainability*
David Wield, *critical reader*
Helen Yanacopulos, *co-ordinator and author, Technology and Knowledge*

BBC STAFF

Jenny Bardwell, *Series Producer July 2000–May 2001*
Gail Block, *Audio Producer*
Giselle Corbett, *Production Manager*
Phil Gauron, *Series Producer*
Julie Laing, *Series Personal Assistant*
Andrew Law, *Executive*
Jenny Morgan, *Freelance Director*
Claire Sandry, *Audio Producer*
Mercia Seminara, *Audio Producer*

SUPPORT STAFF

Carolyn Baxter, *Course Manager*
Sylvan Bentley, *Picture Researcher*
Philippa Broadbent, *Print Buying Controller*
Kevin Brown, *Picture Researcher*
Penny Brown, *QA Software Testing Assistant*
Daphne Cross, *Print Buying Co-ordinator*
Sue Dobson, *Web Designer*
Tony Duggan, *Learning Projects Manager*
Peta Jellis, *Course Manager July–November 2000*
Alison George, *Web Designer*
Richard Hoyle, *Graphic Designer*
Lori Johnston, *Editor*
Roy Lawrance, *Graphic Artist*
Cathy McNulty, *Course Secretary*
Katie Meade, *Rights Editor*
Lynda Oddy, *QA Software Testing Manager*
Pauline O'Dwyer, *Course Secretary*
Katharine Reedy, *Library Online Adviser*
Janice Robertson, *Editor*
John Taylor, *Copublishing Manager*
Mark Thomas, *Team Leader, Online Applications Web Team*
Pamela Wardell, *Editor*

EXTERNAL ASSESSOR

Dr K. Bezanson, *Institute of Development Studies, University of Sussex*

CONSULTANTS

Tim Allen, *author and co-editor of the Course Book*
Seife Ayele, *Poverty and Inequality*
Jo Beall, *Sustainability*
Flemming Christiansen, *Transitions*
Ben Crow, *Sustainability*
Vandana Desai, *Displacement, and Study Guide to the Course Book*
Wendy Fisher, *Technology and Knowledge*
Leroi Henry, *Study Guide to the Course Book*
Ann Le Mare, *Preparing for Development*
Giles Mohan, *Displacement*
Paul Mosley, *Poverty and Inequality*
Njuguna N'gethe, *Study Guide to the Course Book*
Wendy Olsen, *Poverty and Inequality*
Ruth Pearson, *Poverty and Inequality* (video)
Judith Scott, *Poverty and Inequality*
Laixiang Sun, *Transitions*
John Taylor, *Transitions*
David Turton, *Displacement*
Marc Wuyts, *Transitions*

CRITICAL READERS

Henry Bernstein, *Transitions*
Tenkai Bonger, *Sustainability*
Jesimen Chipika, *Poverty and Inequality*
Rachel Marcus, *Poverty and Inequality*
Martin Reynolds, *Sustainability*
Rafal Rohozinski, *Technology and Knowledge*
AbdouMaliq Simone, *Displacement*

WEB TESTERS

Alan Brown, Jackie Bush, Christine Cubbitt, Andrew Dakers, Sarah Downham, Alan Foster, Anna Mattarollo, Fahmida Muhit, Eric Needs, Wendy Shaffer, Nigel Shakespear, Phil Talman

U213
International Development: Challenges for a World in Transition

Course texts

Introduction to Transitions

Introduction to Poverty and Inequality

Introduction to Technology and Knowledge

Introduction to Displacement

Introduction to Sustainability

Transitions

Poverty and Inequality

Technology and Knowledge (web-based)

Displacement

Sustainability

Reframing Development